E
A
T

**HIGH-OCTANE
FIFTH
EDITION**

ROUTE
66

ADVENTURE
HANDBOOK

SANTA
MONICA
PRESS

Published by:

Santa Monica Press LLC
P.O. Box 850
Solana Beach, CA 92075
1-800-784-9553
www.santamonicapress.com
books@santamonicapress.com

Printed in the United States

Santa Monica Press books are available at special quantity discounts when purchased in bulk by corporations, organizations, or groups. Please call our Special Sales department at 1-800-784-9553.

This book is intended to provide general information. The publisher, author, distributor, and copyright owner are not engaged in rendering professional advice or services. The publisher, author, distributor, and copyright owner are not liable or responsible to any person or group with respect to any loss, illness, or injury caused or alleged to be caused by the information found in this book.

ISBN-13 978-1-59580-091-6

Library of Congress Cataloging-in-Publication Data

Names: Knowles, Drew, 1956-
Title: Route 66 adventure handbook / Drew Knowles.
Other titles: Route sixty-six adventure handbook
Description: High-octane fifth edition. | Solana Beach, CA : Santa Monica
  Press, 2017. | Description based on print version record and CIP data
  provided by publisher; resource not viewed.
Identifiers: LCCN 2016059903 (print) | LCCN 2016055734 (ebook) | ISBN
  9781595807977 | ISBN 9781595800916 (paperback)
Subjects: LCSH: United States Highway 66--Description and travel. | United
  States Highway 66--Guidebooks. | West (U.S.)--Description and travel. |
  West (U.S.)--Tours. | Automobile travel--West (U.S.)--Guidebooks. | West
  (U.S.)--History, Local. | United States--Description and travel. | BISAC:
  TRAVEL / United States / General. | TRAVEL / United States / West /
  General. | TRAVEL / United States / Midwest / General. | TRAVEL / Museums,
  Tours, Points of Interest.
Classification: LCC F595.3 (print) | LCC F595.3 .K67 2017 (ebook) | DDC
  917.804/33--dc23
LC record available at https://lccn.loc.gov/2016059903

Cover and interior design and production by Future Studio
Photographs by Drew Knowles. All other images and graphics were culled from the author's personal collection.

Overleaf: Serving hungry travelers in Amarillo, Texas.

CONTENTS

This book is dedicated to all of those
individuals who, by setting out to
explore even a small portion of
Route 66, have kept its mystique alive.
May that spirit of adventure never fade.

—Drew Knowles

FOREWORD

Like so many people who have traveled it in recent years, Drew Knowles fell in love with the Mother Road. I don't mean "love" in the popular, overused sense, but a real love and respect for something very dear. Yet he is not just another enamored router. Far from it. He has spent many years on and off the road digging into every nook and cranny so he could write this important guide.

As Drew takes you down America's most legendary highway, he tempts you with just enough historical details to make you want to search for more. He shares his secrets for finding unmarked stretches so you can become an informed explorer. He challenges you to travel beyond the route itself so you can enjoy even more of our country's texture.

If you read and use this guide, there is a very good chance you will change your attitude towards motoring. Rather than simply driving to a location, your trip will become the destination. In fact, this attitude is relatively new in our country. When I was growing up, nearly every trip we took was a series of dots and dashes. You dashed from one dot to the next, then bragged about how quickly you got there. The advent of super highways was our dream come true. So were franchise operations because you could always count on them to be the same. This was what we wanted and it was what tourists from other countries came to see. But today, every country in the civilized world has more than its share of

Opposite: **At the Lake Overholser bridge, west of Oklahoma City.**
GPS: 35.51462,-97.66260
Overleaf: **Lots of Route 66 roadies are also classic car buffs.**

Nothing but vacancies at motels like this one in Seligman, Arizona.

these "modern" conveniences.

Enter the "Heritage Tourist." These foreign and domestic tourists are more interested in experiencing the roots of America than the rides at its theme parks; and what better way to do that than to travel Route 66—the route to our roots. As it passes by vintage motels, bustling cafés, colorful trading posts, and through picturesque villages, three time zones, dozens of cultures, and numerous geographic and weather changes, the old road is a microcosm of historic roadside America that every age can enjoy.

So, it's time to do something different. Pack up the car, put this guide in the glove box, strap that water bag on the front, and get ready for a serious love affair.

David Knudson
Executive Director
National Historic Route 66 Federation

INTRODUCTION

I was fortunate to grow up in the 1950s within easy striking distance of Route 66. Throughout the heyday of that fabled highway that Steinbeck appropriately dubbed "The Mother Road," my family, like so many others, used the artery of concrete and asphalt to our advantage.

It was a time when just the act of getting there was an important part of the vacation experience. We didn't want to be gypped out of a single moment, so we made the drive an indispensable component of the overall trip. There was an assortment of manmade and natural attractions to visit, tourist traps to survive, detours to avoid, and truck stop meals to consume.

Times may have changed, but Route 66—the highway some folks believed dead and gone—is alive and kicking like never before.

The old road (at least a major percentage of it) survived the attempts of five interstate superslabs that tried in vain to take its place. Today's rendition of Route 66 is a grizzled veteran—tried and true—but with the allure and prestige of an aging celebrity. Some time ago the highway achieved American icon status, and not just because of the physical roadbed or all the historical and cultural treasures that litter its shoulders from Chicago to Santa Monica. The road is a much-more-than-remarkable example of commercial archeology, diverse natural and fabricated attractions, and gentle curves tailor-made for a purring Harley or speedy Corvette.

Most of all, Route 66 is about people. That is what the road has always been about, and that is why it remains active and relevant to this day.

It is inspiring to realize that Route 66 truly is America's highway, just

Postcards such as this one are highly sought after by collectors.

as it has been ever since 1926. Other venerable roads, longer or older than Route 66, crisscross the land, but the reality is that none of them measures up to the Mother Road. Not even close. Through the years, this celebrated highway has persevered, despite attempts to do away with it. Route 66 has become a destination in and of itself.

Although it seems there is something for everyone on Route 66, there are some exceptions. It is not a road for those who like cookie-cutter culture, food in Styrofoam boxes, or sprawling shopping malls filled with indistinguishable people pawing through look-alike merchandise. Even though franchise restaurants, chain stores, and homogenized fast-food joints have invaded the old highway, the true Route 66 crowd does not fully embrace them.

Route 66ers want kitsch that often is so bad it is good. They go for window decals, refrigerator magnets, salt and pepper shakers, and the other kinds of merchandise sold at the best tourist traps. They crave real hash browns, milk shakes, and berry pies made from scratch and on the premises. They like nothing but open road ahead of them. They do not mind taking chances.

Since 1990, when the Route 66 resurgence really began, tens of thousands of enthusiasts from around the globe have discovered that this road is not just another American highway. Nor is it a romanticized corridor of nostalgia that only allows people to return to the so-called good old days. True, Route 66 serves as the definitive symbol of certain key segments of the nation's past, but it is also very much part of the present, as well as of the future.

Today, people from around the globe continue to take the open road—the free road. I enjoy showing these travelers the distinct layers of history along the highway. Their numbers are growing. I meet with them in diners and curio shops, at Smithsonian lectures, in university class-rooms, and all along the old road. Through these many people and their enthusiasm, my sense of pure adventure and my passion for the highway and its people remains strong. The old road has again become an import-ant part of the nation's cultural scene. Route 66 fans range from commer-cial archeologists, historians, and American culture buffs to motorcycle club members, students, and the RV crowd.

Still, after they have listened to my stories and words of advice, every traveler needs a good guidebook to help show them the way.

Through the years, there have been many books published about Route 66, including guidebooks that have helped legions of travelers tra-verse the Mother Road.

This particular book, so carefully written by Drew Knowles, is unlike any other. Drew's writing is as smooth as a cup of fresh custard and cap-tures the adventure and excitement of traveling the open road.

The *Route 66 Adventure Handbook* exposes a true slice of America—a nation of movement and energy. This book shows us people living in secret corners and hidden towns that can still be found if travelers merely dare to exit the interstate highway. To do that, they have to believe that life begins at the off-ramp. Then, with the windows rolled down and the ra-dio playing, they can open their eyes to the past and, just maybe, discover something of themselves.

It is a journey worth taking.

Enjoy the ride.

Michael Wallis
Author of *Route 66: The Mother Road*

AUTHOR'S PREFACE

I f you are reading this, I hope it means that you intend to take a Route 66 trip with this book alongside you.

When I published the first edition of the *Route 66 Adventure Handbook* in 2001, I wanted it to fill a void that I saw in every other Route 66 book I'd seen. Those other books did an adequate job of describing features of the road itself, but all of them seemed to ignore the fact that, in the highway's 2,000-mile-plus course across the continent, it came into contact with literally thousands of interesting places, some of them worthy of being considered destinations in their own right. I wanted those many attractions to take a far more prominent role in any discussion of Route 66.

In the years since, the *Adventure Handbook* has been revised repeatedly. In each case, I've tried to improve the book not only by bringing old information up to date, but also by adding new features that make it even more valuable, such as more and better photographs, graphics to illustrate certain features of the highway, and maps and other directional aids to help the Route 66 traveler navigate some of the more challenging areas.

This latest edition, the fifth, is no exception. I've updated many of the photos and added even more to the collection, and I've increased the number of maps as well. And since many travelers today just plug locations into their phones or navigation devices, I've also noted the addresses and painstakingly recorded the latitudinal and longitudinal

Opposite: Dry Creek Station, Newberry Springs, California. GPS: 34.81901,-116.64042

figures for hundreds of sites so that today's adventurer will have no difficulty finding even the most isolated destinations (Owl Rock in New Mexico, for example).

My sincere hope is that the *Route 66 Adventure Handbook* will be of valuable service to you as you explore Route 66 yourself, and that you will come to appreciate America's Main Street as much as I do.

See you on the road!

Drew Knowles
Fort Worth, Texas

ABOUT THE 1957 ATLAS

Throughout this book, you will see mention of something I refer to as "my 1957 atlas." It's a twelve-by-sixteen-inch paperbound road atlas, published by Rand McNally in 1957 and containing individual road maps for all fifty states (plus Canada and Mexico).

It was in 1956 that President Eisenhower signed the bill which launched what we now call our Interstate Highway System, and which also started the slow decline of the *old* system of interstate highways, of which U.S. 66 was a part. Therefore, my 1957 atlas depicts Route 66 and her sisters at their zenith, just before our nation's road-building energies were diverted to the creation of a decidedly different type of highway.

I obtained my treasured 1957 road atlas at a local antique mall/ flea market, and it has been invaluable to me in my quest to explore everything Route 66 has to offer. To peruse its pages is to take a step back in time, and that's been a journey well worth taking.

At the former Pioneer BBQ,
Wellston, Oklahoma.
GPS: 35.68110,-97.05213

WHAT IS ROUTE 66, ANYWAY?

In the early years of the twentieth century, America was crisscrossed by a collection of disorganized and poor-quality roads (often no more than dirt paths). That was considered adequate when most travel occurred via horse and buggy or railroad. However, the development of the automobile—and especially its mass-production in the 1910s—fueled a demand on the part of the American public for more and better roads.

Construction of more and better roads did begin; however, it occurred at a local or regional level, and so development was spotty and haphazard. Naming and marking conventions also varied considerably, making cross-country travel confusing at best.

In 1926, the now-familiar numbered federal highway system was launched. This facilitated the marking of highways consistently across state and regional boundaries. Furthermore, in order to qualify for federal funding and inclusion in the new scheme, highways had to meet standards for surface quality and other criteria. In the beginning, the U.S. highways—including Route 66— were established as such, simply by posting the well-known black-and-white numbered shields at strategic

Holdovers like this old sign are getting rarer and rarer on the Route 66 roadside.

At the Capri Motel, Duarte, California. GPS: 34.13984,-117.95383

points along pre-existing roads to act as guides. The roads thus connected, then became part of a "route," even though they had not been originally built as such.

Numbers ending in zero, such as 60, were reserved for the major
coast-to-coast routes (as they still are in today's interstate system). The
highway between Chicago and Los Angeles, considered to be of lesser
importance, was designated U.S. 66.

That highway, which we now commonly refer to as Route 66, began its ascension into America's cultural lore when John Steinbeck made
mention of it in his famous 1939 novel, *The Grapes of Wrath*. It was there
that he gave the route one of its many nicknames, "the Mother Road."
The highway received another boost in public awareness when, just after
World War II, Bobby Troup penned his popular song "(Get Your Kicks

on) Route 66" while driving to California for a shot at a career in show business. At about that same time, Jack Rittenhouse, realizing that the post-war years would mean increased auto travel in America, published his book, *A Guidebook to Highway 66* (see bibliography).

During the late 1940s and throughout the 1950s, America became a much more mobile society, and lots of people began to have first-hand experience using Route 66 either on business, while taking family vacations, or simply moving their households. It was during those years that Route 66 experienced its most prodigious growth, and simultaneously gained its reputation for tourist traps such as snake pits, trading posts, and roadside zoos. Countless Americans today still have fond memories of family trips to Disneyland and other Southern California destinations via the Mother Road.

Then, in the early 1960s, a national television series was produced, called simply *Route 66*. Although the series was seldom filmed on the highway for which it was named, it served to reinforce the highway's place in popular culture, and in fact is indicative of the status the highway had already achieved.

Beginning in the late 1950s, the United States began building a new set of cross-country highways that would change highway travel profoundly. For a variety of reasons, the new highways (which we now refer to as "interstates") were constructed as limited-access freeways, with only a relatively small number of access ramps, and no roadside driveway access whatsoever. This was the death knell for small roadside businesses all over the country, including those flanking Route 66.

The entire length of Route 66 was functionally replaced by a series of interstates paralleling it—in some cases only yards away from the older highway, but in the majority of cases making it next to impossible for the modern motorist to gain access to the multitude of businesses left high and dry.

An adventure on Route 66 is an opportunity to see exactly what those interstate highways cast aside so many years ago.

WHY TRAVEL ROUTE 66?

You're wearing a pair of tight, ill-fitting shoes. Sure, they're stylish, and they look pretty sharp with that suit of clothes you're wearing, but the fit is not right. They're confining. Furthermore, it's been a long day and you've been in those shoes so long and become so acclimated to their shortcomings that you've stopped paying attention to them. You've repressed your pain and forgotten what it feels like to be barefoot on a soft, cool carpet of green grass.

Now take off those shoes. Right away, good things begin to happen. The blood vessels in your feet begin to open up, allowing an influx of fresh oxygen and nutrients. The pores of your feet open up and bre-e-e-eathe for the first time in a long time. Even the rhythm of your own breathing becomes less strained, and your mind is sharpened. You flex your toes with enthusiasm and think: "Ahhh, now that's more like it!" And you wonder how you could have put up with your discomfort for so long.

If you've never driven old Route 66, you're in for a similar sensation. And the analogy is far more apt than you might imagine.

For decades now, highway travelers—you included—have been subjected to an onerous set of circumstances which are, by and large, passively accepted. Furthermore, this condition has been accepted for so long that many of us have either forgotten that things weren't always this way, or—even scarier—may never have known anything different.

That set of ill-fitting restrictions I'm referring to is of course part and parcel of today's Interstate Highway System. Now, before you accuse me

Opposite: **In the mining town of Oatman, Arizona.**

of wrongly condemning America's most ambitious peacetime engineering project in its history, hear me out.

Admittedly, the interstates—like the ill-fitting shoes—are not entirely without practical benefits. They are, after all, designed with graceful, high-speed curves, and enable us to travel from point A to point B in minimal time. We accomplish this with greater fuel efficiency, thanks to the ability to move with unvarying speed. And, a limited-access highway is safer from the standpoint that there are no driveways for irresponsible motorists to pop out of unexpectedly. These qualities are quite attractive, particularly to the long-distance truckers among us.

But what are those features costing us? That snazzy pair of oxfords does have a few important drawbacks. Did you ever stop to think of what a tremendous misnomer the word "freeway" is? There's not much freedom in interstate travel. Consider that you are shielded and encapsulated against the world at large. Sealed in your fast-moving mobile cocoon, your perception of the world is distorted. You are cut off from

Retired road warriors like this one litter many parts of the Mother Road.

sound and smell by your tightly sealed windows. Open the window, and the buffeting and roaring of the air will cut you off from your senses just as effectively. Visually, the interstate corridor offers only the barest glimpse of the surrounding countryside. Your visual stimulation is often limited to mile markers, exit signs of uniform appearance, and perhaps a grove of trees to block your view of anything outside the world of the superslab. This isolation is partly due to the enormous amount of land which America's interstates have taken as their own. There are enormous swaths of acreage on both sides of the interstate, in the medians, and still more locked up in the countless clover leafs, flyovers, and other interstate-grade interchanges. All of that empty acreage contributes to the interstate traveler's isolation from his or her surroundings.

Furthermore, there are restrictions which make it *unlawful* to attempt to squeeze a little more gusto from the experience. There are minimum speeds which must be maintained, preventing you from taking advantage of whatever paltry visual stimuli might actually be available. There are also prohibitions against non-emergency stopping or slowing, and against turning your vehicle around. No wonder it's hard to stay awake.

Ah, but Route 66. Now there's highway travel for you. Kick off your shoes, because the above restrictions do not apply.

On Route 66, there is healthy stimulation for all the senses, and conditions encourage you to take full advantage. Sensory experience is in no way out of fashion on the Mother Road. Smell the new-mown hay and the honeysuckle. Hear the clamor of children playing softball in a nearby park, or the tolling of a church bell. Feel the breeze on your face and know that the coolness signals a change in elevation, or even a new climate zone.

Visually, the difference is even more dramatic. There are schools and stores and mountains and crosswalks and downtowns and trains and depots and rivers and billboards and murals and cafés and menus and humanity.

Don't forget: you can pull over and stop at almost any time to savor it a little more. You can travel Route 66 by bicycle, on horseback, or even on foot, so as not to miss a single nuance—don't try doing that on the interstate!

One of the knocks against Route 66, which eventually led to its demise, was a call for increased efficiency. The inter-states are considered efficient because they transport us with a maximum of speed

Part of the roadside in Tulsa, Oklahoma.

in a minimum amount of time. That's well and good. But my point is this: the interstates have had some unforeseen and undesirable side effects, because at the same time that they minimized the *amount* of our time in getting to our destination, they also minimized the *quality* of our time on the road by placing us in an experiential vacuum.

That quality of experience is what you'll put back in your life when you kick off those shoes and travel Route 66.

Tucumcari, New Mexico, used to offer thousands of motel rooms back in the day. Several of those motels are still open for business. GPS: 35.17193,-103.71632

GET THE MOST FROM YOUR ROUTE 66 ADVENTURE

Ask several people what you should bring with you on your Route 66 Adventure, and you'll likely get several different answers. One well-meaning friend might mention such practical travel items as maps, a compass, a pen or pencil, a notebook, a camera, and sunglasses. Another person's suggestion might emphasize such things as proper footwear, layers of clothing, and sunblock. Someone else might recommend an ice chest with bottled water and plenty of trail mix. Oh—and don't forget your mobile phone and credit cards.

I travel with most of those things, too. But there is one thing which is far more important than all of the above *combined* when it comes to getting the most enjoyment out of your trip on old Route 66. And that one thing is a Spirit of Adventure. I never take a road trip without it.

In a nutshell, I urge you not to plan to take charge of your Route 66 experience too precisely; instead, plan for the Adventure on Route 66 to take charge of you.

As much as possible, I encourage you to simply "go with the flow." Don't set an itinerary which requires you to make it to city "X" by a certain time of a certain day. Keeping to such a schedule will inevitably cause you to hurry through certain portions of your journey, and there's no way of knowing how much you'll miss by doing so.

Move as the spirit moves you; pause and take in the sights and the sounds of your Adventure as they present themselves to you. Your reward will be a trip like no other.

Dare to dare. Try new food and drink, meet some strangers, turn

Relic on the outskirts of Lebanon, Missouri. GPS: 37.73096,-92.60077

down a road just because it looks interesting or because you're curious what's there. This is the stuff of which lifelong memories are made.

Things can change rapidly out on Route 66. What you see today might be gone tomorrow or soon after. Keep your camera ready and use it liberally. Don't scrimp, and don't worry whether the resulting photographs will be worthy of a museum exhibition or not. If you don't consider yourself an artist, then be a documentarist. Just record what you see that interests you. It's far too easy to think to yourself: "Well, it's been standing there for fifty years now; I'm sure it'll be there for a few more." Sadly, too often this is not the case. Don't fall into that trap. This is a lesson I've learned again and again over the years, both on and off Route 66.

Bring this book with you. Your navigator can read aloud from it as various points in your journey are reached. Even if you elect to skip a certain side trip, the modest background information can enrich your trip in unexpected ways, sometimes by giving you an appreciation of other features of the countryside.

Incidentally, I certainly don't expect you to take in every feature that I've chosen to make mention of in this handbook. Just pick out some of the ones which most tickle your fancy, or are most compatible with other attractions you intend to visit, and leave the rest for some other time. A continent is not fit for properly exploring in one outing.

Be cognizant of the fact that the information about various features and attractions is not meant to be authoritative. My objective is primarily to whet your appetite for investigation and exploration. If I provide too much detail in this handbook, it may lessen your own desire to find out more on your own. The key is for you to experience things first-hand, not simply to absorb someone else's research.

Similarly, the lists of attractions and trivia associated with various places are not meant to be complete—they constitute more of a random sampling. How could one hope to compile a list of all of the noteworthy events or personalities associated with Chicago, for example? One of the limiting factors I've used is to eliminate some of the more commonly known attractions which are either already familiar to most people or are featured prominently in published visitors' guides to the areas in question. Also, the few attractions shown plotted on the maps are of course just a small sampling of the many things there are to see in each Route 66 town. I encourage you to explore.

Another point about things changing rapidly in 66-land: it took years for me to travel all of the route, and things have been changing the whole time. I have witnessed the disappearance and/or destruction of many distinctive features over the years. Do not be surprised if you find that by the time you use this handbook on your own Adventure, not everything will remain as I've described it. Just consider that a part of the Adventure, and let it make the Mother Road that much more precious to you.

A Spirit of Adventure. Please don't waste your time on Route 66 without it.

HOW TO USE THIS HANDBOOK

This handbook is here to fulfill one objective—to help you get the maximum possible enjoyment from your Adventure on Route 66. That's all. With that in mind, here are a few simple suggestions:

Don't keep your head buried—either in this book or in any other. That's why it's not designed as a "guide" focused on intricate maps and turn-by-turn descriptions that require close scrutiny. I've tried to keep the navigational information short and to the point. Most of the time, you can follow what's left of Route 66 on your own after reading the "How to Find Route 66" section of this book. That way, you won't miss anything due to trying to drive and read at the same time—plus, it's obviously much safer that way!

Keep this book close at hand at all times. What this book *does* have is a wealth of information on nearby attractions, historical background, fun trivia, and side-trip ideas. As you approach a new town or other landmark, have your navigator (if you've got one) read aloud some of the information from that area, so that both of you will know what to be on the lookout for and can make decisions on whether you're "passing through" or want to stop and take in some of the nearby features more fully. Some towns will have simple maps showing where some of those local attractions can be found. If you're traveling alone, you can just pull to

Opposite: **Part of the distinctive ambiance at the Old Town Museum complex in Elk City, Oklahoma. GPS: 35.41180,-99.43632**

the road's shoulder or into a friendly looking driveway and quickly read about the nearby attractions yourself. That's one of the real advantages of Mother Road driving versus interstate driving—on Route 66, it's okay to slow down, pull over, smell the roses, etc.

You're the boss, so customize your trip based on your own passions and interests. Don't slavishly follow anyone's advice, not even mine. This road trip Adventure is all about *your* enjoyment, right? That means that after you've briefed yourself on the area you're entering, make some personal decisions about the things that most intrigue you. For some people, that will mean making it a point to seek out each and every architectural treasure mentioned in this entire handbook. But your own tastes might run more toward historic sites or natural wonders or trivia or folk art or whatever—there's something for everyone. So spend *your* time doing what *you* enjoy the most. Ignore the rest, or save it for your *next* Route 66 safari.

Immerse yourself. As you travel Route 66, remember that you are surrounded by the remnants of an enormous support system developed for the transcontinental motoring public in the mid-twentieth century. I urge you to make full use of it. That support system included—and *still* includes—motels, cafés, fuel stations, general stores, and roadside attractions of every description. While this book *does not* attempt to offer a list of these support-system establishments—they are, after all, subject to frequent change—you should nevertheless take advantage as the need arises. Many of those old Route 66 businesses today have a marginal bottom-line, and would sincerely appreciate your patronage. The other support resource I encourage you to make use of is comprised of the local residents and business operators all along the Route. Inquire locally for advice or directions to local attractions, and I know you'll be pleasantly surprised at the helpfulness of the response.

Enjoy!

HOW TO FIND ROUTE 66

U.S. 66 no longer officially exists—emphasis on the word "officially." The numerical highway designation system adopted in the 1920s was a system in which pre-existing roads were linked together by being given the same number. A traveler could, then, by following signs bearing that number, arrive at any of the destinations on that highway's route, or gain access to any of the other numbered highways which crossed paths with it. When a given route is no longer needed, for whatever reason, the signs can be removed and the route is no longer recognized as such.

But in most cases, the road itself remains. Although it may no longer carry the federal designation, it is unusual for the pavement to actually be removed and the ground returned to nature. Often, the road is re-numbered by the state or county in which it occurs; other times, the older roadway serves duty as an access road to the limited-access thruway, which may have brought about its obsolescence.

Officially, Route 66 ceased to exist when the federal highway authorities ordered the signs removed. But keeping in mind that the route was created in 1926 by the installation of signs marking the way, the only thing preventing a traveler from using the old road today is a lack of knowledge on where to find it without the benefit of all those signs at every turn—thousands in all.

While this book does include plenty of maps and other navigational guidance, it will *not* tell you exactly where each and every turn ought to be made in order to drive old Route 66. Other writers have already attempted this. As the old adage goes, "Give a man a fish and he eats for a day; teach a man to fish and he feeds himself for a lifetime." Similarly, my objective here is to share with you sufficient basic knowledge to be able to fend for yourself. A significant advantage to this strategy is that this knowledge will apply for years to come, with little or no regard to how local conditions might change over time. Another advantage is that you will begin to see and discover other old routes in your travels which have undergone the same processes of construction, use, upgrade, re-routing, bypassing, and de-certification as Route 66. I think you'll find that some of those other routes, though not as famous as the Mother Road, are also worthy of exploration, and you'll be well-equipped to do so.

HOW TO FISH

In the broadest terms, Route 66 ran (or runs) southwestward from Chicago, Illinois to Los Angeles (technically Santa Monica), California. The next thing for you to take note of is which modern-day highways currently carry that same Chicago-to-Los Angeles traffic. Look at a road map of the overall continental United States if you have one. Today's traffic is borne by a huge network of interstate highways. It turns out that Route 66 was replaced by not one, but five modern highways, none of which bears the number 66. The series which supplanted Route 66 is: I-55 from Chicago, Illinois, to St. Louis, Missouri; I-44 from St. Louis across the state of Missouri and all the way to Oklahoma City, Oklahoma; I-40 from OKC to Barstow, California; I-15 from Barstow to San Bernardino, California; and I-10 from there to the Pacific coast at Santa Monica. This is the general corridor in which you'll be traveling in order to experience Route 66.

This brings us to the first rule in learning to fish: be on the lookout for secondary roads which more or less parallel the interstate highways mentioned in the paragraph above. This goes for roads which take us to a destination city—a city formerly on old Highway 66—and not necessarily a road which literally runs alongside the freeway within sight of it. The main narrative section of this book points out most of those Route 66 towns. Your strategy, then, in keeping to the old route, should be to avoid the interstate when possible, and move from one town to the next using secondary roadways. In many cases, this is authentic Route 66 pavement.

The second consideration is the simplest and most obvious: the placement of "Historic Route 66" signs. In the last several years, the eight states along Route 66 have made great strides in getting the old road marked. Unfortunately, there are considerable gaps in sign placement, so that relying solely on them will get you off-course fairly quickly in many cases. However, you'll find that by keeping on the lookout for those friendly brown-and-white signs, you'll more easily keep to the route and be able to enjoy the sights and sounds thereof, without having your nose perpetually buried in a mile-by-mile guide or map. In places where the old road has been buried or otherwise obliterated, and you are forced to use the interstate, quite often the next exit which includes a stretch of Route 66 will have the Historic 66 symbol on the big green exit sign. This enables you to travel a minimum amount of the sleep-inducing superslab before returning to the central theme of your trip.

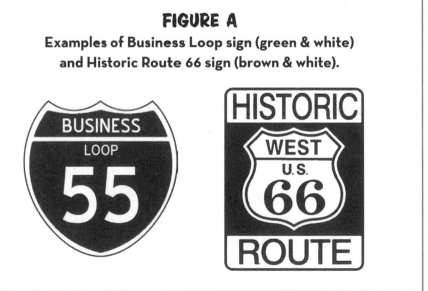

FIGURE A
**Examples of Business Loop sign (green & white)
and Historic Route 66 sign (brown & white).**

**The neon still glows at the Blue Swallow Motel, Tucumcari, New Mexico.
GPS: 35.17193,-103.71632**

Very closely related to the foregoing is the third fishing strategy: "business loop" routes. Again, this is helpful when you have been forced to use the interstate for a distance. In many of the larger cities on Route 66, the old route through town will be designated as "Business Loop X," where the "X" stands for the number of the interstate that supplanted 66. For example, in the city limits of Albuquerque, New Mexico, and Amarillo, Texas, the path of Route 66 is marked with green signs designating it Business Loop I-40. Similarly, in Springfield, Missouri, Route 66 is marked Business Loop I-44. Keep in mind that in larger cities such as these, the path of Route 66 in most cases changed several times over the years. The alignment marked in this way is typically the last alignment of 66 prior to its demise as an official route. The earlier alignments will go either unmarked, or may bear the brown-and-white "historic" signs. Exploration is the order of the day.

Some of the rest of our fishing tips are a little more subtle, and will draw upon your powers of reasoning and observation a little more. This makes locating a vintage stretch of old 66 all the more satisfying, however.

For reasons of economy and expediency, most routes of any kind are established along the paths of previously-existing routes. Just as immigrant trails often followed older trade routes of Native Americans or trappers, Route 66 and others like her were constructed along right-of-way corridors established earlier by the railroads. Railroad tracks, then, are often an excellent guide to where the earlier alignments through a region are to be found. Given a choice between two alignments which will eventually reach the same destination, in most cases the one physically following the railroad tracks more closely is the older route. Over time, as the highway has been widened or otherwise upgraded, the newer alignment tends to be placed farther from the tracks. An instructive example of this can be found along the stretch of Route 66 between Sayre and Erick, Oklahoma. Two lanes of Route 66 were originally c onstructed just a few yards to the south side of the railroad right-of-way. Later,

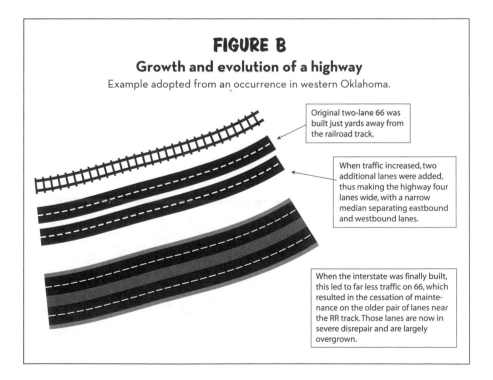

FIGURE B
Growth and evolution of a highway
Example adopted from an occurrence in western Oklahoma.

Original two-lane 66 was built just yards away from the railroad track.

When traffic increased, two additional lanes were added, thus making the highway four lanes wide, with a narrow median separating eastbound and westbound lanes.

When the interstate was finally built, this led to far less traffic on 66, which resulted in the cessation of maintenance on the older pair of lanes near the RR track. Those lanes are now in severe disrepair and are largely overgrown.

the highway was increased to four lanes by the addition of a median and two east-bound lanes further still to the south. Then, when Interstate 40 was constructed, it was placed much farther south. The presence of I-40 resulted in diminished traffic on the older highway, and it was downgraded to two lanes by ceasing maintenance on the oldest two lanes near the railroad track. This is what the visitor sees very clearly today in traveling these several miles in western Oklahoma, and it's one of my favorite features. It's as though one can literally read the historical journal of the highway in this area.

Another tip-off to the location of old Route 66 has to do with some of the ancillary structures associated with it. In more urban areas, this means being observant of buildings—and building remains—which seem to have travelers' needs as their focus. Examples are motels, cafés, and gasoline stations, which originate in the era when the old road was in its development (1930s) and growth (1945–55) stages. In small towns that were not crossed by other major highways, this is often

Many miles of Route 66 are within the Mojave Desert. GPS: 35.37480,-113.72288

simple. In larger cities, which may have been hubs for more than one major highway, it becomes more difficult to discern one from another, especially in light of the fact that multiple routes would often follow the same streets for a portion of their journey through town.

Central Avenue, Albuquerque, New Mexico.

In more rural areas, bridges can be an excellent indication of a Route 66 alignment. The federal highway system, Route 66 included, was originally formed in the 1920s from pre-existing roads. Shortly thereafter, efforts were undertaken to improve these roads, many of which were not even paved at first. In the late 1920s and throughout the 1930s, many small bridges were constructed during the process of improving the country's network of highways. The bridges constructed during this period are not only often quite distinctive in design, they also sometimes bear a small plaque or medallion indicating the year of construction. Many of these were projects of the Works Progress Administration, and, in keeping with their dates of origin, exhibit an almost Art Deco appearance. A case in point is that often there will be an access road on either side of the interstate, and you might suspect that one of these might be old enough to be Route 66. One of the clearest indications is the type of bridges built for each of the two candidates. Often, one of the two will have bridges which appear to be 60 or more years old, while the other will have bridges of a decidedly more modern, less embellished style. The latter may have been

Just as in covered-wagon days, not every attempt at crossing the continent is successful.

constructed at the time of the interstate's construction for practical reasons, such as access to properties on that side of the freeway.

Somewhat related to the last point about structures to be found on old 66 has to do with construction methods used in building the highway itself. Road-building methods in the early- to mid-twentieth century were not as advanced as in later years, nor were funds as readily available. This is evident in the fact that the older highways such as Route 66 appear to follow the contours of the landscape more closely than more modern roads. Route 66 tends to rise and fall with the shallow hills and depressions in its path, and also tends to curve around prominent geographic features, such as mesas. Modern highways—the interstates especially—tend to exhibit considerable modification of the terrain. Blasting of hills and filling of depressions occur more regularly, while curves tend to be fewer and more gradual than in the case of the older highways, such as 66.

This results in a very important fact: there are many, many miles of Route 66 which have literally been cut to pieces by the interstates. Because the old highway took more turns and curves, while the modern interstate is much more direct, old portions of legitimate Route 66 are often found on both sides of a stretch of interstate highway, having been severed by the straighter cut of modern building methods. So, sometimes you'll need to keep the superslab to your left, and then you might need to cross to the other side and keep it to your right awhile in order to travel authentic Route 66 miles.

Another structural difference you're sure to note in many parts of Route 66 is the use of sectioned concrete rather than the continuous asphalt so prevalent today. This leads to a reassuring *thump, ka-thump, ka-thump* as your tires repeatedly hit the expansion seams in the roadway. You will find some excellent stretches of this type. For me, it evokes a nostalgia for road trips long past.

Finally, one last indication of an old highway alignment. In some cases, when a section of the Mother Road was taken out of service, the pavement was actually taken up and hauled away, leaving a scar in the

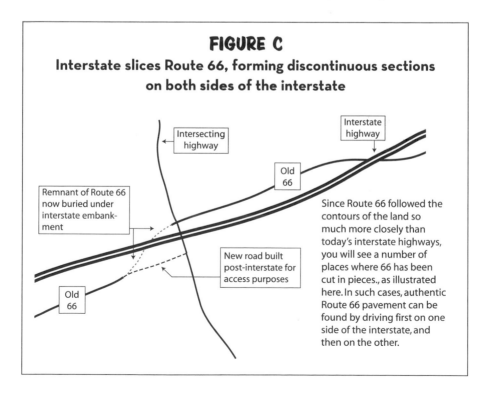

FIGURE C
Interstate slices Route 66, forming discontinuous sections on both sides of the interstate

Intersecting highway

Interstate highway

Old 66

Remnant of Route 66 now buried under interstate embankment

New road built post-interstate for access purposes

Old 66

Since Route 66 followed the contours of the land so much more closely than today's interstate highways, you will see a number of places where 66 has been cut in pieces., as illustrated here. In such cases, authentic Route 66 pavement can be found by driving first on one side of the interstate, and then on the other.

earth. There are several places between Chicago and Los Angeles where you can see evidence of this. In many cases, even decades later, the grass or other vegetation, which re-populates the old roadbed, exhibits a different color or texture than that on the undisturbed ground. This can be particularly pronounced in the more arid western portions of the route, where soil breakdown and other changes take place much more slowly than in the east. Keep your eyes peeled for swaths of vegetation that look just a little different than their surroundings, are one-to-two lanes wide, and alternately approach and diverge from the pavement on which you're driving. These are the ghosts of extinct roadways.

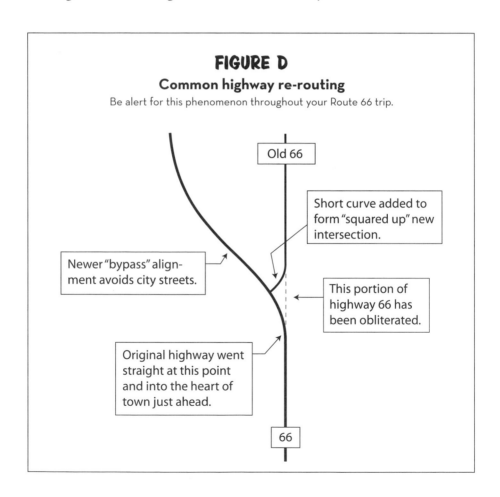

FIGURE D
Common highway re-routing
Be alert for this phenomenon throughout your Route 66 trip.

Old 66

Short curve added to form "squared up" new intersection.

Newer "bypass" align-ment avoids city streets.

This portion of highway 66 has been obliterated.

Original highway went straight at this point and into the heart of town just ahead.

66

TO SUMMARIZE OUR FISHING TIPS:

- Be aware of the general direction and next destination town of the highway. Look for older, less-used roads which take you to that next Route 66 town.

- Look for, and take advantage of, the brown-and-white Historic Route 66 signs. These are found not only in rural stretches, but sometimes as a feature of an interstate exit sign.

- In larger cities, be aware that the green Business Loop signs often are used to designate old 66 through town, albeit only the most recent alignment. But also note that following these signs strictly will always return you to the interstate. As you near the interstate after having passed through such a city, be on the lookout for a more authentic route by way of which you could continue without the need to return to the interstate.

- Original stretches of highway are often very close to the shoulder of the railroad tracks in the area. As a general rule, the closer to the railroad, the older the alignment.

- Look for telltale period structures. The prime years of Route 66 occurred prior to the mid-1950s, so look for travel-oriented businesses (or buildings which used to house such businesses) dating from the same era. Other helpful indications include small bridges crossing ravines, especially if constructed in the WPA era.

- Look at the character of the road itself. Older highways such as Route 66 followed the lay of the land, rising and falling with the natural contours, with little or no evidence of large-scale earth-moving. Also be observant of the road surface itself; a road constructed of poured concrete may be vintage Route 66.

- Finally, look for telltale signs in the local vegetation for evidence of old roadbed that is either severely overgrown or has had the pavement completely removed.

Keep the above recommendations in mind, and in no time at all you'll be ferreting out old alignments of Route 66 like a pro. Now, let's get to it!

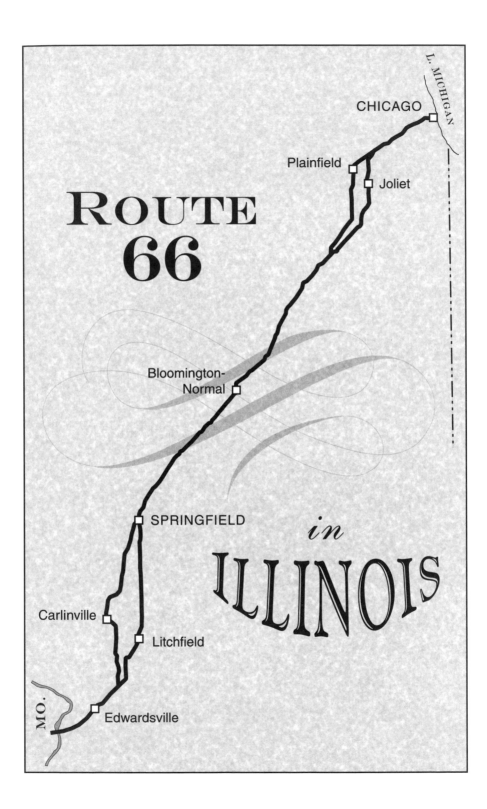

ILLINOIS

Route 66 begins in Illinois, near the shore of Lake Michigan. Of course, one can just as easily begin a tour of Route 66 from its western terminus in California, but there are good reasons not to. Traditionally, the Mother Road runs westward, from Chicago to Santa Monica, just as the United States of America has always been a westward-moving nation.

The U.S. began as a small grouping of states huddled along the Atlantic coast. To the west, the future states of Kentucky and Tennessee were wildernesses. Ohio and Indiana were settled by a few intrepid farmers for the value of their soil. Illinois was at that time considered the Northwest, and about as far west as any "American" semblance of civilization that existed. Over the generations, more and more of that West has been tamed, and the outposts of civil society have moved westward as well.

Traveling Route 66 from east to west, then, you will be following the well-worn path of this country's very development. The countryside will unfold before you—just as it did for the American people in their conquest of the continent several generations ago—almost as though you've mastered time travel. You will be richer for the experience, because you will come away feeling a kinship for the brave souls who pushed America's boundaries and made her what she is today.

Inseparable from the story of westward movement is the availability of water, as both transportation and sustenance. The development of

Overleaf: **One of many street corners that aren't as busy as they used to be. This one is in Dwight, Illinois. GPS: 41.09160,-88.43961**

Chicago as the outpost of civilization that it came to be was largely due to its location at the far end of a string of lakes and other navigable watercourses. For many reasons, water sources are conducive to settlement, while a scarcity of water is a severe hindrance to any development. It is no accident, then, that Chicago, St. Louis, and Los Angeles are the largest cities on Route 66—they are located at the route's three largest water sources: Lake Michigan, the Mississippi River, and the Pacific Ocean, respectively.

As you move westward on Route 66, the story of water is one which the observant traveler will read all along the way. West of St. Louis, there is a gradual decrease in water availability and a simultaneous decrease in population density. The rivers that Highway 66 encounters are smaller, and the cities that dwell on the banks of those rivers are proportionately smaller as well.

CHICAGO

The famous Chicago fire of 1871, which may or may not have been caused by Mrs. O'Leary's cow, utterly destroyed the city. Afterward, the city made a conscious effort to rebuild using more durable materials and

superior building methods so that the new Chicago would stand the ravages of time and nature. More than a century later, the city continues to take pride in its architecture. If you are at all interested in the art and science of architecture, it is worth your while to take advantage of some of the countless tours available. Some of the most well-known tours take place on the water, and launch from either the Chicago River or Lake Michigan. Other tours, which can be taken by bus, air, trolley, or bicycle, are also available.

Route 66 in Chicago originally began at the corner of Lake Shore Drive and Jackson Boulevard, right at the edge of Lake Michigan. At the time, Jackson ran both east and west. These days, however, Jackson is eastbound-only, except for the portion between Lake Shore and Michigan Avenue. This means that, for westbound travelers, your first couple of blocks will be on Jackson, but then you'll have to jog over to Adams Street for several blocks. As always, when Route 66 splits onto two one-way streets, I recommend backtracking in the other direction so you don't miss anything you'll be sorry about later.

Chicago was the scene of the World's Columbian Exposition in 1893, the grounds of which were designed by Frederick Law Olmstead, who also designed New York's Central Park, the Stanford University campus, and other acclaimed outdoor spaces. It was at the 1893 Exposition that George Washington Gale Ferris introduced the now-familiar Ferris wheel. The original was 250 feet tall and had 36 cars, each with a capacity of 60 passengers. That original wheel was later moved and used at the 1904 World's Fair in St. Louis. The two lions that graced the Exposition's Palace of Fine Arts building have since been made a part of the Art Institute of Chicago, near the spot where westbound Route 66 begins.

The Exposition of 1893 made some other memorable or even permanent imprints. It was there that Cracker Jack was first introduced, later immortalized in the 1908 song "Take Me Out to the Ball Game." Little Egypt, otherwise known as Catherine Devine, scandalized the fair by performing the hoochee-coochee in scanty attire (some say in the nude). The model for Aunt Jemima, a woman named Nancy Green, was a cook who advertised food products at the Exposition. Visitors enjoyed the first-ever public use of electric lighting at the Exposition, and it was also the scene where hot dogs were first served on buns. The vendor, A. L. Feuchtwanger, handed out white gloves with the sausages so that his customers' hands wouldn't be scalded. To his initial dismay, the gloves were not being returned as he had intended, and so he began substituting bread instead.

Chicago once had a less-than-savory reputation as the home of the underworld. Gangland slayings were not uncommon. The infamous St. Valentine's Day Massacre occurred in 1929 at the SMC Cartage Company

CHICAGO FIRE

The Chicago fire of 1871 is a well-known event. What most people don't know is that on the same date in nearby Peshtigo, Wisconsin, a forest fire consumed more than a million acres and claimed 1,182 lives. That's more than four times the lives lost in the Chicago fire (250). Over 400 of the dead were buried in mass graves due to the fact that, in many cases, there were not enough survivors left to identify the bodies.

at 2122 Clark Street. The building was demolished shortly after its use as the set for the 1967 film starring Jason Robards and George Segal.

Outlaw John Dillinger was gunned down by law enforcement officials on July 22, 1934, outside the **Biograph Theater** (2433 N. Lincoln Avenue). Dillinger had just viewed a gangster film there called *Manhattan Melodrama*. There is a plaque at the site to mark the occasion. The leader of the FBI contingent was Melvin Purvis, who committed suicide in 1960 using the same pistol given to him by his fellow officers to commemorate Dillinger's violent end.

Poster from Chicago's 1933 Century of Progress celebration.

In 1933, Chicago played host to the Century of Progress Exposition. It was there that Sally Rand made her splash by riding a white horse to the fair "attired," more or less, as Lady Godiva. Her main act consisted of an essentially nude dance routine, which included the strategic use of ostrich feathers. This caused such a sensation that she was able to parlay it into a career which lasted some thirty years.

The 1933 Exposition also brought the first aerial tramway, the first public demonstration of stereophonic sound reproduction, and the debut of Grant Wood's now-famous painting, *American Gothic*. A former student at the Art Institute of Chicago, Wood intended for his painting to be a sort of spoof of the Holbein style.

CHICAGO HOME-GROWN

Chicago gave birth to the mail-order catalog business about 100 years ago. This is the home of Sears Roebuck, Montgomery Ward, and Spiegel.

Other famous commercial names centered here include Marshall Field, Hertz Rent-A-Car, Wrigley, Yellow Cabs, Kimball Pianos, Schwinn Bicycles, J. L. Kraft, and Oscar Mayer. It was Gustavus Swift, of Swift & Company meat packing, who made the famous remark that he used every part of the pig but the squeal. The Oscar Mayer wienermobile first appeared here in 1936. It was the Chicago stockyards, and some of the deplorable conditions therein, that inspired Upton Sinclair to write his classic book *The Jungle*, which later resulted in the Pure Food and Drug Act of 1906.

In 1896, the zipper was invented in Chicago by Whitcomb L. Judson, who called it the "hookless fastener." In 1930, the pinball machine was invented here by the In & Outdoor Games Company, and the world-famous Twinkie was invented in nearby Schiller Park by James Dewar, manager of the Continental Baking Company's Hostess Bakery. Chicago was home to Scott Foresman and Company, publishers of the Dick and Jane readers, beginning in 1909. Brach's Candies originated in Chicago; in 1977, the heir to the Brach fortune checked out of the Mayo Clinic and was never seen or heard from again. With a fortune estimated at $45 million, she is considered the richest woman ever to have disappeared without a trace.

Ernest Hemingway and Edgar Rice Burroughs grew up in nearby Oak Park. Walt Disney was Chicago-born, but moved to Marceline, Missouri, as a young child because the neighborhood here was considered too rough. Chicago was the birthplace of Raymond Chandler, creator of the Philip Marlowe detective character, and known for works such as *The Big Sleep* and *Double Indemnity*. Nat "King" Cole grew up in Chicago after moving here from Montgomery, Alabama, as a child. In 1931, Dick Tracy was created by Stephen Gould for the *Chicago Tribune*.

CHICAGO ATTRACTIONS

Following is just a small sampling of local offerings that you might find interesting if you plan to spend significant time in America's "Second City" and its immediate surroundings.

Chicago Avenue Water Tower (Palmolive Building in Rear).

34   Chicago   60797

This postcard depicts Chicago's water tower, one of very few structures that survived the Great Fire of 1871.

The **Chicago Water Works** (163 E. Pearson St.) tower was one of the few structures in Chicago to survive the 1871 fire. It now houses a visitor center where you can purchase half-price day-of-performance theater tickets. There is also a gallery of photographs by some of Chicago's own native talent, as well as other welcome amenities.

The **Chicago History Museum** (1601 N. Clark St.) is the city's oldest cultural institution, established in 1856. The museum traces the city's development from outpost through the present day, with a permanent display pertaining to America in the Age of Lincoln. Also included is a passenger car from 1893, on which the public traveled to the World's Columbian Exposition that year.

Dearborn Station (47 W. Polk St.), a National Landmark in the Romanesque style dating to 1885, has been converted to a mall and marketplace.

The **Charnley-Persky House Museum** (1365 N. Astor St.), formerly a residence, was a joint project by Louis Sullivan and protégé Frank Lloyd Wright in the early 1890s.

Dating from the early 1880s, the **Pullman Historic District** is the country's first planned industrial community. Guided walking tours are available at the Historic Pullman Visitor Center (11141 S. Cottage Grove Ave.) Within the district are the **Greenstone Church**, the **Hotel**

Florence Museum, and the **A. Philip Randolph Pullman Porter Museum Gallery**. The Pullman Porter Museum features an outstanding collection of historical photographs.

The **Prairie Avenue Historic District** includes the **Clarke House Museum** (1827 S. Indiana Ave.), a Greek Revival design built in 1836 that is the oldest residence in the city. The **Glessner House Museum** (1800 S. Prairie Ave.) is nearby.

The residences in the 3800 block of **Alta Vista Terrace** are a little bit peculiar. Each house on one side of the street has a twin (with only minor variations) on the opposite side of the street, in exactly the same order. However, since the two series begin at opposite ends of the block, only in the center of the block do the designs directly across from one another match.

Chicago's **Hotel Intercontinental** (505 N. Michigan Ave.) started out in 1929 as the Medinah Athletic Club, and its world-class, lavishly decorated swimming pool is where Olympic gold medalist Johnny Weissmuller did some of his training during his years portraying Tarzan on the big screen.

The **Tribune Tower** (435 N. Michigan Ave.), which houses the famous newspaper, was completed in 1925 following a design competition among several distinguished architectural firms. The building includes fragments of some 120 architectural icons from around the world embedded in its walls, including the Taj Mahal, Palace of Westminster, and Great Wall of China.

Accessible through a subway-like entrance across from the Tribune building is the **Billy Goat Tavern** (430 N. Michigan Ave.), made famous by *Saturday Night Live*'s "cheese-boiga" routine.

Speaking of eateries, Chicago has myriads of them. But one of the more out-of-the-ordinary ones is the **Weber Grill Restaurant** (539 N. State St.). All meals are prepared on actual Weber-manufactured grills, much like one you may have at home. They're fired by charcoal, just like yours, and you can watch your food being prepared in "backyard" fashion. Surrounding the patio is a railing made from Weber grill cooking grates.

The **Polish Museum of America** (984 N. Milwaukee Ave.) tells the story of Polish immigration to the New World, and to Chicago in particular, said to be the home of the largest Polish population in the world outside of Warsaw.

The **National Italian American Sports Hall of Fame** (1431 W. Taylor St.) pays tribute to those Italian Americans making their mark in the world of sports. Inductees include the obvious, like Phil Rizutto and Rocky Marciano, but also some surprises such as Mary Lou Retton and Phil Mickelson.

The **International Museum of Surgical Science** (1524 N. Lake Shore Dr.) is housed in a landmark lakeside mansion constructed by one of the heirs to the Diamond Match Company fortune. The museum, which launched in 1954, features more than 10,000 display items and traces the art and science of surgery from its primitive beginnings to present day.

The long-closed **Castle Car Wash** (3801 W. Ogden Ave.), in the North Lawndale section of town, was an early automotive business (1925) that resembles a crenellated medieval castle.

GREATER CHICAGO

Nearby Oak Park is the home of the **Frank Lloyd Wright Home and Studio** (951 Chicago Ave.). Oak Park features more than twenty of Wright's designs and, of course, tours are available.

Oak Park was also the boyhood home of Ernest Hemingway. The **Ernest Hemingway Foundation of Oak Park** includes the famous author's birthplace (339 N. Oak Park Ave.) and a museum (200 N. Oak Park Ave.) containing first editions and Hemingway's diary. Visitors are encouraged to begin their tour at the museum; Hemingway's birth home is just a short walk away.

Within Greater Chicago is Des Plaines, home of the first franchised McDonald's restaurant. (The very first McDonald's, run by the McDonald brothers themselves, was in San Bernardino, California.) This was the first one run by Ray Kroc, a former salesman who liked the McDonalds' concept and bought them out. Closed in 1983, it reopened a couple of years later as the **McDonald's Museum** (400 N. Lee St.). Of course, McDonald's is the organization which started the demise of so many mom-and-pop enterprises, and so is actually antithetical to Route 66.

In the community of Niles is the **Leaning Tower of Niles** (6300 W. Touhy Ave.), a half-size replica of the world-famous Leaning Tower of Pisa. It was constructed in the 1930s, and is located on the grounds of the local YMCA.

THE BEGINNING OF ROUTE 66

Route 66 begins in downtown Chicago, by the shore of Lake Michigan. This end of Route 66 presents an immediate challenge, since eastbound and westbound lanes are actually on separate streets. Westbound 66 follows Adams Street, while eastbound 66 is a block to the south, on Jackson. Since you don't want to miss a thing, I suggest you drive on both streets to find as much of the old highway's flavor as possible prior to leaving downtown.

Some of that flavor is to be found at **Lou Mitchell's Restaurant** (565 W. Jackson Blvd.), a downtown Chicago eatery established in 1923, with its name spelled out in neon. It's on eastbound 66 (westbound travelers can turn left off of Adams at DesPlaines, then turn left again onto Jackson). Don't stop at Lou's if you're on a diet—patrons munch on free Milk Duds while waiting to be seated.

The easternmost end of Adams Street has the **Art Institute of Chicago** (111 S. Michigan Ave.) as its landmark,

Art Institute of Chicago poster from the 1930s.

where countless American artists have received formal training. The Art Institute includes such famous works in its collection as Edward Hopper's *Nighthawks* and Grant Wood's *American Gothic*.

When you're ready to leave Chicago and Lake Michigan, begin your adventure by proceeding west on Adams Street. Like all of the larger cities on Route 66, Chicago itself will not reveal much in the way of that Mother Road feel you are looking for—at least not when compared with the hundreds of smaller towns ahead of you. Cities like this were plotted out in the days well before automobile travel, so you and your car do not feel entirely welcome here.

Westbound Route 66 angles left (southwest) at Ogden Avenue, which is named for Chicago's first mayor, William B. Ogden. He took office in 1837, at the time the city was first incorporated.

Continuing on Ogden, you will pass through the communities of Cicero and Berwyn.

CICERO-BERWYN

Here in Cicero once stood a large muffler man figure holding a hot dog in front of Bunyon's. He was relocated to Atlanta, Illinois, a few years

Ogden Avenue, Cicero, Illinois. GPS: 41.8335, -87.77485

Ogden Avenue,
Berwyn, Illinois.
GPS: 41.82524,
-87.79866

ago, but there's still Henry's Drive-In, with a sign featuring a hot dog with fries.

There's not a great deal that differentiates Berwyn—it's suburban Chicago. But do check out **Berwyn's Toys & Trains** (7025 Ogden Ave.).

Berwyn is also home to a **Route 66 Museum** (7003 W. Ogden Ave.) that will help you kick off your Mother Road journey. There's even an electric-vehicle charging station right out front.

LYONS-McCOOK

Standing on what was once Highway 66 in Lyons is the **Hofmann Tower**, a circa-1908 concrete structure built by a local brewer as part of a recreational park, which today is home to the **Lyons Historical Commission Museum** (3910 Barry Point Rd.). Also in Lyons is the **Chicago Portage**

Route 66 spirit with Las Vegas flair.
GPS: 41.80014,-87.82993

National Historic Site (4800 Harlem Ave.), sometimes referred to as "Chicago's Plymouth Rock."

McCook now features a distinctive **city sign** patterned after the one made famous by Las Vegas, Nevada.

A short time after turning onto Joliet Road, you'll be forced to enter I-55. Interstate 55 follows the course of primary 66, which went toward the town of Plainfield but ultimately bypassed it.

For a time, Route 66 split into two separate routes northeast of Plainfield. The rightmost fork was the primary route when my 1957 atlas was printed, and went towards the city of Plainfield. The left fork was designated ALT 66, and headed south toward Joliet. Even at this early date, Route 66 was being realigned to bypass most cities and their associated traffic. At this time, the older ALT 66 passed directly through towns such as Joliet, Elwood, Wilmington, and Braidwood. At the same time, the map shows the newer primary route passing near, but not through, Plainfield and other towns, much as I-55 does today. The two alignments later converged again just southwest of the town of Gardner.

Both Plainfield and Joliet were on the Lincoln Highway (U.S. 30), an east–west artery that passed through here. So whichever path you take (and I recommend you explore both), it is here that you cross one of many routes of significance on your way west on 66. The Lincoln Highway was established in 1915, and was the first American transcontinental highway conceived with automobile travel in mind. Later, in the 1920s, when such interstate routes were designated with numbers, the Lincoln Highway officially became U.S. 30, but lovers of history still refer to it more commonly by its original name.

PLAINFIELD

If you enjoy hot rods and custom cars, Plainfield has them. This is the home of **Midwest Hot Rods** (23533 W. Main St.). They can either work with what you've got, or you can explore their inventory.

From I-55, exit Joliet Road toward Romeoville, where you'll soon merge with Highway 53 for the run into town.

ROMEOVILLE

Keep an eye out for the **White Fence Farm** (1376 Joliet Rd.), a sort of grand catering enterprise right beside the highway. They even have kiddie rides and a petting zoo on-site. There was a very large fiberglass chicken on a flatbed truck parked on the grounds the first time I passed through here.

Part of the décor at White Fence Farm.
GPS: 41.67522,-88.05698

Between Romeoville and Joliet is the **Stateville Correctional Center** (16830 Rte. 53). The grounds cover a huge, well-manicured expanse, and when you first glimpse it, you'll be excused for thinking you've come upon a university campus of some prestige.

Continue into Joliet on Highway 53, which will entail a left turn at Ruby Street and across the Des Plaines River. Note that 53 is one-way through a portion of town, so you'll want to explore the other half of it (northbound) a couple of blocks to the east (Scott Street).

JOLIET

Once nicknamed the City of Spires due to its many houses of worship (some 122 at one time), Joliet has in recent years taken a liking to gaming, and is now very much a center for casino gambling. Even the local

East of the Des Plaines River, Joliet, Illinois.
GPS: 41.54152,-88.08514

JOLIET
ILLINOIS

A - JOLIET AREA HIST. MUS. (incl ROUTE 66)
B - RIALTO THEATER

to Elwood, Wilmington

Joliet Prison (1125 Collins St.) has what might be called spires, though. The first prisoners were received within its depressing walls in 1858. Among the prison's more notorious prisoners were the duo Leopold and Loeb, who in 1924 murdered their victim solely for the challenge of committing the perfect crime. In the world of fiction, Joliet Prison gave John Belushi's character his nickname, Joliet Jake, in the movie *The Blues Brothers.*

There's another building in town that looks like a prison but is actually **Joliet Central High School** (201 E. Jefferson St.). Built in 1901, it has what some would call a Gothic flavor. In 2010, restoration work was completed on the four original 109-year-old front doors, with plans to tackle the other forty-one exterior doors in the near future.

In the past few years, Joliet has begun billing itself as the "Gateway to Route 66." The idea has merit since, as mentioned earlier, there's not much Mother Road flavor to be had in Chicago. Roadies from overseas, in particular, seem interested in the small-town experience that begins somewhere west of Chicago.

In 1940, the Dairy Queen ice cream chain was established, with its first store in Joliet. The now-familiar confection was actually first offered to the public two years earlier in a special "taste trial" in nearby Kankakee. Today, you can indulge the same impulse at **Rich & Creamy** (920 N. Broadway St.), a walk-up ice cream stand embedded within a linear park with walking paths. The place even includes figures of Jake and Elwood Blues, which have been installed on the roof.

The Rialto is a truly luxurious theater, sometimes called the "Jewel of Joliet." GPS: 41.52613,-88.08157

JOLIET ATTRACTIONS

Popularly known as the Jewel of Joliet, the **Rialto Square Theatre** (102 N. Chicago St.) is a restored 1926 vaudeville theater on the National Register. It contains the largest hand-cut chandelier in the U.S., and the inner lobby area was fashioned after the Hall of Mirrors at the Palace of Versailles. Tours are available.

Explore Joliet history at the **Joliet Area Historical Museum** (204 N. Ottawa St.), where there is a permanent

The Joliet Area Historical Museum inhabits a former church building in the heart of Joliet. GPS: 41.52832,-88.08315

Downtown Joliet. GPS: 41.53064,-88.08309

Route 66 exhibit and welcome center. The museum is located within a former Methodist church building, where old 66 crossed paths with the Lincoln Highway.

Take a free tour of blast furnace ruins at the **Joliet Iron Works Historic Site** (75 Columbia St.). This is also an access point for the 12.5-mile Illinois & Michigan Canal Trail, which connects Joliet's City Center to the Centennial Trail in Cook County.

In the South East Neighborhood Historical District on a street that was once called "Silk Stocking Row" is the **Jacob Henry Mansion** (20 S. Eastern Ave.), a forty-room manor house that was built in 1873 and decorated in lavish style. Today, it specializes in weddings, receptions, and similar events. The house is especially well turned-out at Christmastime.

ELWOOD

This is a very small community just south of Joliet. Was this the inspiration for the name of Joliet Jake Blues's brother, Elwood?

WILMINGTON

Wilmington has been nicknamed the Island City because the Kankakee River runs through town, forming an island, which is home to Island Park.

Wilmington is known among Route 66 fans as the home of the **Gemini Giant** (S. East St.). He's one of those giant figures, formerly muffler men, that used to populate American highways in the 1950s and '60s. This one has been decked out like an astronaut and stands in front of the

MUFFLER MEN

The Gemini Giant at Wilmington is a notable example of what are commonly referred to as "muffler men." Over twenty feet in height, muffler men were once plentiful across the American landscape, proliferating from the late 1950s to the early '60s as roadside icons for automotive muffler shops. Early on, some owners of these figures personalized them by customizing their clothing or even their facial features. In the case of the Gemini Giant, the oversized muffler held in the figure's hands was replaced by something else. Today, he holds a model rocket.

The Gemini Giant, as he appeared in better days. GPS: 41.31040,-88.13858

former Launching Pad Drive-In restaurant, where he has been attracting attention since 1965. Since the restaurant closed, both the building and the giant outside have been deteriorating. Make a visit before it's too late.

Fans of architectural curiosities might want to drive by the octagonal

Schutten-Aldrich House (600 Water St.). It dates from 1856, and is said to have sheltered runaway slaves as part of the famous Underground Railroad. The house is a private residence, so please be respectful.

FURTHER AFIELD

About halfway between Wilmington and Kankakee to the southeast is the **Kankakee River State Park** (5314 W. State Route 102), consisting of over 2,700 acres strung out along 11 miles of the river. This area takes its water seriously, offering canoe rentals and hosting an annual fishing derby, as well as the Kankakee River Valley Regatta each Labor Day.

Leaving Wilmington, you're still on Highway 53, and you'll have the railroad tracks running right alongside to let you know you're on an early alignment of highway.

BRAIDWOOD-GODLEY

Running through these neighboring towns are two versions of old 66 (Washington and Front Streets) separated by a set of railroad tracks right in-between.

Route 66 slices through the southeast corner of Braidwood. There is an annual cruise held here every August that's sponsored by the 1950s-themed **Polk-A-Dot Drive-In** (222 N. Front St.). The restaurant features figures of a few famous personas outside.

Some famous faces can be found at the Polk-A-Dot Drive-In, Braidwood. GPS: 41.26538,-88.21001

Godley is a tiny village right on the Will County-Grundy County line.

BRACEVILLE

According to my atlas, the town of Braceville was just west of Highway 66 in 1957. Today, it sits in a narrow corridor between old 66 and I-55, which is just to the west.

GARDNER

Gardner has a sort of "bypass" loop that skirts the southeast side of town and is easy to follow, but I recommend you enter town on Washington Street and meander through downtown, just as old 66 once did. The town of Gardner features a **two-cell jailhouse** (E. Mazon St.) dating from 1905.

 After Gardner, Route 66 runs directly alongside Interstate 55 toward Dwight.

> Approaching Dwight, be on the alert for a left turn just as the road you're on starts peeling away from the railroad track. That left turn takes you on the early alignment directly toward downtown, where there's much to see. The main highway will completely bypass the town of Dwight.

DWIGHT

In 1940, Eleanor Jarman was serving a 199-year sentence at a women's prison in Dwight for her involvement in several hold-ups. On August 8 of that year, "the Blond Tigress" escaped, never to be seen or heard from again. Although the **Dwight Correctional Center** (23813 E. 3200 North Rd.) closed in 2013, the facility is still standing.

On old Route 66 itself (not the bypass), near the corner of Chippewa, is a retired **service station** now displaying a collection of vintage gasoline pumps and signage. The décor has changed significantly over the years.

A - GAS STATION "DIORAMA"
B - AMBLER'S TEXACO STATION

DWIGHT
ILLINOIS

DWIGHT ATTRACTIONS

On the west side of town is **Ambler's Texaco Gas Station** (W. Waupansie St. and W. Mazon Ave.), a 1930s-era building restored in 2007 that now serves as the town's visitor center.

Downtown at the old Keeley Institute—now the **William Fox Developmental Center** (134 W. Main St.)—are five Tiffany-style windows, each of them portraying one of the five senses. Next door is the **First National Bank** (122 W. Main St.), designed by none other than Frank Lloyd Wright around 1905. Nearby is an impressive Romanesque railroad depot listed on the National Register, now housing the **Dwight Historical Society Museum** (119 W. Main St.).

Dwight's railroad depot, which now houses offices. GPS: 41.09276,-88.42821

The **Bank of Dwight** (132 E. Main St.) dates from 1855 and features a mural inside by Viennese artist Oskar Gross. Also notable is the windmill on the grounds of the **Prairie Creek Public Library** (501 Carriage

Roadside sight in Dwight, Illinois. GPS: 41.09158,-88.43971

House Ln.), which dates from 1896.

Every September, Dwight hosts a basset hound parade called the **Basset Waddle** that benefits Basset Rescue, an organization specializing in finding homes for neglected or abused dogs.

 Shortly after passing the Mt. Olivet Catholic Cemetery south of town, you'll find yourself running right beside I-55 again.

> Just as you did at Dwight a little earlier, be on the lookout for a left turn that keeps you parallel to the railroad tracks—that's the old route that'll take you through the heart of town.

ODELL-CAYUGA

When I first passed through Odell in the 1990s, the old fuel station here was sagging and dilapidated. But thanks to the efforts of donors and volunteers, Odell's **Standard Station** (400 S. West St.) has since been restored for your enjoyment. Don't fail to stop and take some photographs.

A few years ago, a **tunnel** was discovered (or re-discovered) that used

Once in ruins, this station was beautifully restored by dedicated volunteers.
Odell, Illinois. GPS: 41.00201,-88.52872

to run beneath Route 66 so that schoolchildren and churchgoers could cross the busy street safely. Today, you can plainly see the entrance. Odell is small enough that you can take some time and thoroughly explore most of its streets.

Between Odell and Cayuga, there are several instances of old retired lanes of Route 66 running beside you. Just north of Cayuga is a **restored barn** bearing a Meramec Caverns advertisement.

Cayuga, Illinois. GPS: 40.94101,-88.58265

You know how to do this now—as you approach the northern outskirts of Pontiac, the road you're on will start to wander away from the railroad tracks. Be alert for a left turn that more closely follows the railroad tracks in order to maximize your adventure. At that junction is the Old Log Cabin Inn.

Advertising barn near Cayuga, Illinois. GPS: 40.94326,-88.58144

PONTIAC

The first thing you'll see when you enter Pontiac from Cayuga is the **Old Log Cabin Inn** (18700 Historic Rte. 66). This place has gained some renown for not giving up when the highway was re-aligned and the new Route 66 was at their back door. The owners actually picked up and rotated the building toward the new road, barely missing a beat. The older roadway can be seen behind the present orientation, near the railroad tracks, as befits an early highway alignment.

At the **Pontiac Correctional Center** (700 W. Lincoln St.), inmates manufactured Route 66 shields to meet public demand following the highway's decommission in Illinois in 1977.

PONTIAC ATTRACTIONS

The **Route 66 Association of Illinois Hall of Fame & Museum** (110 W. Howard St.) was established here in 2004, in an old city hall/firehouse complex. Featured in the museum's collection are several artifacts from the now-demolished Wishing Well Motel, which for years did business in suburban Chicago. Includ-

Old Log Cabin Inn, at the northern outskirts of Pontiac, Illinois. GPS: 40.89834,-88.62368

ed are both the original sign and the iconic wishing well itself. Also in the museum's collection is Bob Waldmire's modified school bus, on which the artist logged many Mother Road miles and even lived in at times. Bob passed away in 2009, but his postcards and other artwork are still popular up and down the route. He even left a partially completed mural here at the museum.

Pontiac's Route 66 Museum is something you won't want to miss. GPS: 40.88086,-88.62911

In 2009, a group called the Walldogs painted several murals scattered throughout town. One year later, the town showed its appreciation by opening the **International Walldog Mural and Sign Art Museum** (217 N. Mill St.). The museum pays tribute to the history and evolution of mural and sign art.

The **Pontiac-Oakland Museum and Resource Center** (205 N. Mill St.), established in 2011, is a relative newcomer to Pontiac's collection of

Artist and Route 66 advocate Bob Waldmire is immortalized on this mural in downtown Pontiac. GPS: 40.88067,-88.62868

museums. A collector of Pontiac automobiles thought it would be appropriate to move his collection to the town of Pontiac for display, and we are beneficiaries of that decision.

The **Jones House** (314 E. Madison St.) is the second brick home built in Pontiac, completed in 1858. It bears the name of Henry C. Jones, newspaper publisher and founder of the Pontiac Light, Heat, and Power Company. The house is currently owned and operated by the Livingston County Historical Society.

The **Catharine V. Yost Museum & Arts Center** (298 W. Water St.) is a Queen Anne-style home from the 1890s, containing most of the Yost family possessions, some of which are much older than the house itself.

A Buick in Pontiac.

CHENOA

Chenoa is home to the **Matthew T. Scott House** (227 N. 1st Ave.), the home of Matthew Scott and his wife, Julia. Matthew was an enterprising farmer, businessman, and town founder, and Julia held office in the Daughters of the American Revolution. Organized in 1890 and chartered by Congress in 1896, the DAR offers membership to "any woman eighteen years or older, regardless of race, religion, or ethnic background, who can prove lineal descent from a patriot of the American Revolution."

The **Chenoa Historical Society Museum** (239 Green St.) houses a collection of artifacts that includes a very large, forty-five-star U.S. flag, with each star measuring about nine inches across.

LEXINGTON

There's an old alignment of Route 66 close to the railroad tracks called Memory Lane, but it's only open to auto traffic during special events. You can pay a visit, however, by turning east on Wall Street and driving for a couple of blocks.

Part of the Memory Lane display in Lexington, Illinois. GPS: 40.65040,-88.77953

Lexington has an old neon sign announcing itself upon your arrival in town. On the north side of Lexington, Route 66 fans have created a sort of **"Memory Lane" exhibit** (Parade Rd.), with a stretch of old 66 roadway set aside and enhanced with period billboards, reproductions, and even a Burma Shave sign.

Downtown Lexington. GPS: 40.64156,-88.78521

The **Patton Cabin** (near the intersection of N. Cherry St. and Harrison St.) is a log structure, parts of which date from 1829. It was used as an official polling place as early as 1831, and is the oldest building in the county. Originally located about a mile and a half southeast of its current spot, the cabin was reassembled in Keller Park in 1969.

The southern edge of Lexington.
GPS: 40.63672,-88.79412

TOWANDA

Towanda is small, so explore it thoroughly; there are fragments of old 66 on both sides of the main alignment. In recent years, a walking/biking path called **Route 66 Linear Park** has been set up beside the newer bypass alignment of 66.

BLOOMINGTON-NORMAL

Unfortunately, Route 66 has been broken up where it enters town from the northeast. Although the route used to follow the railroad tracks for a fair distance in the early days, the downtown alignment was bypassed many years ago and some of the old alignment has been obliterated. Today you're faced with a "stair-step" effect if you want to stay close to the more colorful early alignment. From Shelbourne, try taking a left at Henry and a right onto Pine, then a left on Linden, right on Willow, and left onto Main Street.

NORMAL
ILLINOIS

SHELBURN

A - TUDOR STATION
B - McCLEAN CO. HIST. MUSEUM

BLOOM-INGTON
ILLINOIS

to
Shirley

When two towns have to coexist this closely (they share the same Main Street), it's natural for a rivalry to develop. Normal is home to Illinois State University, and Bloomington has Illinois Wesleyan College.

Bloomington seems to be able to claim more famous sons than Normal. These include the fictional Colonel Henry Blake from *M*A*S*H*; author and publisher Elbert Hubbard, who perished on the Lusitania; and Pawnee Bill, a.k.a. Gordon W. Lillie, who produced Wild West shows in the first decade of the 1900s, similar to what Buffalo

Pine Street in Normal, Illinois.
GPS: 40.51771,-88.98050

Bill became famous for. Adlai Stevenson also grew up here; feel free to view the **Adlai Stevenson home** (901 N. McLean St.) during your visit. Bloomington is also the birthplace of the Republican Party, which was organized here at a convention in 1856.

> The route in Bloomington is split between northbound and southbound streets, with Center Street carrying the westbound traveler and Main Street carrying eastbound traffic.

NORMAL ATTRACTIONS

Sprague's Super Service (305 Pine St.), a Tudor-style gas station from the 66 era, has been placed on the Nation Register of Historic Places. It's unusual in that it includes a caretaker's apartment upstairs.

Check out the Art Deco-influenced **Normal Theater** (209 W. North St.), which first opened its doors in 1937. It's on the National Register and has been fully restored to its original beauty.

Normal also has a one-room 1899 schoolhouse, the **Eyestone School** (N. Adelaide St.), that you can tour.

BLOOMINGTON ATTRACTIONS

Bloomington is home to the **Beer Nuts plant** (103 N. Robinson St.). Invented here in the 1930s and originally called "Virginia Redskins," Beer Nuts were a rousing success from the get-go. You can't actually view them being made at the plant, but you can visit the gift shop and watch a video about them.

Also in Bloomington is the **David Davis Mansion State Historic Site**

David Davis Mansion, Bloomington, Illinois.
GPS: 40.48280,-88.98062

(1000 Monroe Dr.). The twenty-room Victorian home, named Clover Lawn, was built in 1872 for U.S. Supreme Court Justice David Davis. Decorated by his wife, Sarah, the home features original furnishings and stencil work. It also has features which were quite luxurious at the time, such as indoor plumbing and a central heating system. You are urged to allow at least ninety minutes to tour this gem.

The **McLean County Museum of History** (200 N. Main St.) is in the former courthouse, which was constructed from 1901 to 1903. The museum includes a hands-on area where visitors can experience such age-old tasks as beating a rug and pushing a steel plow.

The **Prairie Aviation Museum** (2929 E. Empire St.) includes several restored aircraft and a collection of Charles Lindbergh memorabilia, and also offers flight simulation.

At the south end of town, just after Center and Main Streets rejoin one another, turn right onto I-55 Business Loop (S. Veterans Parkway) to continue your journey west. Many travelers enter I-55 just outside of town and then exit in a few miles, near the town of Shirley. However, follow this route if you want to stay off the superslab: from S. Veterans Parkway, turn right onto Fox Creek Road, cross over I-55, and then take the first left turn onto the west frontage road/Beich Road. This will take you into Shirley.

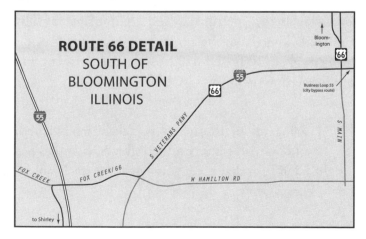

ROUTE 66 DETAIL
SOUTH OF
BLOOMINGTON
ILLINOIS

A subtle reminder that cross-country travel did not always involve automobiles.
Shirley, Illinois.

SHIRLEY

In Shirley, we have the **Funk Prairie Home and Funk Gem & Mineral Museum** (10875 Prairie Home Ln.). The Funk Prairie Home was built from 1863 to 1864, and includes the first-ever electric kitchen island (added a bit later, of course). The Funk Gem & Mineral Museum is located on the same twenty-seven-acre property and features a collection of gemstones, fossils, and petrified wood accumulated by Illinois state senator and cattle king Lafayette Funk II. Tours are by prior arrangement, so call ahead at (309) 827-6792 for an appointment and detailed instructions for getting there.

Leaving town, Route 66 is tightly sandwiched between I-55 on the left and railroad tracks on the right. A few miles past Shirley, look for a right-hand turn that takes you across the tracks into the sleepy community of Funks Grove.

FUNKS GROVE

Here you'll see the remains of a **small country store** and a **tiny old rail-road depot** (Funks Rd.) that was relocated from nearby Shirley. The Funk family has been tapping trees and making what they call "sirup" for well over 100 years. Stop in at the store and pick some up.

Funks Grove, Illinois. GPS: 40.35618,-89.11749

McLEAN

One of two towns named McLean on Route 66 (the other is in Texas), the Illinois McLean is home to the **Dixie Travel Plaza** (400 Dixie Rd.), a truck stop that started life as a much more humble travel amenity in 1928. Across from the Dixie is a small **railroad depot** (200 E. Dixie Rd.) that has been restored, and now contains a shop for train hobbyists.

Exit McLean on the highway that parallels the railroad tracks.

Heading into Atlanta, the railroad tracks are on your right. After the road begins to veer left and away from the tracks, look for a right turn to take you through the heart of downtown (Sycamore Street, which will turn into Arch Street).

ATLANTA

Atlanta was at one time called Xenia, as evidenced by the modest **Xenia Park** in the heart of town.

ATLANTA ATTRACTIONS

The centerpiece of downtown Atlanta is now a giant muffler man, called the **Bunyon Giant** (103 SW Arch St.), that was moved here from Cicero a few years ago. Across the street from the muffler man are the **Route 66 Arcade Museum** (108 SW Arch St.) and the **Atlanta Museum** (112 SW Arch St.). The Arcade Museum features several vintage arcade games, all of which can be played for twenty-five cents each (when they're in working order). The Atlanta Museum specializes in local history, including lots of 66-related memorabilia.

The distinctive **Atlanta Public Library** (100 Race St.)

Downtown Atlanta, Illinois.
GPS: 40.26078,-89.23143

Atlanta's public library is distinctive for having eight sides.
GPS: 40.26043,-89.23199

was built with an eight-sided plan. The circa-1909 Seth Thomas clock tower standing beside it came from a near-by school building. Unlike most of its electrified peers, the clock is still wound by hand.

Atlanta was fortunate enough not long ago to host a sort of mural-making festival. You'll see a number of buildings throughout the town that have had **murals** added to their sides. This project was spearheaded by a group of signmakers calling themselves Letterheads.

The town also boasts the circa-1904 **J. H. Hawes Grain Elevator Museum** (301 SW 2nd St.). The museum claims that the grain elevator is standing on its original site, and describes it as a "skyscraper of the prairie." The museum is set up to actually demonstrate some of the arcane workings of the place, so you may want to take in the tour and lecture. I'll bet every grade-schooler around here remembers coming here on a field trip.

Atlanta's latest attraction is the restored **Palms Grill Café** (110 SW Arch St.), a combination restaurant and museum that has been restored to look and feel just like the original 1934 location.

You can't get lost in a town like this, so I recommend doing some exploring.

Atlanta, Illinois. GPS: 40.26023,-89.23169

LAWNDALE

Lawndale is a very small community beside Route 66, where the highway crosses Kickapoo Creek.

 Again, the railroad tracks are to your right. Just before arriving in town, take a left onto Kickapoo Street.

LINCOLN

This is said to be the only town named after Abraham Lincoln while he was still alive. Upon hearing of this plan, Lincoln remarked that he never knew of anything named Lincoln that amounted to much. He was personally involved in drawing up the legal papers establishing the town, and he also practiced some law here in the 1850s. For a time, there were actually two separate towns here, Postville and Lincoln, which were officially merged in 1865.

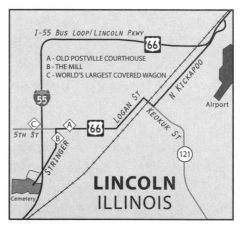

LINCOLN ATTRACTIONS

While in Lincoln, look for **The Mill restaurant** (738 S. Washington St.) on the far side of town. The Mill dates from the early days

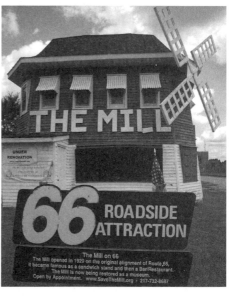

The Mill restaurant, Lincoln, Illinois.
GPS: 40.14357,-89.38295

Lincoln, Illinois, is home to the World's Largest Covered Wagon. GPS: 40.14877,-89.38680

of the route (1929), and features a lighted, revolving Dutch-style windmill. There is a long-range plan afoot to restore the building and include a museum inside.

Lincoln is now home to the **World's Largest Covered Wagon** (1750 5th St.), recognized as such by the *Guinness Book of Records*. The wagon was built several years ago, and after completion it was displayed for a time in the Divernon area with a huge figure of Abraham Lincoln in the driver's seat. It now has a permanent home on the grounds of the Best Western Lincoln Inn.

Reconstructed in 1953 on the site of the original is a replica courthouse at the **Postville Courthouse State Historic Site** (914 5th St.). The original, constructed in 1840, was frequented by Abraham Lincoln during his years of practicing law in the area. In 1848, however, the county seat was moved to Mount Pulaski, and a new courthouse was erected there. The old Postville Courthouse was acquired in 1929 by Henry Ford, who dismantled it and reassembled it in his Greenfield Village complex in Dearborn, Michigan. The replica you see today was created in the 1950s.

Postville Courthouse, Lincoln, Illinois. GPS: 40.14732,-89.38097

Incidentally, Greenfield Village is of interest in itself, having more than 200 historic buildings of all sorts spread over an eighty-one-acre tract.

At the **Heritage In Flight Museum** (1351 Airport Rd.), barracks that once housed German prisoners of war are now a museum filled with aircraft and other artifacts dating as early as World War I.

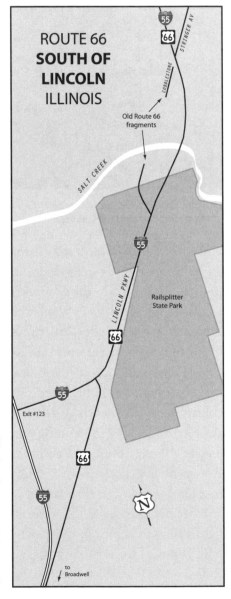

FURTHER AFIELD

Southeast of Lincoln (or due east of Springfield, if you prefer) is the city of Decatur. It was in Decatur that the Lincoln family first settled after coming to the state from Indiana. Scattered through Decatur are several Lincoln statues: *Finding the Biggest Man* (101 N. Water St.); *Lincoln's First Speech* (N. Main at Merchant St.); *Wake Up Lincoln* (130 N. Water St.); and *The Railsplitter Candidate* and *Troosting Lincoln* (both on S. Park St.).

The **Macon County History Museum and Prairie Village** (5580 N. Fork Rd.) includes a train depot and print shop, as well as a log courthouse dating from 1830 where Lincoln is said to have tried some cases.

The **James Millikin Homestead** (125 N. Pine St.) was built in 1876 in an ornate and rather Gothic style, which contrasts sharply with the more austere homes surrounding it, some of which seem to have been inspired by Frank Lloyd Wright's Prairie School. The home, which is open on weekends, has been fully restored and is listed on the National Register.

The Muellers, a family of German immigrants who lived in Decatur, played a significant role as inventors in both the nineteenth and twentieth centuries. The list of things they either invented or improved includes plumbing fixtures, roller skates, soda fountains, auto parts, and munitions. Visit the **Hieronymus Mueller Museum** (420 W. Eldorado St.) while you're in town.

Decatur was also the original home of the Chicago Bears professional football team, originally known as the Decatur Staleys.

Leaving Lincoln, you'll rejoin I-55 Business Loop. But just before merging onto Interstate 55, you should take a left turn onto a frontage road that closely follows the railroad tracks toward Broadwell.

BROADWELL-ELKHART

Broadwell is the former site of the **Pig-Hip Restaurant and Motel** (100 N. Frontage Rd.). The owner, Ernie Edwards, had turned it into a museum post-retirement, but unfortunately it burned down in 2007. Today there

is a large monument stone with a commemorative plaque.

Continue to parallel the railroad tracks through Elkhart.

Former site of the Pig Hip, Broadwell, Illinois. GPS: 40.06720, -89.44456

WILLIAMSVILLE

The railroad tracks are to the left. Take a left turn onto Taylor Street in order to explore downtown. However, not only does "old" Route 66 not pass completely through town due to fragmentation, but even the newer bypass alignment has been broken off. You'll need to backtrack toward the middle part of town and enter Interstate 55 using Stuttle Road to leave Williamsville and continue on your way west.

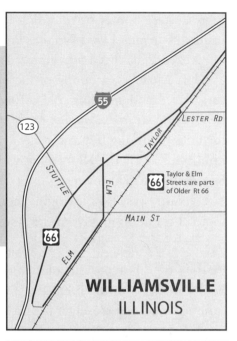

WILLIAMSVILLE
ILLINOIS

The **Williamsville Historical Museum** (104 S. Elm St.) was fashioned from a pair of railroad cars. Next door is the old railroad depot, which is now home to the **Williamsville Public Library** (217 N. Elm St.).

After passing through and exploring Williamsville, you'll be forced to enter the interstate for a short distance. Exit again at the I-55 Business Loop in order to pass through the town of Sherman.

SHERMAN

You probably won't be able to tell from the highway where Sherman's

Sherman, Illinois. GPS: 39.85678,-89.61617

business district is. If you want to see it, make a left turn onto E. Andrew Road and then a right onto 1st Street, where you'll find a small central district of only about four square blocks.

After passing through Sherman proper, you'll encounter **Carpenter Park**, which includes a quarter-mile section of pre-1936 Mother Road pavement near its eastern edge. That stretch of road has been closed to vehicular traffic since that time, so it's more of an archaeological site for Route 66, including some bridge abutments where it crossed the Sangamon River.

After Carpenter Park, you'll enter Springfield via N. Peoria Road/ N. 9th Street.

SPRINGFIELD

There is a very early (pre-1930) alignment through town that leaves the city on what is now Highway 4. However, because that alignment was superceded so early, most roadies traverse Springfield via the later alignment, which uses 5th and 6th Streets downtown and has more surviving Route 66-era places of business.

The Illinois state capital was moved here from Vandalia in 1857, by a group which included Abraham Lincoln. Today, Springfield is still the

Now closed, the former Shea's Gas Station Museum still beckons to Route 66 travelers in Springfield. GPS: 39.82928,-89.63793

center of the Lincoln universe, as well as being nearly the exact geographic center of the state (the precise center being about twenty-eight miles northeast, in Logan County).

Springfield boasts more Lincoln sites than any other city, which is not at all surprising when you consider that the man lived and worked here for many years before departing to pursue the presidency. Several of these Lincoln sites can be taken in rather conveniently via **Springfield Trolley Tours** (229 W. Allen St.)

According to numerous sources, "the only home Mr. Lincoln ever owned" is at 8th and Jackson Streets. Tour tickets for the home are free at the **Lincoln Home National Historic Site Visitor Center** (426 S. 7th St.). While you're in town, be sure to also visit Lincoln's law office, the **Lincoln-Herndon Law Office** (1 SE Old State Capitol Plaza). The railroad depot here in Springfield, the **Great Western Depot** (930 E.

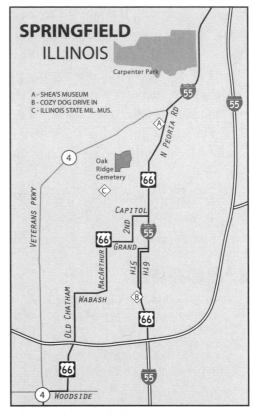

Another Illinois giant, this one in Springfield. GPS: 39.76416,-89.68002

Monroe St.), is where Lincoln gave his eloquent departure speech before leaving permanently to assume the presidency. And the Lincoln family tomb is at the **Oak Ridge Cemetery** (1441 Monument Ave.), where you

Oak Ridge Cemetery, final resting place of our sixteenth president, Springfield, Illinois. GPS: 39.81996,-89.65415

can walk the solemn halls of the mausoleum and rub the nose of Lincoln's bronze likeness for luck, as many have before you. The cemetery even offers a souvenir kiosk where you can indulge your lust for more Lincoln memorabilia. Topping it all off, the **Abraham Lincoln Presidential Library and Museum** (112 N. 6th St.), which opened in 2004, houses the largest collection of Lincoln artifacts ever assembled.

For Route 66 followers, the hands-down centerpiece of Springfield is the **Cozy Dog Drive-In** (2935 S. 6th St.). Ed Waldmire, who established a small chain of restaurants here, invented the corn dog while serving military duty at Amarillo, Texas (also on Highway 66). After the war, he started serving his treat—which he originally wanted to call the "Crusty Cur"—in his hometown of Springfield in 1949. Today, the Cozy Dog on Route 66 (just north of its original location) is still open, and still run by members of the Waldmire family.

SPRINGFIELD ATTRACTIONS

The **Illinois State Military Museum** (1301 N. MacArthur Blvd.) salutes the Illinois National Guard through exhibits of uniforms, equipment, weaponry, and photographs housed in a Civilian Conservation Corps structure. By far the most notable item in the museum's collection is the wooden leg worn by General Santa Anna. The story goes that the general and a small group of his men were having a lunch of roasted chicken when an Illinois detachment surprised them. The general had just enough time to mount his horse and escape, but was forced to leave behind his artificial leg and the remains of the chicken. Fortunately for him, he had a spare one just like it elsewhere—the leg, that is.

In front of the Illinois Exhibits building at the state fairgrounds is a thirty-foot-tall statue of a clean-shaven Abraham Lincoln entitled *The Rail Splitter* (801 Sangamon Ave.). It was created in 1968 by Carl W. Rinnus, a Springfield native.

Old Courthouse, Springfield. GPS: 39.80169,-89.64856

The **Old State Capitol State Historic Site** (S. 6th St. and E. Adams St.) is where President Lincoln delivered his famous "House Divided" speech, and where he lay in state following his assassination in 1865. It was also the scene of the 1858 Lincoln-Douglas debates.

The **Dana-Thomas House** (301 E. Lawrence Ave.) is a home designed by Frank Lloyd Wright in 1902. It still has most of its original furnishings, including art glass, and is considered one of Wright's earliest experiments in what would later become known as his Prairie Style. Every year on October 8, citizens turn out to celebrate the birthday of the lady of the house, socialite Susan Lawrence Dana, with an open house, live music, and more.

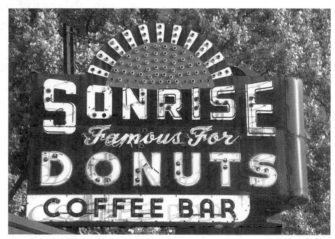

The **Executive Mansion** (410 E. Jackson St.) is the nation's third-oldest, continuously occupied governor's residence. Many rooms are open to public viewing, including the state dining room, library, ballroom, and the Lincoln bedroom.

Roadside evangelism, Springfield, Illinois.
GPS: 39.79029,-89.64395

The **Vachel Lindsay Home** (603 S. 5th St.) is the birthplace of the native Springfield artist and poet Vachel Lindsay, who resided there until his death—by suicide—in 1931.

The **Oliver P. Parks Telephone Museum** (529 S. 7th St.) houses a collection assembled by a longtime Ma Bell employee. At last count, there were 117 phones on display here, including such classics as wooden wall-mounted phones, candlestick models, early coin phones, and even a switchboard.

The interior of the **Lawrence Memorial Library** (101 E. Laurel St.) was designed by Frank Lloyd Wright, and has been restored to its original luster.

The **Route 66 Twin Drive-In Theater** (1700 Recreation Dr.) shows two features nightly (when in season), beginning at dusk. The theater is actually part of a larger recreational complex called Knight's Action Park, which includes a water slide, driving range, picnic areas, pedal boats, and more.

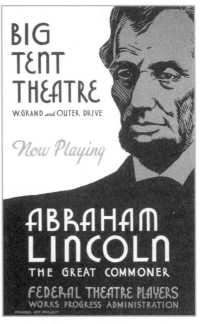

Back on 66: Leaving Springfield, you have a treat—there are two distinct Route 66 alignments here to enjoy. The more modern route takes you south out of town paralleling I-55,

Depression-era artwork featuring Springfield's most prominent citizen.

through towns including Divernon, Litchfield, and Mount Olive. This was the course of the highway during most of its years of existence. However, there is an older alignment, passing through Auburn, Carlinville, and Gillespie—and today bearing the number 4—which carried traffic in the 1920s. In fact, that road predated Route 66 and was a major thoroughfare in the area years earlier. Because of the very early realignment (1930), the older highway does not have much surviving 66-era road architecture, and is harder to follow. However, it is certainly worth driving, as it is easier to imagine yourself in an Illinois long gone. If you follow Highway 4, keep alert for a **section of very old, brick-paved roadway**, just over a mile long, north of Auburn.

The narrative immediately following takes you on the older alignment along Highway 4. If you choose to take the more modern route through Litchfield (my personal preference), you can pick up the account for that segment at the town of Glenarm.

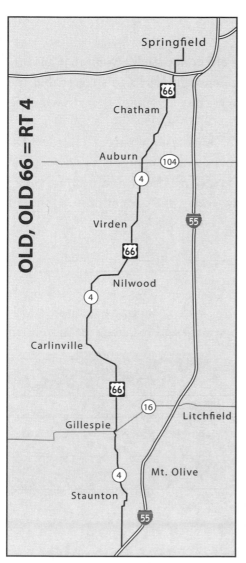

OLD, OLD 66 = RT 4

Springfield
66
Chatham
Auburn 104
4
Virden 55
66
Nilwood
4
Carlinville
66
16 Litchfield
Gillespie
4 Mt. Olive
Staunton
55

CHATHAM-AUBURN

Between Chatham and Auburn, be on the lookout for a right turn onto Snell Road, and then a left onto Curran. This is an example of an old section of highway that predated Route 66, then became part of 66 from 1926 to 1930, and then was bypassed in favor of a more direct alignment to the east. The bricks were not added to the roadway until 1932. According to the Auburn Historical Society, the town did not have paved streets until 1928.

One of Auburn's esteemed sons was Emil "Dutch" Leonard, who was a major league baseball pitcher for twenty years in the 1930s, '40s, and '50s. He is buried in **Auburn Cemetery** (15125 Kennedy Rd.).

THAYER-VIRDEN-GIRARD

In 2010, Girard lobbied hard to win the title of "Single Best Town in America" in a contest sponsored by Kraft Foods. Although it was among the finalists, Girard ultimately lost out to Three Lakes, Wisconsin. While in Girard, consider a stop at **Doc's Soda Fountain** (133 S. 2nd St.), a circa-1880 former pharmacy that is now a soda fountain and pharmacy museum.

NILWOOD-CARLINVILLE

Nilwood is known for its **stretch of old concrete highway** that has turkey tracks imprinted in it. There are enough tracks to suggest that the turkey was not just crossing the street, but dancing or shadow-boxing instead.

Carlinville's **town square** and adjacent areas are part of a historic district recognized since 1976. The town's spiritual center is a gazebo in the center of the square, built on the same spot as a former courthouse where Abraham Lincoln once practiced law. Today, the gazebo hosts a series of concerts held during the summer months.

CARLINVILLE ATTRACTIONS

The **Macoupin County Courthouse** (200 E. Main St.), a.k.a. the Million-Dollar White Elephant Courthouse, is said to have cost more than

This nineteenth-century jail was still in use as recently as 1988. Carlinville, Illinois.
GPS: 39.27870,-89.87954

ten times its original estimate, taking more than two years to build and forty years to pay for. It has some rather overwrought features, including iron doors (some weighing in at over a ton) and interior trim made of either iron or stone throughout. It was at one time the largest courthouse in the United States. The courthouse project also included a new jailhouse that also has some interesting features, such as a crenellated roofline and leftover cannonballs embedded in the walls (construction was completed in 1869, not long after the Civil War). The jailhouse, amazingly, was still in use as recently as 1988.

Nearby is the **Loomis House** (118 E. Side Sq.), a fifty-room former hotel by the same architect who designed the town's courthouse and jail. The Loomis has been preserved and today contains a number of local businesses.

More on the pragmatic side is **Carlinville's Standard Addition**, a housing subdivision comprised of one of the largest aggregates of Sears Roebuck catalog homes to be found anywhere—more than 100 of them. This community has inspired a number of books and documentaries.

The **Macoupin County Historical Museum** (920 W. Breckenridge St.) is in the 1883 Anderson Mansion, which features a stained glass window purchased at the 1893 Columbian Exposition in Chicago. A schoolhouse, church, and blacksmith shop are also on the property.

There is a small stone marker in front of Carlinville's **United Methodist Church** (201 S. Broad St.) designating the spot where Abraham Lincoln delivered a speech in 1858 while campaigning for a Senate seat against Stephen A. Douglas.

GILLESPIE-BENLD-SAWYERVILLE

These three communities share a mining heritage; at least three coal mines were established in this area to serve the needs of the railroads in the first decade of the twentieth century. A paved recreational path—the **Benld-Gillespie Bike Trail**—connects these two towns along what was once an interurban rail line. To find it in Gillespie, turn left onto Clark

Street from Highway 4 (on the south side of town) and go about two and a half blocks. The trail entry is on the right.

Benld's strange name comes from the first five letters of the name of its founder, Ben L. Dorsey. He and his son of the same name are buried in the city cemetery.

STAUNTON

Staunton is the home of **Henry's Rabbit Ranch** (1107 Historic Rte. 66), which features a sign that pays subtle homage to the billboard at the Jackrabbit Trading Post (see page 371) many miles to the west in Arizona. Look for the Campbell's "Humpin' to Please" truck trailer here, along with lots more roadie stuff on display. Also adding to the ambience is **VW Ranch**, a display of four-wheeled rabbits upended as a salute to the Cadillac Ranch in Texas (see page 289). By the way, they really do raise rabbits here—the four-legged variety. The sign for the Stanley Cour-tel,

Henry's Rabbit Ranch, Staunton, Illinois. GPS: 39.00394,-89.78176

Part of the collection at Henry's Rabbit Ranch, Staunton, Illinois. GPS: 39.00394,-89.78176

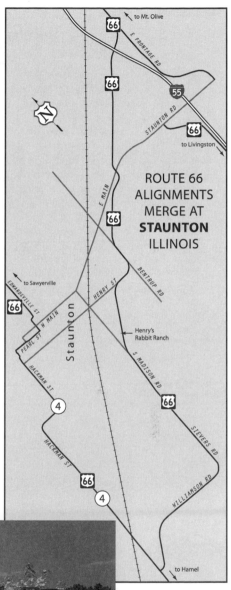

ROUTE 66
ALIGNMENTS
MERGE AT
STAUNTON
ILLINOIS

a tourist lodging that succumbed to the wrecking ball in greater St. Louis, has also found a more or less permanent home here at Henry's.

If you've been following the old alignment, Highway 4, then the next town you'll come to is Hamel. Skip ahead to page 100 to find the Hamel section.

This sign formerly stood in St. Louis, Missouri, but found a new home here at Henry's. GPS: 39.00394, -89.78176

If you elected to skip the old Highway 4 alignment in favor of the more modern route out of Springfield, continue on to the Glenarm section below.

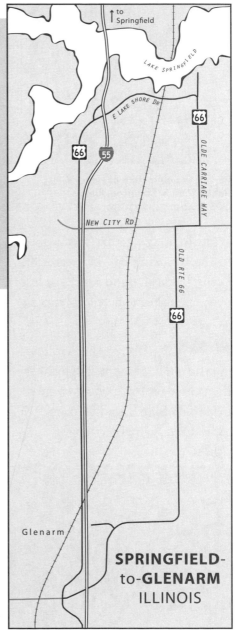

SPRINGFIELD-
to-GLENARM
ILLINOIS

The conventional way to get to Glenarm is along the most modern Route 66 alignment, which runs right beside I-55. However, if you're interested in something a little more "off the beaten path," you can use an alignment older than the modern "55" corridor but newer than the Highway 4 corridor explained earlier. In either case, your first step is to leave southbound I-55 at exit #88. Then, turn either right (onto a late 66 frontage road) or left (onto Lake Shore Road), depending on your preference (see the Glenarm-area reference map).

GLENARM

Adjacent to Pioneer Park is the restored **Sugar Creek Covered Bridge** and shady picnic grounds (located where Sugar Creek meets Covered Bridge Road).

 You'll be forced to enter I-55 at interchange #82 to continue on your way, but you'll be able to exit again at #80 for the town of Divernon.

Near Glenarm, Illinois, is a small park which includes this covered bridge.
GPS: 39.64042,-89.66161

DIVERNON-FARMERSVILLE-WAGGONER

All three of these communities are just to the west of the highway (both I-55 and Route 66, the west frontage road). Divernon has a nice, quiet little town square that features a few **vintage advertising murals** on some of the buildings. Look for the **Mother Road-era sign** at Art's Motel in Farmersville, and the **Our Lady of the Highways Shrine** (22353 W. Frontage Rd.).

Farmersville, Illinois.
GPS: 39.44381,-89.64492

South of Waggoner, Illinois. GPS: 39.33269,-89.64327

 South of Waggoner, the west frontage road comes to a "T" at N. 16th Avenue. Turn left to cross I-55 and then right (south) onto the east frontage road for the approach to Litchfield.

North of Litchfield, you should be traveling on the western frontage road. Cross over to the east side of the interstate via County Road 1600 N./N. 16th Avenue. Turn south toward Litchfield, where both Sherman Street (now officially designated Old Route 66) and Columbian Boulevard carried Route 66 traffic.

LITCHFIELD

The **Sky View Drive-In Theater** (1500 Historic Rte. 66 N.) has been in continuous operation since 1951, right on

You can still watch movies from your car in Litchfield, Illinois. GPS: 39.18593,-89.66471

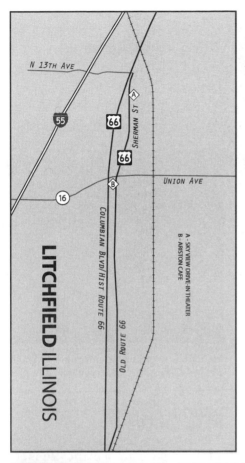

LITCHFIELD ILLINOIS

N 13TH AVE

55   66

SHERMAN ST

66

16

UNION AVE

COLUMBIAN BLVD/HIST ROUTE 66

OLD ROUTE 66

A - SKYVIEW DRIVE-IN THEATER
B - ARISTON CAFE

66 on the north outskirts of town.

A longtime Route 66 stopping place is the **Ariston Café** (413 Historic Rte. 66 N.), which has been in business in its present location since 1935. The café's first location was in Carlinville, established in 1924, on the old alignment of the route (Highway 4). When Route 66 was re-routed around 1930, the café's owners, the Adam family, started up anew in Litchfield, first opening their café across the street before moving to the current location in 1935. When Route 66 was re-aligned yet again (from the street in front of the café to the one in the rear), the Ariston simply added some signage on the back side for the new traffic flow.

A newer addition to town is the **Litchfield Museum & Route 66 Welcome Center** (334 Historic Rte. 66 N.), with a restored "Gas for Less" sign outside.

The Ariston Café has been serving locals and travelers alike since the 1920s. GPS: 39.17749, -89.66667

Relatively new to the scene in Litchfield is this museum. GPS: 39.17723,-89.66666

Between Litchfield and Mt. Olive, you'll be traveling old Route 66 with the railroad tracks immediately to your left. Look for a left-hand turn just as the main highway begins to veer away from the tracks to keep you on 66 into the heart of town.

Inside Litchfield's museum and welcome center. GPS: 39.17723,-89.66666

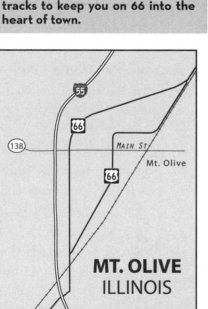

MT. OLIVE
ILLINOIS

MT. OLIVE

Make a stop to see the **Russell Soulsby Shell Station** (710 W. 1st South St.), a restored jewel originally constructed in the 1920s.

Union Miners Cemetery (Old Reservoir Rd.) in the northwest corner of town includes the gravesite of Mother Jones (Mary Harris), the famous mining activist and labor organizer who died in 1930.

Soulsby Station,
Mt. Olive, Illinois.
GPS: 39.07119,-89.73524

At the I-55 exit #41 Interchange, you'll need to cross from the eastern frontage road to the western frontage road, which will take you to Livingston.

Gravesite of labor leader Mother Jones, Mt. Olive, Illinois. GPS: 39.08069,-89.73314

LIVINGSTON

By the time Route 66 was realigned to take in Livingston, it was no longer standard highway practice to take a motorist through the central part of town. Route 66 only nudged Livingston along its southeast edge in my 1957 atlas, just as the interstate does today.

Just as you're about to leave the city limits, be on the alert for the **Pink Elephant Antique Mall** (908 Veterans Memorial Dr.), which can be relied upon for having some interesting items displayed on their grounds. Over the years, these have included muffler men, mock spaceships, and even a small, ancient Ferris wheel.

After exploring Livingston, continue on the west frontage road toward Hamel.

HAMEL

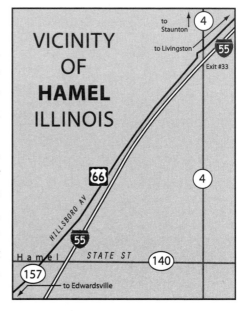

Before you reach Hamel proper, keep an eye out for **St. Paul Lutheran Church** (6969 W. Frontage Road), with its blue neon cross.

Weezy's (108 Historic Rte. 66) first started serving highway travelers in Hamel in the 1930s under the name Tourist Haven, offering sleeping accommodations upstairs. Rumor has it that Al Capone and some of his minions stayed here back in the day.

 Continue southwest on Route 66 (now marked Highway 157/Hillsboro Avenue) to Edwardsville.

EDWARDSVILLE

In Edwardsville, Route 66 continues under the guise of Highway 157, entering town from the northeast on Hillsboro, then cutting westward on Vandalia and St. Louis, and finally leaving town headed southwest via West Street and N. Bluff Road.

The unassuming town of Edwardsville was the scene of some social experimentation in the late 1800s. **LeClaire Village** was a test community founded by industrialist N. O. Nelson on the principles of profit sharing and Britain's cooperative movement, and survived as such into the early years of the twentieth century. In the 1930s, it was annexed by the city of Edwardsville, and is now listed as an official historic district. The area is roughly bounded by Longfellow Avenue to the west, Madison Avenue to the east, Hadley Avenue to the south, and Wolf Street to the north.

The **Madison County Historical Museum & Archival Library** (715 N. Main St.) is housed in the 1836 Weir home, with period furnishings, historical costumes, and other exhibits.

FURTHER AFIELD

Directly south of Edwardsville, via Highway 159, is the city of Collinsville. Called the Horseradish Capital of the World, the town holds a **horseradish festival** each spring, with horseradish-eating contests, cook-offs, and a horseradish toss competition.

Collinsville is also the home of the **World's Largest Ketchup Bottle** (800 S. Morrison Ave.), at the old Brooks Foods plant. Built as a water tower, the bottle is about 70 feet tall and stands atop a 100-foot base. Brooks closed years

Collinsville, Illinois.
GPS: 38.66295,-89.98250

ago, but the bottle replica, constructed in 1949, remains.

Just west of Collinsville is the **Cahokia Mounds State Historic Site** (30 Ramey St.). Located here are the ruins of a prehistoric city, inhabited from about A.D. 700 to 1400 and covering nearly six square miles. There are several mounds here, the largest of which is called Monk's Mound and is approximately 100 feet high. You will also find the remains of a sort of wooden stockade, which has been nicknamed Woodhenge, due to its astronomical similarity to the world-famous Stonehenge. Partial reconstruction of the site allows for dramatic effects at the time of the equinoxes. Cahokia is considered the largest prehistoric society on this continent, north of Mexico.

Further west is the town of Cahokia. The **Cahokia Courthouse** (107 Elm St.), originally constructed as a residence in about 1740, was completely disassembled in 1901 and displayed at the 1904 World's Fair across the river in St. Louis. It was then sold at auction and relocated to Chicago, where it was reassembled and stood for many years. In the 1930s, it was reacquired by the citizens of Cahokia and reassembled on its original foundation with the aid of historic photographs. The courthouse is part of the Colonial Cahokia State Historic Sites complex, which also includes the **Jarrot Mansion** (124 E. 1st St.) and the **Martin-Boismenue House** (2110 1st St.) in neighboring East Carondelet. The Jarrot Mansion was completed in about 1810, and is the former home of one of Cahokia's most prominent citizens. The Martin-Boismenue House, built in 1790, is a rare surviving example of French-Creole construction. Both the Jarrot and the Martin-Boismenue hold open houses twice per year; at other times, an appointment for a tour can be arranged by calling (618) 332-1782.

Old 66/Highway 157 forms a junction with S. University Drive east of Mitchell, and it's here that you'll have the option of taking westbound Chain of Rocks Road, which will take you through Mitchell and also to the well-known **Chain of Rocks Bridge** (now closed to vehicular traffic).

The Chain of Rocks Bridge now carries foot and bicycle traffic over the Mississippi River. West of Mitchell, Illinois. GPS: 38.76018,-90.17522

MITCHELL

What's left of the **Bel-Air Drive-In Theater** (1117 E. Chain of Rocks Rd.) is on the outskirts of Mitchell, next to the Highway 111 junction. The screen is gone; only the marquee remains, and who knows for how long.

Further west in Mitchell, be on the

Mitchell, Illinois.
GPS: 38.76168,-90.08851

lookout for the **Luna Café** (201 E. Chain of Rocks Rd.), an authentic roadhouse that predates Route 66, with a neon martini glass incorporated into its sign.

If you intend to visit the Chain of Rocks Bridge, be advised that just west of the Luna Café the road encounters a pretzel-like interchange with I-270, which can be confusing. As a stranger to the area, it could take you more than one attempt to get to the bridge.

FURTHER AFIELD

Lovers of petroliana may want to take a side trip to Wood River, Illinois, less than ten miles north of Mitchell. Here you'll find the **Wood River Refinery History Museum** (900 S. Central Ave.), in what was formerly part of a refinery on State Highway 111. The complex dates from 1918, when it was operated by Shell Oil Company; after some eighty years, ownership passed to Phillips Petroleum. In addition to the usual pumps, globes, and advertising examples, the museum has on display a number of authentic vehicles, such as an oil tanker and fire truck, that actually serviced the refinery.

The community of Wood River is also the proud home of several **Sears catalog homes**, though this collection, of course, is not as large as Carlinville's. If you're interested, check with the folks at the **Wood River Museum and Visitors Center** (40 W. Ferguson Ave.).

According to my 1946 map of Illinois, Route 66 split at the town of Mitchell, with "City 66" veering southwest through Nameoki, Granite City, Madison, and Venice, with a subsequent crossing of the river into the central city of

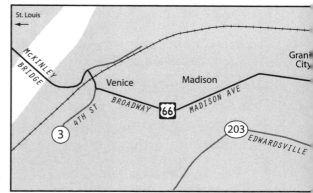

St. Louis via the McKinley Bridge. That road is still driveable, and is named Nameoki Road/Highway 203 (see the accompanying map).

The simple "66" designation belonged to what is now Highway 270, which bypassed *urban* St. Louis in favor of a beltway route. This is the favored route today, which in the old days crossed the Mississippi via the Chain of Rocks Bridge. You can continue west to the Chain of Rocks Bridge, but it no longer carries traffic over the Mississippi. To cross the river, most 66 travelers take I-270, which is just to the north of the closed bridge. If you take that path, which bypasses St. Louis, I recommend that you double back to take in some of the city's many attractions.

I find the older "City 66" to be enjoyable: from E. Chain of Rocks Road, veer left onto Nameoki Road/Highway 203, then angle right onto Madison Avenue through Granite City and Madison; the road then becomes Broadway and takes you into Venice, which then joins Cedar Street and crosses the Mississippi River into central St. Louis via the McKinley Bridge.

Granite City was once known as Six Mile, due to its distance from the Mississippi River. The **Old Six Mile Museum** (3729 Maryville Rd.) is housed in the Emmert-Zippel mansion, which dates from the 1830s.

The Illinois prairie is now behind you. Just ahead is the mighty Mississippi River. And beyond that, you and Route 66 will get much better acquainted.

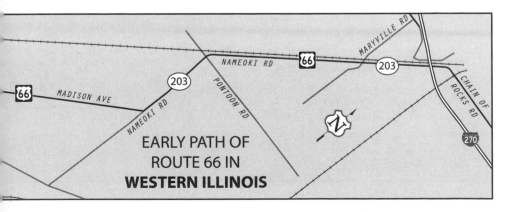

EARLY PATH OF
ROUTE 66 IN
WESTERN ILLINOIS

MISSOURI

Long before there were roads in the modern sense, there were river roads. Look at any map of any country and be reminded that the older, more established cities—if not on a coastline—were

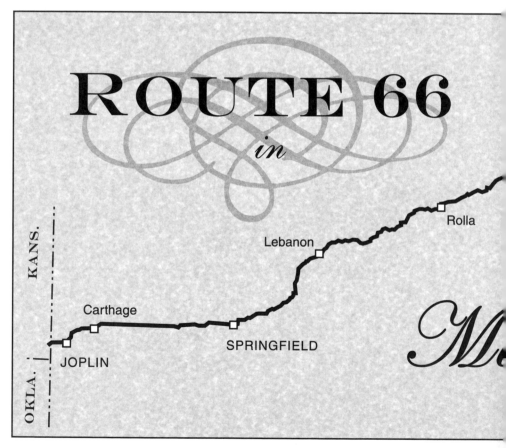

founded on the banks of rivers, whose currents and near-frictionless surfaces made for quicker and more economical transportation than the available land-based modes of transport. Yet while rivers have been conducive to transportation and settlement along their lengths, they have at the same time presented barriers to movement where bridges have been few and far between. And so arises their age-old role as natural borders.

The Mississippi is just such a barrier-road, fostering settlement and commerce while at the same time creating a sort of natural pause in America's relentless westward movement. As you cross the Mississippi River, you pass over one of the North American continent's most vital arteries, one which served to nourish and sustain generations of mankind long before the invention of asphalt and the proliferation of the internal combustion engine. What is more, you leave behind the older and more established portion of the American experience, and you pass both physically and spiritually into one of America's most important chapters: westward expansion.

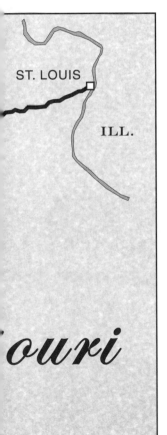

Missouri—first at St. Louis, then later at Independence—was long the staging ground for that westward impulse. Situated at the threshold of an enormous, uncharted wilderness, this was the last bastion of civilization and the last chance to prepare and outfit for the rigorous journeys that lay ahead. Just as Chicago is the starting point for Route 66, Missouri is the starting place for the famous migratory trails of history that made settlement of the West a reality: the Overland, Oregon, and Santa Fe trails all had their origins here on a Missouri riverbank. And, under the sponsorship of President Thomas Jefferson, a corps led by Meriwether Lewis and William Clark set out from here on the Voyage of Discovery in 1804, eventually finding its way to the Oregon coast.

As for U.S. Highway 66, it crossed the Mississippi River into the Show Me State at several places over the years. Today, you may want to avoid the older alignments, which crossed the river directly into the central part of St. Louis.

Unfortunately, those alignments of the highway pass through sections of the city that are congested and do not always feel safe. For that reason, and also because urban alignments tend to fragment over time and become very hard to follow, you may prefer to approach St. Louis via the "bypass" route, which used to take the traveler across the Chain of Rocks Bridge.

Today, the Chain of Rocks Bridge is closed to auto traffic, but it has been turned into a recreational attraction open to pedestrians and is also the scene of frequent special events. The bridge is just south of Highway 270 and Riverview Boulevard, and is touted as "the world's largest bicycle and pedestrian bridge." Earlier in its history, a popular park named Riverview sat near the end of the Chain of Rocks Bridge on the Missouri side of the river. There, St. Louisans gathered for picnics, skating, swimming, and softball. Riverfront Trail now connects the bridge with the Gateway Arch to the south. Up on the bluff overlooking the bridge and the site of

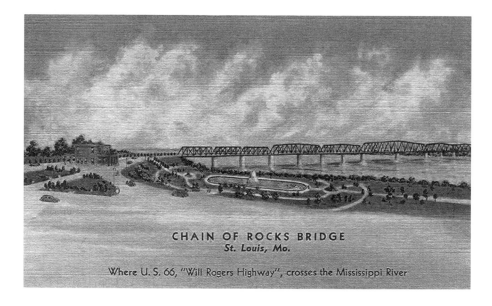

CHAIN OF ROCKS BRIDGE
St. Louis, Mo.

Where U. S. 66, "Will Rogers Highway", crosses the Mississippi River the old park, there used to be a fairly elaborate amusement park called Fun Fair Park. Fun Fair Park and its sundry attractions failed to survive the competition from Six Flags Over Mid-America, which opened just to the west, near Eureka, in the early 1970s.

Opened to traffic from 1929 until the late 1960s, the former toll bridge with the distinctive bend in the middle was used in the filming of 1981's *Escape from New York*. It is here that Adrienne Barbeau's character meets her demise, while Kurt Russell makes good his own escape.

 Today's Mother-Roader usually crosses the Mississippi just a little north of the Chain of Rocks Bridge on Highway 270. This modern-day loop highway has replaced the old route for several miles along here. Exit Highway 270 at Highway 67 and go south to follow the course of 66 as it once skirted the city. Head due south on 67 until you meet up with the city alignment of 66 at Watson Road (now numbered 366) near the community of Kirkwood. Turn to the east here to take in some of what St. Louis has to offer before continuing your 66 odyssey west.

As an alternative, you can also drive from Illinois into Missouri via an older alignment of Route 66 that crossed over the McKinley Bridge. That route is described near the end of the Illinois chapter.

ST. LOUIS

> Route 66 took several paths around and through St. Louis over the years. As with other urban areas, 66 originally passed through the downtown business district, but was later re-routed to avoid central-city congestion by creating beltline or bypass routes. For most of its life, U.S. 66 was marked to offer the driver two or more choices in traversing the area, depending on his or her objectives. There's plenty to do and see in St. Louis, so today's roadie will want to stray from the standard alignments anyway.

The city of St. Louis attained what many consider to be its high-water mark in the first decade of the twentieth century. In 1904, the city hosted the World's Fair and summer Olympic Games. The fair was timed

to coincide with the centennial of the Louisiana Purchase. The following year, 1905, St. Louis had the dubious distinction of being the city with the first recorded auto theft. At the end of the twentieth century, St. Louis was the fastest-shrinking major city in the U.S., with its population declining by more than twelve percent during the 1990s.

The 1904 World's Fair (or St. Louis Exposition) enjoyed a number of distinctions, having played a role in the evolution of ice cream, hamburgers, and iced tea. It was there that ice cream was first served in cones when a Syrian immigrant named Ernest Hamwi came to the rescue of an ice cream vendor who had run out of serving dishes. By the end of the fair, it was reported that several vendors were selling ice cream in folded waffles.

That same fair was also the scene of the mass introduction of the hamburger served on a bun, a development which had originated just a little earlier in New Haven, Connecticut. This fair was also where an English tea concessionaire named Richard Blechyden determined that the weather was simply too hot for his tea to sell well. His solution was to ice it down, thus creating the

St. Louis, Missouri.
GPS: 38.59046,-90.25376

decidedly un-English iced tea.

The 1904 World's Fair was held at **Forest Park**—then the nation's largest urban park at over 1,300 acres—which is still very much a part of present-day St. Louis. Forest Park contains the **St. Louis Zoo** (1 Government Dr.), the **St. Louis Art Museum** (1 Fine Arts Dr.), and the **Missouri History Museum** (5700 Lindell Blvd.). There are also some giant turtle sculptures on the south side of the park.

A replica of Charles Lindbergh's famous airplane, the *Spirit of St. Louis*, is at the Missouri History Museum. The *Spirit of St. Louis* was so named because Lindbergh's backers for the trans-oceanic flight consisted of the *St. Louis Globe-Democrat* newspaper and a group of local businessmen who wanted to promote their city as a center of aviation. Earlier, Lindbergh had approached the American Tobacco Company with the idea of naming the craft after their Lucky Strike cigarettes (Lindbergh had already been nicknamed "Lucky" Lindy by that time), but the company refused to back the venture. The replica at the Missouri History Museum was manufactured by the same firm that made the original, and it was used in the Jimmy Stewart movie.

In 1944, Judy Garland starred in a musical entitled *Meet Me in St. Louis*, which portrayed the year the world came to visit the city for the

fair (the title song, "Meet Me in St. Louis, Louis" actually dates from the year of the Exposition). It was during the filming of that movie that Judy Garland became romantically involved with her future husband, Vicente Minelli.

Betty Grable, pin-up girl par excellence during World War II, was from St. Louis and lived at the **Forest Park Hotel** (4910 W. Pine Blvd.). Vincent Price graduated from **St. Louis Country Day School** (101 N. Warson Rd.). Miles Davis and Chuck Berry were both born here in St. Louis. Another St. Louis native, the moody T. S. Eliot, won the 1948 Nobel Prize in Literature; well after his death, one of his lighter works, *Old Possum's Book of Practical Cats*, inspired the Broadway musical comedy *Cats*. You will be amazed at the number of St. Louisans who have made it big in the world and have been inducted into the city's Walk of Fame on Delmar Avenue (see the Attractions section below).

Here in St. Louis, there's a Route 66 institution still going strong that you simply must pay a visit to: **Ted Drewes Frozen Custard** (6726 Chippewa St.). The building itself is an important landmark, but the crucial thing is that this business still believes in the older values of a quality product and personal service. They've never "sold out" for a fast buck, and their adoring public appreciates it. Their list of mouthwatering toppings is printed right on the side of the building to stoke your anticipation. Stop by some morning before opening time and watch the people begin to flock in from all over. In no time at all, the place will be mobbed, and it happens virtually every day. And check to see if there's still a mannequin peering out from one of the upstairs windows.

Before leaving St. Louis and hitting the road once again, consider heading down to the riverfront area that the Highway 270 alignment avoided on your way in. The **Jefferson National Expansion Memorial** (11 N. 4th St.) includes the Gateway Arch and the Museum of Western Expansion at its foot. Eero Saarinen's famous 630-foot archway aptly symbolizes the area's role as a gateway to the West. The arch contains a pair of elevator-trams that swivel as they ascend to the top, sort of like a Ferris-wheel car, constituting a feat of engineering in and of themselves. There is a terrific panoramic view from the top of the arch, and there

Ted Drewes Frozen Custard is still a popular stop for both roadies and St. Louisans, as it has been since the heyday of Route 66.
GPS: 38.58960,-90.30767

is also a film, *Monument to the Dream*, which details its construction (the arch was completed in 1965). The adjacent museum, which is as large as a football field, presents information about the Louisiana Purchase and the Jefferson-sponsored Lewis and Clark Expedition. Also part of the memorial complex is the Old Courthouse. This building originates from 1839, and was the site of the early trials of the Dred Scott case, which was ultimately decided by the United States Supreme Court in 1857.

Elsewhere downtown, the old **Union Station railroad depot** (1820 Market St.) has been nicely converted into a luxury hotel and eclectic shopping venue.

ST. LOUIS ATTRACTIONS

You can spend a considerable amount of time at the **Blueberry Hill Restaurant** (6504 Delmar Blvd.), just admiring the great memorabilia on display that includes posters, album covers, and vintage toys. However, a more "gut" reason to come in is the restaurant's extraordinary burgers. The Blueberry Hill also plays host to the largest annual dart tournament in the United States, with approximately 500 entrants each year.

At **Fitz's Root Beer** (6605 Delmar Blvd.), you can enjoy your meal and watch root beer being bottled at the same time. The equipment dates from the 1940s, and is visible from the main dining area.

In the 6100 through 6600 blocks of Delmar is the **St. Louis Walk of Fame**. Here there are stars embedded in the sidewalk on both sides of the street, honoring nearly a hundred men and women who are connected to St. Louis and have made an impact on the world at large. They run the gamut, from Yogi Berra and Josephine Baker to William Burroughs and Virginia Mayo. In 2009, this same stretch of Delmar became the home of the **Delmar Loop Planet Walk**, a walkable (2,880 feet) "model" of the solar system, where representations of the sun and planets are proportionally spaced according to their real-world relationships.

During Prohibition, the local Anheuser-Busch brewery sold non-alcoholic brews from the **Bevo Mill** (4749 Gravois Rd.), a replica of a Dutch-style windmill built in 1916. The mill still stands, and was recently refurbished for its new life as a special-events venue. Across the street is the **Miniature Museum of Greater St. Louis** (4746 Gravois Rd.).

St. Louis's **City Museum** (750 N. 16th St.) is located in the heart of the loft and garment district, and is more offbeat than its name would imply. It is housed in the International Arts Complex, which was formerly the home of the International Shoe and Rand Shoe companies, two of the leading shoe manufacturing firms of yesteryear. Included among the exhibits is the Tiny Trailer of Tragedy, once owned by Elvis and Priscilla Presley, as well as the world's largest pair of underpants. The museum has also added a rooftop water park.

Formerly on display at the City Museum, but relocated to the Brown Shoe Company headquarters, is the **Shoe of Shoes** (8300 Maryland Ave.). It consists of hundreds—perhaps thousands—of life-sized, cast-metal shoes welded together in the shape of one enormous woman's pump. This city used to be so well-known for its shoes that at one time wags used to say of St. Louis: "First in shoes, first in booze, and last in the American League." Of course, that was when the St. Louis Browns were still playing America's pastime.

Not on the route, but well worth a look. St. Louis, Missouri. GPS: 38.58157,-90.26688

Faust Park (15185 Olive Blvd.) includes an 1820 estate home, historical village, and butterfly house, as well as a restored Dentzel carousel formerly owned by the second governor of Missouri.

The **Anheuser-Busch Brewery** (1127 Pestalozzi St.), the world's largest brewery, offers tours, beer tastings, and brewing demonstrations. And don't forget its world-famous Clydesdales.

Calvary Cemetery (5239 W. Florissant Ave.) covers more than 400 acres and includes the gravesites of such notables as playwright Tennessee Williams, General William Tecumseh Sherman, and Dred Scott. There is also a large crucifix marking the location of a mass grave; at the time of the cemetery's establishment, earlier burials of American Indians were

collected and reinterred at that spot. Adjacent to Calvary is **Bellefon-
taine Cemetery** (4947 W. Florissant Ave.), where explorer William
Clark and other notables are buried.

The **Ulysses S. Grant Historic Site** (7400 Grant Rd.) was the Grant
family residence from 1854 to 1858 and is known as White Haven. Adjacent to it is **Grant's Farm** (10501 Gravois Rd.), a ranch that includes
an 1856 log cabin, free-roaming animals, breeding Clydesdales, and a
fence made from Civil War rifle barrels. The property was purchased by
the Busch family in 1903.

The **Campbell House Museum** (1508 Locust St.), the first home
built in the elegant Lucas Place neighborhood, has been restored to its
1880s prime and is open for tours Wednesday through Saturday. The
home still has many of its original furnishings, including some of the
family carriages.

Canine lovers won't want to miss the **American Kennel Club Museum of the Dog** (1721 S. Mason Rd.). The permanent collection includes
a great many oil paintings and other works of art devoted to man's best
friend, some by household names like William Wegman. Rotating exhibits have included matchbook cover art portraying dogs.

The **Eugene Field House & St. Louis Toy Museum** (634 S. Broadway) is the former home of the Field family and features a book collection spanning 250 years, as well as antique and collectible toys. The son
of a prominent attorney, Mr. Field was known as the Children's Poet, as
well as Father of the Personal Newspaper Column.

The **St. Louis Car Museum** (1575 Woodson Rd.) has more than 150
legendary vehicles on display.

Take a tour of the **Samuel Cupples House** (3673 W. Pine Blvd.)
on the grounds of St. Louis University. The forty-two-room mansion
was built in 1888, and features gargoyles, ornate stonework, and twenty-two fireplaces. It also boasts Tiffany glasswork and other decorative
arts dating from the fifteenth century onward. On the third floor is a
special exhibit, the Turshin Fine Arts Glass Collection of American and
European Art Glass.

Also open for tours is the **Scott Joplin House State Historic Site** (2658 Delmar Blvd.). Here, Joplin and his wife kept a modest flat that was built circa 1902. There is a music room with an operating player piano so visitors can experience first-hand the type of ragtime piano that Joplin used himself.

The **Cherokee-Lemp Historic District** is a south-side neighborhood with two nineteenth-century mansions (the Lemp and the DeMenil), as well as the Lemp Brewery, which was once the largest in the world. The Lemp Mansion (now an inn and restaurant) is said to be haunted by the spirits of four family members who committed suicide in the house, and a fifth who died there under the proverbial "mysterious circumstances." The district is bounded by the streets of Cherokee Street, Lemp Avenue, Utah Street, and DeMenil Place.

Jasper's Antique Radio Museum (2022 Cherokee St.) has over 10,000 radios in its collection, making it the largest in the world. The owner, Jasper Giardina, has a stated goal of repairing and restoring any radio that crosses his path. You'll see everything from fully restored examples to basket cases fresh from the attic, and everything in-between. Many are for sale.

Open only on the first Saturday of the month, the **Compton Hill Water Tower** (S. Grand Blvd. and Russell Blvd.) was built in 1898, in a style described as French Romanesque. The observation deck offers a 360-degree view after a climb of 198 steps.

The **Kemp Auto Museum** (16955 Chesterfield Airport Rd.) specializes in Mercedes-Benz automobiles, with specimens from as early as 1886.

The **Moto Museum** (3441 Olive St.) is a collection of motorcycles representing more than a dozen countries of manufacture.

FURTHER AFIELD

Just northwest of St. Louis is the city of St. Charles. Be sure to check out the **St. Charles Visitors Bureau** (230 S. Main St.) while you're here. The city's central business district was named the "Williamsburg of the West" by a national magazine.

St. Charles is where Lewis and Clark began their long journey of discovery after camping here in the spring of 1804. You can see the departure point for Lewis and Clark's expedition—Bishop's Landing—at the **Lewis & Clark Boat House and Nature Center** (1050 S. Riverside Dr.). Replicas of the vessels used in the voyage can be seen on the lower "boathouse" level, while the museum level above has extensive exhibits of other kinds.

In the St. Charles historic district is the **First Missouri State Capitol Historic Site** (200 S. Main St.). This federal-style row house is where the territorial government met from 1821 to 1826 to reorganize into a state system of government. Sessions were held here until the new capitol building in Jefferson City was ready for use, in October of 1826. Included are legislative chambers, two residences, a dry goods store, and a carpentry shop, all of which have been restored to period appearance.

St. Charles is also home to the Missouri wing of the **Commemorative Air Force** (6360 Grafton Ferry Rd.). The CAF is dedicated to preserving WWII-era aircraft in flying condition as "a tribute to the men and women who built, serviced, and flew them in the defense of democracy." This is the same organization formerly known as the Confederate Air Force; the name was changed for the sake of political correctness, but of course they never had anything to do with the War Between the States, anyway. Stop in and browse the collection of vintage warplanes on Thursdays and Saturdays.

If you've still got some time to spend in St. Charles, there's the **Shrine of St. Rose Phillippine Duchesne** (619 N. 2nd Street), site of the first free school west of the Mississippi River. It was established in 1818 by Missouri's only saint, who was canonized in 1988.

When Route 66 was first born, it followed what is now Highway 100/Choteau Avenue out of downtown. That highway passes through such communities as Maplewood, Manchester, and Pond before

An old roadhouse in Pond, Missouri. GPS: 38.58140,-90.66012

meeting up with the more modern and well-traveled route at Gray Summit to the west. That alignment, however, has become quite urbanized over much of its length, and it forces you to skip several communities that you really shouldn't miss. After exploring what St. Louis has to offer, I recommend that you take the later route, starting with . . .

KIRKWOOD

Kirkwood, while once a distinct community, has been more or less absorbed by its sprawling neighbor, St. Louis. There is a very nicely restored **railroad station** (110 W. Argonne Dr.) in the old Kirkwood business district. The downtown business district in general has also undergone some nice work to make a pleasant, pedestrian-friendly area.

A few blocks south of the railroad depot is the **Magic House** (516 S. Kirkwood Rd.), a children's museum that now occupies a former mansion built by George Lane Edwards, a director of the St. Louis Exposition, in 1901.

In the Sugar Creek area of Kirkwood, you'll find a **Frank Lloyd Wright residence** (120 N. Ballas Rd.), one of only five Wright-designed structures in the entire state of Missouri. Built in the 1950s, the house is particularly notable in that it is virtually 100 percent authentic, right

Kirkwood, Missouri. GPS: 38.57900,-90.40645

down to the original furnishings. Tours are available, but must be arranged in advance by calling (314) 822-8359.

Kirkwood is also home to the **Museum of Transportation** (3015
Barrett Station Rd.). The museum has an automobile pavilion, as well as
several tracks of locomotives and other railroad stock for you to tour and
enjoy. The autos include a 1963 Chrysler Turbine, and a custom-built
aluminum car made in 1960 and used in the Bobby Darin movie *Too
Cool Blues.* Among the railroad exhibits are the last steam locomotive
to operate in Missouri, a wooden caboose, a complete passenger train,

One of the many displays at the Museum of Transportation, Kirkwood, Missouri.
GPS: 38.57303,-90.46295

a tank car, and the "Big Boy," the world's largest-ever steam locomotive. Also on display are a tow boat and a C-47 military transport, which flew in the Second World War. But most important to Route 66 fans is the façade from one of the Coral Court Motel units, on exhibit inside. The Coral Court was a very special example of highway architecture from the heyday of postwar travel, and it stood not far from here until "redevelopment" took it in 1995. Thankfully, a small part of it has been preserved for your enjoyment. Built in 1941 of glazed hollow brick and glass block in the Streamline Moderne style, the Coral Court, even when new, was evocative of another time. Legend has it that bank robbers once stashed loot in the hollow walls of one or more units, of which the Coral Court once boasted more than seventy.

TIMES BEACH

Times Beach was a planned community established about 1925, just on the eve of the birth of the federal highway system. Lots were sold or given away by the *St. Louis Star-Times* newspaper as part of a promotion, hence the name.

What happened at Times Beach, however, shouldn't happen to anyone. Residents were forced to evacuate decades later when it was determined that the ground on which the community sat had been contaminated with dioxins, which had been present in the materials used to spray the roads for dust control. That evacuation occurred in 1982. Fortunately, the site was the object of cleanup efforts for years, and has since been turned into the **Missouri Route 66 State Park** (97 N. Outer Rd. E. #1), with trails, picnic areas, and river access. The visitor center includes Route 66 exhibits, and is housed in a vintage roadhouse building that dates to 1936.

 After visiting the Missouri Route 66 State Park, leave the interstate again at exit #264 and cross to the south side. Follow Eureka's W. Main Street out of town toward Allenton.

EUREKA

West of Eureka is **Six Flags Over Mid-America**, a large-scale theme park that adds immeasurably to the traffic in this area.

South of I-44 at exit #264 in Eureka is the **Black Madonna Shrine and Grottos** (100 St. Josephs Hill Rd.). Built entirely by hand by a Franciscan brother, the grottos are "dedicated to the Black Madonna, Our Lady of Czestochowa, Queen of Peace and Mercy." These ornamental works of faith have become known far and wide.

Founded by Dr. Marlin Perkins of Wild Kingdom fame, the **Endangered Wolf Center** (6750 Tyson Valley Rd.) at the Washington University Tyson Research Center has sought to protect and preserve endangered wolf species through educational programs and captive breeding since 1971.

ALLENTON-PACIFIC

About a mile east of Pacific is the Red Cedar Inn, a café and former hotel that first started serving travelers on this stretch of road around 1934. It's been closed for years, and although many citizens wanted to see it adapted for re-use, none of those ideas came to fruition.

Pacific, Missouri. GPS: 38.48158,-90.71783

When I last visited, the Red Cedar had been leased out to a heating and air conditioning company using it for offices and equipment storage.

When it's time to leave Allenton, cross to the north side of the railroad tracks to I-40 Business Loop/66.

One of the more distinctive features of Pacific is the presence of some prominent **bluffs** along the north side of the highway. These were considered interesting enough that they found their way onto many an early postcard of the area. There are several cave-like cavities here that resulted from silica mining.

GRAY SUMMIT

This town is best known for its association with Ralston-Purina. Just north of Gray Summit is **Purina Farms** (200 Checkerboard Dr.). This compound holds canine events through most of the year, which include agility trials, herding competitions, all-breed shows, and racing. One of my personal favorites is Jack Russell Fun Days, sponsored by the Missouri Earth Dog Club. These dogs are incredibly enthusiastic about racing around, rooting things out of holes in the ground, and just all-around cavorting. Aside from being fun for pets and owners alike, many of the events presented at Purina Farms are educational as well. There are workshops in

Gray Summit. GPS: 38.48298,-90.82262

West of Gray Summit, Missouri. GPS: 38.48093,-90.83157

dog obedience training, for example. You can also learn how to milk a cow or operate a simulated pet food manufacturing machine.

South of the interstate and right on Historic 66 is the 2,500-acre **Shaw Nature Reserve** (Hwy 100 and I-44), an extension of the Missouri Botanical Garden, where prairie flora and fauna are preserved, and a visitor center, historic home, and several miles of hiking trails await.

VILLA RIDGE

Near Villa Ridge is the former **Gardenway Motel**, a colonial style motel that probably graced the front of many a postcard in its prime. Notice the glass-block detailing in the roadside sign. A little farther west is what remains of the **Tri-County Truck Stop**.

West of the Tri-County is the **Sunset Motel** (225–289

**Villa Ridge, Missouri.
GPS: 38.46448,-90.86891**

Historic Rte. 66), which has a unique neon sunburst-style sign that was restored and ceremonially re-lit in 2009.

ST. CLAIR

This town was formerly known as Traveler's Repose, but it's said that the townsfolk grew tired of being thought of as a cemetery. For many years, St. Clair was the home of **Ozark Rock Curios**, a purveyor of interesting geological specimens to Route 66 tourists.

Between St. Clair and Stanton, if you follow the road paralleling the railroad track (W. Springfield Road) on the south side of I-44, you'll be taken on an old alignment of the highway through Anaconda. The town is about midway between St. Clair and Stanton, and was named Morrellton when my 1946 road map was printed. By the time my 1957 atlas was published, the town had been completely bypassed by the new alignment, and it bore the current name of Anaconda. Unfortunately, that road no longer continues to Stanton. Instead, use the later incarnation of Route 66, which today means the north I-44 service road.

STANTON

This community is best known as the gateway to the Meramec Caverns to the south (see the Further Afield section).

STANTON ATTRACTIONS

Here in Stanton you'll find the **Jesse James Wax Museum** (I-44, exit #230), a true roadside attraction. The museum focuses on the theory that Jesse James didn't really die of a gunshot wound in 1881, as the authorities have been telling us all these years—he actually lived to a ripe old age

Stanton, Missouri. GPS: 38.27270,-91.10760

under another name and died in 1952! There are even wax figures of the conspirators featured in the retelling of this diabolical plot to mislead the public. The museum staff will enthusiastically heap evidence upon you of their version of Jesse's life, such as a list of physical traits (scars, etc.) shared by the original Jesse and the mystery man who survived well into the Route 66 era.

East of Stanton is the **Riverside Wildlife Center** (275 Hwy W), where you can see a wide variety of native and non-native snakes and other reptilians, as well as big cats.

FURTHER AFIELD

Just a few miles southeast of Route 66 is one of the route's most widely known attractions, **Meramec Caverns** (1135 Hwy W). In fact, a trip to Meramec Caverns is more a required pilgrimage than a side trip for any-one traveling the Mother Road. That's largely because clever marketing made this cave a part of almost any trip down 66. First of all, when Lester Dill opened Meramec Caverns commercially in 1935, he successfully managed to portray his caverns as a former hideout of Jesse James, even though the evidence for this is fairly thin. Secondly, he paid to have the

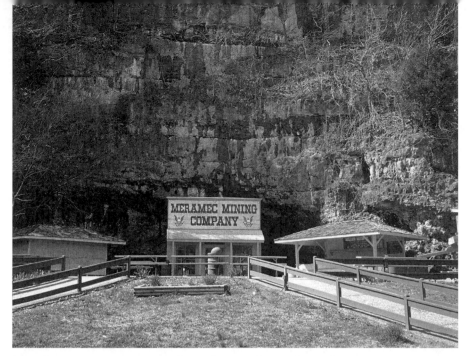

Part of Meramec Caverns, a traditional tourist destination on Route 66, near Stanton, Missouri. GPS: 38.24765,-91.08852

sides and roofs of barns all over the country painted with his "logo" so that motorists far and wide were made aware of Meramec Caverns. These barns dotted the countryside, not just along Route 66, but on roadsides all over the Midwest (some estimates place the number at around 350). Thirdly, each visitor to Meramec Caverns became an advertisement for the attraction. That's because the Dill clan pioneered the bumper sticker. Youngsters were paid to ensure that each vehicle in their parking lot left with a Meramec Caverns tag tied to their rear bumper. The combination of these strategies made Meramec Caverns not just one of the best-known caves in the country, but one of the most-recognized attractions of any kind whatsoever.

Inside the caverns, in addition to the usual underground formations, there is a neon sign marking the "Jesse James Hideout." Nearby is Loot Rock, where facsimiles of Jesse and his gang divide the spoils of their latest heist. Also included is a "moonshiners' cave." The tour climaxes with a light show projecting the Stars and Stripes onto a structure called the Stage Curtain—the largest such formation in the world—while a recording plays of Kate Smith belting out "God Bless America."

Adjacent facilities include a motel, campground, gift shop, restaurant, and canoe rentals (with shuttle service).

Note on barn painting: Well-informed roadies will know of an attraction near Lookout Mountain, Georgia, which began painting barns back in 1936. Those barns, once numbering about 900, covered 19 states with the "See Rock City" message. Many of those barns remain, and Rock City itself is still going strong.

Very near Meramec Caverns as the crow flies is the much lesser-known **Fisher's Cave** (2800 S. Highway 185), on the grounds of Meramec State Park. You'll need to approach it via Highway 185 from a junction just east of Sullivan. Visitors use handheld lanterns to explore these caves during a ninety-minute tour on paved walkways. This cave is said to have been in use since the 1860s, when then-governor Thomas Fletcher organized a celebration there.

Meramec and Fisher are just the first of several caves that will be within striking distance of Route 66 as we sweep through Missouri. For cavers, Missouri is a paradise. At last count, there were more than 5,400 registered caves in the state.

Leaving Stanton, use S. Outer Road (not Springfield Avenue). The road will hug the interstate all the way to Sullivan, eventually becoming Springfield Road.

SULLIVAN

George Hearst, whose son, William Randolph, later made his name in the publishing business, was born on a farm near Sullivan. George made his fortune in mining. In the **Odd Fellows Cemetery** (N. Church Street) is the grave of Jim "Sunny" Bottomley, Hall of Fame baseball player for the St. Louis Cardinals.

Leaving Sullivan, you should be on the south service road of I-44, which will take you through the community of St. Cloud and all the way to . . .

BOURBON

The town slogan? "Make Our Bourbon Your Bourbon." The town's water tower has become a popular photographic subject. Past Bourbon, keep your eye out for what remains of the **Bourbon Lodge**, a former tourist complex on the southwest edge of town.

A former roadside business, Bourbon, Missouri. GPS: 38.14101,-91.25898

About two-thirds of the way from Bourbon to Cuba, right where the railroad track sidles up close to the south side of I-44 and just east of exit #210, is the site of a town called Hofflins. Although it was a full-fledged town in the 1940s, my 1957 atlas chose to omit it completely. That same atlas shows U.S. 66 in this vicinity, already as a four-lane divided highway. That highway growth, nearly on its doorstep—along with the concomitant traffic—likely made Hofflins unlivable for its residents. Today, little remains.

After Hofflins, old 66 wanders away from the interstate and towards the town of Cuba.

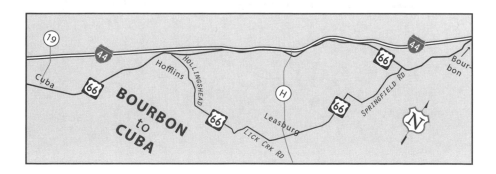

CUBA

Cuba has adopted the nickname "Mural City," thanks to more than a dozen **outdoor artworks** scattered throughout the town. One of those murals adorns the side of a restored Phillips 66 station at the corner of Washington and Franklin Streets. The station is at an intersection known locally as the "Four-Way." Washington Boulevard is the former U.S. 66, while Franklin Street is Highway 19, the first designated "scenic route" in the state.

The most important feature of Cuba to a Route 66 traveler is the **Wagon Wheel Motel**

The Wagon Wheel Motel is a truly successful restoration project. Cuba, Missouri. GPS: 38.06450,-91.39576

Downtown Cuba, Missouri. GPS: 38.06287,-91.40358

(901 E. Washington Blvd.), which is still in operation and looks every bit as inviting as the day it opened for business. If you haven't stayed in a good old-fashioned mom-and-pop motel yet on this trip, this is an excellent place to do so, since the current ownership has restored it to excellent condition. If you'll be moving on, then just stay around long enough to snap a few photos and appreciate the one-of-a-kind sign, with its neon-trimmed wagon wheel suspended over the road.

The **Crawford County Historical Society Museum** (308 N. Smith St.) occupies a two-story 1934 building across from the library. Just north of town on Highway 19 is the **19 Drive-In Theater**, which has been showing films since 1954.

FANNING-ROSATI

West of Cuba, you'll encounter the small community of Fanning. At the site of the former Fanning US 66 Outpost stands the Guinness-certified **World's Largest Rocker**. Constructed in 2008, it is more than forty feet tall, making for an outstanding photo opportunity.

The area around Rosati is known for its grape vineyards. Years ago, the area was thick with vendors offering grapes from small roadside stands. Today, there are a number of operating wineries in the vicinity.

U.S. 66 Outpost & General Store, Fanning, Missouri. GPS: 38.03717, -91.46924

Wine district, near Rosati, Missouri. GPS: 38.02906,-91.53617

ST. JAMES

Route 66 becomes James Boulevard through town. After exploring St. James, drop down to Springfield Road—the old route toward Dillon and Rolla. Once you reach the Highway V junction, site of the Mule Trading Post, cross to the opposite side of I-44 and use N. Outer Road to continue.

Opened in 2009, the **Vacuum Cleaner Museum and Factory Outlet** (3 Industrial Dr.) is an offshoot of local vacuum maker Tacony Manufacturing. The museum exhibits models from as early as 1910, and the displays are organized by decade, with carpeting and furniture of each era adding to the atmosphere.

FURTHER AFIELD

About eight miles southeast of St. James, via Missouri State Highway 8, is **Maramec Spring Park** (21880 Maramec Spring Dr.). Maramec [sic] Spring proper is a National Natural Landmark, and it exudes some 96 million gallons of water each day from the base of a bluff. This spring used to provide the power for the Maramec Iron Works, established circa 1857, the ruins of which can still be seen within the park.

Leave St. James on Springfield Road, which becomes St. James Road as you approach Dillon (see the reference map). As you leave

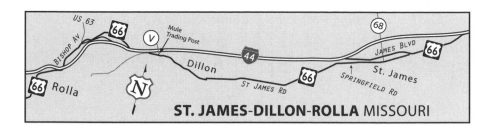

ST. JAMES-DILLON-ROLLA MISSOURI

the vicinity of St. James and continue your southwesterly trek across Missouri, you are leaving the Big Prairie section of the state and climbing atop the Ozark Plateau. You will begin to see a change in the topography as you encounter more and more exposed rock outcroppings. The hilly Ozark region, which extends into northwestern Arkansas, is well-known as moonshine territory and home of the Hatfields and the McCoys.

DILLON

South of I-44, Dillon had already been bypassed by 1957 in favor of a faster, four-lane alignment in the corridor now occupied by the interstate. On the opposite (north) side of the interstate, on the frontage road, is **Route 66 Motors** (12661 Historic Rte. 66). At the time I visited, they had an impressive array of signs on display outside, making

Route 66 Motors, Dillon, Missouri.
GPS: 37.98341,-91.69359

for an excellent photo op. Also on hand were gasoline pumps, a power boat, and sundry vehicles in various stages of neglect or restoration.

The **Mule Trading Post** (11160 Dillon Outer Rd.) is still in business near I-44's Highway V exit. The Mule moved here in 1957 from Pacific. In 2007, the Mule's proprietors added a giant hillbilly sign with rotating arms.

NORTHWYE

This village did not appear on my 1946 map, but evidently the U.S. 63/66 junction location spurred growth. By 1957, it had been plotted by the cartographers.

ROLLA

Route 66 enters Rolla from the north along U.S. 63/Bishop Avenue, and for most of its life skirted the west edge of downtown. As always, I recommend exploring downtown, which has plenty to offer, before rejoining Bishop Avenue for parts west.

Rolla was named after the North Carolina capital Raleigh, but spelled more phonetically with a Southern drawl. Rolla has a surprisingly active downtown, with the **Lambiel Jewelry Store** (218 W. 8th St.) and **Alex's Pizza Palace** (122 W. 8th St.) keeping things going. It doesn't hurt that it's a college town.

Rolla, Missouri.
GPS: 37.97807,-91.72170

The **Missouri University of Science and Technology** (300 W. 14th St.) is proud to be not-your-average university. They have their own mine rescue team and an extensive mineral collection, and they've created some works of art using high-pressure water-jet technology, including a scale model of Stonehenge and the Millennium Arch.

ROLLA ATTRACTIONS

The **Dillon House** (302 W. 3rd St.) is a log structure which served as the area's first courthouse circa 1857. The logs used are eighteen feet in length. The 1860 **Phelps County Jail** (500 W. 2nd St.) is on the National Register.

The **Totem Pole Trading Post** (1413 Martin Springs Dr.) moved to the west side of Rolla more than thirty years ago from its original location near Clementine. The carved totem pole, which used to adorn the roof of the old trading post, is now on display indoors at the present location. The building really doesn't look anything like what you think of as a "trading post," with a huge modern overhang sheltering the gas pumps.

Leaving Rolla, you are heading into the heart of Ozark country. Keep an eye

The Mule Trading Post, on the eastern outskirts of Rolla, Missouri.
GPS: 37.97807,-91.72170

Stonehenge replica, Rolla, Missouri. GPS: 37.95638,-91.77655

out for some curbed sections of the highway as you leave town, heading west on Martin Springs Road (the south interstate service road).

The Rolla-to-Springfield portion of Route 66 here in Missouri roughly follows the infamous Cherokee Trail of Tears. There were a number of variants on the route of the forced march from Georgia to Oklahoma, and the Northern Route went through this very corridor, circuitous as it may seem. It began in 1838, when a combination of congressional maneuvering, along with some wholesale trickery, led to the expulsion of the Cherokee people from their homes in Georgia. That year, U.S. troops under the

Inside the Totem Pole Trading Post, Rolla, Missouri. GPS: 37.94241,-91.79297

command of General Winfield Scott began rounding up men, women, and children and herding them hundreds of miles across the country. As implied by the name, many perished along the way.

DOOLITTLE

Route 66 passes through the town of Doolittle under the name Eisenhower Street.

The town was named for air-racer and World War II hero Jimmy Doolittle of Alameda, California. Doolittle set a world speed record in 1932; ten years later, he led the famous attack on Tokyo and other cities via B-25s that were launched from the U.S.S. *Hornet* aircraft carrier. That raid, coming as it did only a few months after Pearl Harbor, was a tremendous boost to American morale, and was later dramatized in the film *Thirty Seconds Over Tokyo*, starring Spencer Tracy. Doolittle also served in Italy, Germany, and North Africa during the war.

Doolittle, Missouri. GPS: 37.94028,-91.88171

Part of the remains of John's Modern Cabins. These ruins get more dilapidated—and hazardous—with each passing day. GPS: 37.93789,-91.94293

Prior to joining I-44 at interchange #176, you can make a short side trip for something you really should stop and see (refer to Arlington map). **John's Modern Cabins** was a tourist abode made up of a set of small wooden cabins. These were some rather primitive accommodations, as evidenced by the remains of an outhouse in the rear. Somewhat ironically, a neon "Welcome" sign glowed in the midst of this rather rustic encampment. A stone's throw away from the cabins is **Vernelle's Motel** (10891 Sugartree Outer Rd.). John's and

West of Doolittle. GPS: 37.93912,-91.94280

Vernelle's were bypassed many years ago, but a more recent realignment of I-44 isolated them even further.

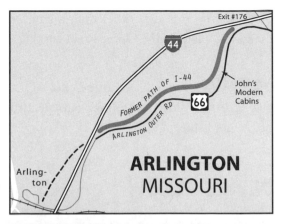

ARLINGTON

On the bank of the Little Piney River, the town of Arlington has been pretty effectively cut off from highway traffic. You might assume that this was a result of the replacement of U.S. 66 by Interstate 44. However, if you read Jack Rittenhouse's 1946 account of his passage through here, you'll learn that Arlington had already been cut off by that time, due to earlier construction. Rittenhouse

Town center of Arlington, Missouri.
GPS: 37.92042,-91.97132

went on to report a rumor that the area had been earmarked for development of a resort, which was never built. Seventy years later, Arlington is a quiet place indeed.

CLEMENTINE

In his notes, Jack Rittenhouse stated that Clementine was "hardly a town," and it does not appear on my 1946 or 1957 maps of the region (nor does Powellville). At one time, this area was characterized by its numerous basket vendors set up beside the highway. Today, there is little to nothing left of these communities, other than a small **cemetery** that can be reached by taking Clementine Outer Road east from exit #169.

 After Clementine/exit #169, you will need to take Highway Z (south side of the interstate) in order to pass through the village of Devil's Elbow.

DEVIL'S ELBOW

> The early Route 66 alignment was extremely convoluted, not only at the river crossing itself, but also for much of its eastern approach to the town. Looking at it closely, it's easy to see why the highway was straightened by construction of the Hooker Cut in order to facilitate the passage of trucks.

The ominous name of Devil's Elbow comes not from any highway hazard, but rather from the fact that there is a severe bend in the Big Piney River here, which caused problems for those whose livelihoods depended on the transport of goods up and down the waterway. There is a 1920s-era bridge that crosses the river here, and carried Route 66 traffic in the highway's early years. However, the narrow bridge and twisting roads in the

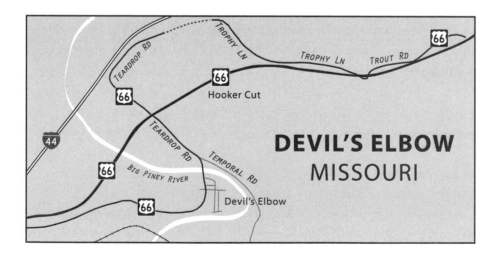

Devil's Elbow, Missouri. GPS: 37.84947,-92.06313

vicinity were considered a real problem when military material was transported back and forth during the war years, so the highway was re-routed
for a straighter course. You can see the wandering course 66 took prior to
the war era by looking at the reference map: old 66 followed Trout Road,
Trophy Lane, and Teardrop Road to the town of Devil's Elbow. That had
to have been some headache for truck drivers.

The Munger Moss Sandwich Shop plied its trade here in the town
of Devil's Elbow in the structure that is currently the **Elbow Inn** (21050

**Detail from the bridge over Big Piney River, Devil's Elbow, Missouri.
GPS: 37.84843,-92.06240**

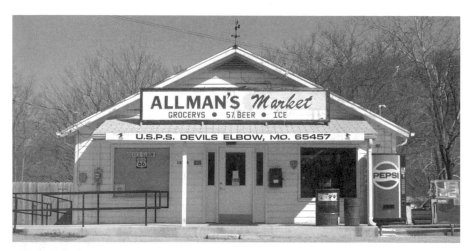

This store has for many years served as the post office for the small hamlet of Devil's Elbow, Missouri. GPS: 37.84642,-92.06134

Teardrop Rd.). However, during the highway's re-alignment in the 1940s, both the town and the restaurant were unceremoniously cut off, and so the proprietors moved to Lebanon and eventually established the Munger Moss Motel there (see page 147).

Devil's Elbow has a combination post office and general store that has changed its name over the years from Miller's, to Allman's, to **Shelden's** (12175 Timber Rd.), but otherwise it has looked very much the same for decades.

 Continue on Highway Z (south side of the freeway) to St. Robert.

ST. ROBERT

St. Robert is a young community by Route 66 standards, having been chartered in 1951. The town seems to have been engendered by the growth in local population, spurred by the establishment of Fort Leonard Wood during the Second World War. There is a small historical museum in the **St. Robert Municipal Center** (194 Eastlawn Ave., Suite A).

The **Pulaski County Tour-ism Bureau** (137 St. Rob-ert Boulevard, Suite A) has brochures describing three self-guided local driving tours for Fort Leonard Wood, Frisco Railroad, and Route 66.

FURTHER AFIELD

There is a turnoff for Fort Leonard Wood at Spur 44/ Missouri Avenue. General Leonard Wood was quite an accomplished officer, and well deserving of having an army post named after him. After the outbreak of the Spanish-Amer-

East of St. Robert, Missouri, you'll see this prehistoric creature standing guard at a retail complex. GPS: 37.82940,-92.10516

ican War in 1898, then-Colonel Wood and his friend Theodore Roosevelt recruited the 1st United States Volunteer Cavalry—the famous Rough Riders—of which Wood was the commanding officer. Meritorious con-duct at the battles of Las Guasimas and San Juan Hill gained Wood a promotion to brigadier general. After the war, Wood served as military governor of Cuba from 1899 to 1902. During this time, he oversaw im-provements in sanitation, education, and policing. He also served as gov-ernor of the Philippines from 1921 to 1927. General Wood even ran for the Republican presidential nomination in 1920, narrowly losing that bid to Warren G. Harding.

At Fort Leonard Wood you'll find the **John B. Mahaffey Museum Complex** (495 South Dakota Ave.). Included are exhibits honoring the army's Engineer Corps, Chemical Corps, and Military Police Corps. There is also information about General Wood's life and career, as well as an area set up as a replica of Fort Leonard Wood as it appeared during the 1940s.

**Former hotel and stagecoach stopover, downtown Waynesville, Missouri.
GPS: 37.82894,-92.20056**

WAYNESVILLE

This town is named after a revolutionary war hero, "Mad" Anthony
Wayne. Located just northwest of Fort Leonard Wood, Waynesville was
the chief recreational center for troops training there during the war
years. During that time, the streets were lined with bars, cafés, and other
businesses that young GIs tend to gravitate toward. This was very much
in evidence immediately following the war, when our friend Jack Rittenhouse came through here.

During the Civil War, Union troops built a fort overlooking the city
in order to protect the telegraph wires between St. Louis and Springfield.
There is a **historical marker** at the fort's location, on Fort Street between
Benton and Dewitt.

At Roubidoux Creek, Route 66 is carried by a five-span concrete arch
bridge that was constructed in 1923 (pre-66) and widened in 1939. A
large open field near the bridge served as a campsite for the Cherokees
during the Trail of Tears march.

WAYNESVILLE ATTRACTIONS

Be on the lookout for **Frog Rock** (a.k.a. W. H. Croaker) jutting out of a hillside on Route 66, on the eastern outskirts of town. Locals decided that the rock outcropping looked a lot like a frog, so it has been painted very nicely now to really look like a frog.

The **Old Stagecoach Stop** (105 N. Lynn St.), a two-story station that has also served as a wartime hospital and a hotel during its 140-year history, is on the National Register.

The **Pulaski County Courthouse Museum** (123 N. Benton St.) is located within the town's 1903 courthouse. The museum's themes include the Civil War, Trail of Tears, pioneer history, and Route 66. Open Saturdays in the town square.

The **Talbot House** (405 North St.) is one of the oldest in town. It now houses an antiques shop, so you don't need to come away from your tour empty-handed.

 After Waynesville, the highway is now marked Highway 17. Stay with it all the way to Buckhorn.

BUCKHORN-LAQUEY-HAZELGREEN

At Buckhorn, continue following Highway 17, which crosses here to the south side of I-44.

Here in Buckhorn, Historic 66 crosses I-44 (at exit #153) under the guise of Highway 17. Buckhorn was named after the Buckhorn Tavern, a former stage stop on the old Wire Road, which displayed a set of antlers. Between here and the Highway 133 junction is an area called Gascozark. That name was coined by a developer in the 1920s, and is a hybrid derived from Ozark and Gasconade (for the nearby river). The old **Gascozark Trading Post** still stands, neglected and overgrown, near where

Buckhorn, Missouri. GPS: 37.78607,-92.26871

Highway 133 crosses I-44, including some former tourist cabins. West of Hazelgreen, Route 66 crosses the Gasconade River on a steel bridge constructed in 1922 (south of I-44).

IMPORTANT NOTE: Recently, Missouri highway authorities closed the Route 66 bridge crossing the Gasconade River west of Hazelgreen, perhaps permanently. Therefore, you'll need to cross to the north side of the interstate at exit #145/Highway 133 to continue your journey west. You'll miss some authentic Route 66 miles unless you do some backtracking. Your next opportunity to return to 66 will be crossing to the south side of I-44 at exit #140. Then you'll need to cross again to the north side of the freeway at exit #135 for the run into Lebanon.

U. S. Highway 66 Bridge over Gasconade River
in the Scenic Missouri Ozarks

Bridge over the Gasconade River, east of Lebanon, Missouri. GPS: 37.75961,-92.45134

LEBANON

Lebanon is home to the **Munger Moss Motel** (1336 Historic Rte. 66), which has a huge, red, porcelain-and-neon sign out front that was manufactured just a little up the road by a firm named Springfield Neon. If you'll be staying the night in the Lebanon area, I highly recommend you do so here at the Munger Moss. The owners really care about Route 66 and roadies like you and me. The lobby is also a combination gift shop and vintage toy display.

Not far from the Munger Moss is **Wrink's Market**. Unfortunately, Glenn "Wrink" Wrinkle passed away in 2005. Wrink started operating the market in 1950, and kept it open until only a few weeks before his death fifty-five years later. After sitting idle for a time, the store was reopened by Glenn's son Terry, but it has since closed again, likely indefinitely.

Opened in 2004, the LaClede County Library houses a great **Route 66 Museum** (915 S. Jefferson Ave.) run by the Lebanon/LaClede County Route 66 Society. The old **LaClede County Jail** (262 N. Adams Ave.) is on the National Register.

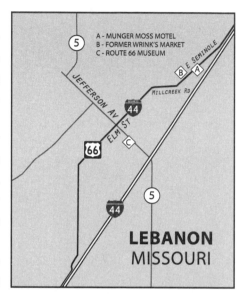

FURTHER AFIELD

North of Lebanon (about twenty-five miles) via Highway 5 is Camdenton. A nearby park, **Ha Ha Tonka State Park** (1491 State

The Munger Moss Motel is a place every Mother Roader should plan to stay the night sometime. Lebanon, Missouri. GPS: 37.68652,-92.63994

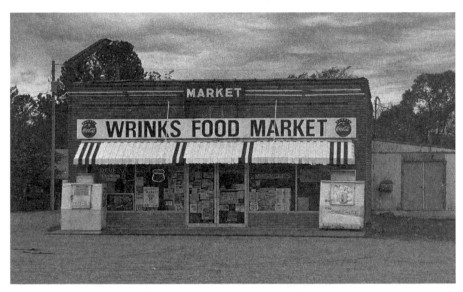

The former Wrink's Market in Lebanon. GPS: 37.68497,-92.64254

Rd. D), includes the remains of a 100-year-old European-style castle. In 1905, a Kansas City businessman named Robert Snyder began construction of a three-story stone castle on 2,500 acres of land that he had acquired for its natural beauty. He intended to create a retreat that would rival any in the world and spared no expense in its creation, hiring the most qualified artisans and obtaining the best materials available. Tragically, Snyder died suddenly in 1906, and the unfinished project was taken over by his sons. The property eventually included the castle, an eighty-foot

Lebanon, Missouri.
GPS: 37.68389,-92.64865

The centerpiece of Ha Ha Tonka State Park is this stone ruin. Near Camdenton, Missouri. GPS: 37.97630,-92.76960

water tower, stables, and several greenhouses. In later years, the family came upon hard times and was forced to lease the property to someone who operated it as a hotel for some years. In 1942, more tragedy struck when a spark from a fireplace spread rapidly and gutted both the main house and the stable. Those ruins now stand stark and haunting atop a 250-foot bluff overlooking the Lake of the Ozarks.

The state of Missouri purchased the estate in 1978 and opened it to the public as Ha Ha Tonka ("Laughing Water") State Park. The park's beautiful natural features confirm Mr. Snyder's good

Castle Hahatonka, Lake of the Ozarks, Missouri

A MISSOURI STATE HIGHWAY PHOTO

taste in obtaining the property. Today, park visitors can enjoy sinkholes, caves, a natural bridge, springs, and, of course, the famous ruins via some fifteen miles of trails. The trails run the gamut from paved, "accessible" paths and boardwalks to strenuous, rocky climbs suitable for overnight backpacking. Some of the caves here—like many others throughout Missouri—are said to have been used as hideouts by criminals during the 1830s. The Ha Ha Tonka visitor center features a relief map of the area carved from a block of stone.

 Back on 66: From Lebanon, take Highway W (west side of I-44) to Phillipsburg.

PHILLIPSBURG-CONWAY-SAMPSON-NIANGUA

Cross to the south side of I-44 at Phillipsburg (exit #118) and join Highway CC (see the reference map).

According to a 1946 oil company road map of Missouri, Conway and Sampson were both Route 66 towns strung between Phillipsburg and Marshfield, with 66 just barely missing Niangua. Since the railroad

Alongside I-40, near Phillipsburg, Missouri. GPS: 37.56701,-92.77635

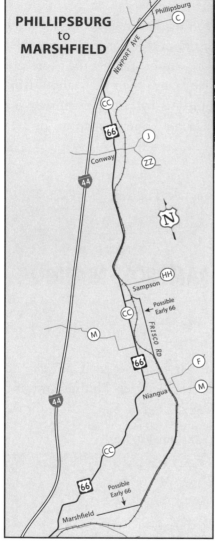

PHILLIPSBURG
to
MARSHFIELD

Phillipsburg, Missouri.
GPS: 37.55545,-92.78909

tracks pass directly through the heart of Niangua, it seems likely that, originally—in the 1920s or '30s, perhaps—the early Route 66 did take in Niangua. By 1957, however, a new four-lane alignment had been constructed that bypassed all of these towns by a few miles and occupied the present-day I-44 roadbed through the region. By then, the village of Sampson was no longer deemed worthy of any mention at all. All of these towns are still there, but you'll have to make a greater effort if you intend to see them (see the reference map).

MARSHFIELD

Marshfield is the hometown of Edwin Hubble, creator of the Hubble Space Telescope. The town has a one-quarter-sized replica of the telescope occupying the west side of the lawn at the **Marshfield Courthouse**

County courthouse, Marshfield, Missouri. GPS: 37.33846,-92.90717

(140 S. Clay St.). Nearby is the **Webster County Historical Museum** (219 S. Clay St.), housed in the old community library that was funded by the Carnegie Foundation in 1911. Outside the museum is a "Walk of Fame" honoring prominent citizens of Missouri.

Hidden Waters Nature Park (716 W. Hubble Dr.) includes springs that form the headwaters of the Niangua River and walking trails that pass other water features, as well as an assortment of gardens. In the park you'll also find the Callaway Cabin, which dates from 1853 and was one of the few structures to survive the tornado that struck the area in 1880.

 Leave Marshfield on Highway OO toward Strafford.

HOLMAN-STRAFFORD

East of Strafford, near the small hamlet of Holman, is the **Wild Animal Safari** (124 Jungle Dr.), one of those zoological parks you can drive through in your car and view hundreds of animals in captivity—some of which may not even know that it is they, and not you, who are in the lockup. Denizens of this paradise include bison, llamas, and zedonks (zebra-donkey hybrid). Unlike most zoological parks of one kind or another, you are not forbidden to feed the animals here. In fact, there is animal feed for sale that you can toss out of your car to entice the animals to approach you. There are also paddle boats and a petting zoo.

 Leave Strafford on Highway 125, paralleling the railroad tracks.

SPRINGFIELD

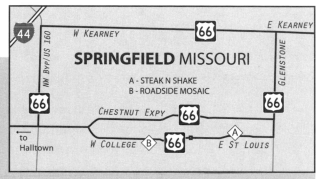

There are multiple Route 66 alignments, so exploration is strongly encouraged. The best-known versions enter Springfield on Kearney Street, turn south on Glenstone, and then head west again after turning onto either Chestnut or St. Louis. Both will take you through the heart of downtown. A later bypass routing continues further west on Kearney before turning south, thus avoiding downtown traffic. There are still a number of classic motels and other vintage businesses to excite your senses. Among the motels are the Rest Haven, Skyline, and Rail Haven, to name only a few.

Established in the 1820s when pioneer John Polk Campbell carved his initials in a tree near the confluence of four springs, and soon thereafter known as the Queen of the Ozarks, Springfield won't disappoint the Route 66 traveler. Upon your arrival, be sure to stop by the **Route 66 Visitor Center** (815 E. St. Louis St.).

Springfield has a special distinction. It was here, in 1947, that Red Chaney opened the first hamburger stand with a drive-thru window: Red's Giant Hamburg. In 1982, a song was written about the place called "Red's" that was recorded by a Springfield band called the Morells. A photo of Red's even appeared on the album cover. Red eventually retired, though, and his landmark was demolished in the 1990s, with more than a few nostalgic souls turning out for the occasion. Today, **Birthplace of Route 66 Roadside Park** (College St. and S. New Ave.) is the town's

The eastern outskirts of Springfield, Missouri. GPS: 37.23933,-93.23490

tribute to Red's.

Another business originating here in Springfield was **Campbell's 66 Express**, the trucking firm which used Snortin' Norton, the "Humpin' to Please" camel, as its trademark.

The Steak 'n Shake restaurant chain still has a sizable presence in Missouri, and in Springfield in particular, a number of the earlier restaurants still remain. The chain's famous directive to "Take Home a Sack" (modified to "Takhomasak") has been echoed many times over by famous burger chains nationwide: White Castle's "Buy 'Em by the Sack," White Tower's "Buy a Bag Full," and Krystal's "Take Along a Sack Full" all encourage us to indulge the same impulse. The **Steak 'n Shake flagship restaurant** (1158 E. St. Louis St.) will make you think you've time-traveled to 1960.

As you pass through town on what is now College Street, be on the lookout for a small embankment beside the road adorned

Springfield, Missouri.
GPS: 37.20879,-93.32302

ED GALLOWAY

Nathan Ed Galloway was born in 1880 in Stone County, near Springfield, Missouri. From a very young age, he showed a talent and propensity for wood carving.

In 1898, Ed joined the U.S. Army and served in the Spanish-American War before being assigned to duty in the Philippines. While there, he came into contact with creatures such as crocodiles and other reptiles that would inspire some of his later art.

After leaving the army, Ed returned to Springfield and pursued his wood carving. He specialized in household objects such as hall trees and smoking stands, which he covered with intricate carvings of animals and other figures. He also fashioned many large-scale items from tree trunks; these, too, were often decorated with human and animal figures.

Ed planned to be an exhibitor at the Panama-Pacific International Exposition in San Francisco, taking place in 1915. Tragically, a fire at his studio destroyed most of his work. Ed managed to salvage a few pieces, including his sculpture known as *Lion in a Cage*, and began making his way west toward California for the exposition. It is said that he had been temporarily waylaid in Tulsa, Oklahoma, when his work was seen and admired by Charles Page. Page was a businessman and philanthropist who had established a home for orphaned children in nearby Sand Springs. He offered Ed a job teaching woodworking to the boys at the Sand Springs home, and Ed remained in Sand Springs in that capacity for the next twenty-plus years.

From 1936 to 1937, Ed and his wife, Villie, bought several acres of land near Foyil, Oklahoma (Villie was from the Bushyhead area), and began the chapter of his life for which he is best known. He began building a stone residence on the property (completed in 1937), as well as a collection of large American Indian-inspired structures. The largest of these structures is a ninety-foot-tall totem pole bearing the date 1948, which took him eleven years to complete.

During this time, Ed also constructed his "Fiddle House," an eleven-sided building created expressly to house the growing collection of fiddles he carved. That collection is said to have exceeded 300.

Ed seems to have been speaking to Mother Road lovers such as you and me when he said: "All my life, I did the best I knew. I built these things by the side of the road to be a friend to you."

Ed died of cancer on November 11, 1962 (Veterans Day). His Foyil property was donated by his family in 1989 to the Rogers County Historical Society, which maintains the present-day Totem Pole Park (see page 202).

with a **Route 66-themed mosaic**. The artwork was created by local artist Christine Schilling with the help of some young students. In 2010, Schilling began restoration of an advertising mural in downtown Springfield that was partially exposed when a vehicle collided with the building. The ad touts Beeman's Pepsin Gum (305 E. Commercial St.).

SPRINGFIELD ATTRACTIONS

Springfield is widely known as the home of **Bass Pro Shops Outdoor World** (1935 S. Campbell Ave.), a veritable theme park of a retail experience for the outdoor set. There's a 140,000-gallon game fish aquarium and a four-story waterfall. If that's not enough, check out the stuffed and mounted bears, antique fishing gear, and wildlife art gallery.

Next door to Bass Pro Shops is **World of Wildlife** (500 W. Sunshine

The Rest Haven Motel in Springfield, Missouri, sports a huge neon sign in excellent condition. GPS: 37.23984,-93.25612

St.), featuring a myriad of authentic wildlife habitats, such as aquariums, aviaries, and even a swamp area.

The **Typewriter Toss** is held each April on Secretaries Day—just in case you thought that was a "holiday" you could live without. On this day, typewriters are thrown at a bullseye from a height of fifty feet.

If pioneer history interests you, check out the **Gray-Campbell Farmstead** (2400 S. Scenic Ave.) in Nathanael Greene Park. Centered around the oldest house in Springfield (circa 1856), the farmstead features a log kitchen, two-crib barn, family cemetery, and Civil War-era artifacts. There are costumed docents on hand to explain the history of the place. Also at Nathanael Greene Park is the **Mizumoto Stroll Garden**, with over seven acres of lakes, winding paths, and other traditional features of Japanese-style gardens.

At the **Missouri Sports Hall of Fame** (3861 E. Stan Musial Dr.), you'll become acquainted with some of the great names that have called the Show-Me State home base: Stan Musial, Whitey Herzog, and Bob Gibson, to name only a few. There's even a cage where visitors can stand behind home plate while 100-mph fastballs come blazing in from the mound.

Springfield, Missouri.
GPS: 37.20885,-93.32372

The **History of Hearing Museum** (628 E. Commercial St.) will take you back to the days of handheld ear trumpets, and explains how the evolution of hearing-aid technology has improved lives.

The restored **Jefferson Avenue Footbridge** (Commercial St. and Jefferson Ave.) was built in 1902, and is a favorite train-watching spot, passing as it does over several sets of tracks. Locals consider the footbridge, which is more than 500 feet in length, to be their largest public sculpture. In fact, it's the longest footbridge in the entire country.

The **Railroad Historical Museum** (1300 N. Grant Ave.) preserves railroading heritage with several different types of railcars on display. Opportunities for kids include exploring a locomotive cab and ringing the bell.

Pythian Castle (1451 E. Pythian St.) was originally constructed by the Knights of Pythias in 1913 as an orphanage. It was commandeered for use by the U.S. Army during World War II, and is said to be haunted. Tours are available of the 55-room, 40,000-square-foot castle, and special events are held there frequently. The **Calaboose** (409 W. McDaniel St.) was built in 1891 as a jail, but now serves as a police substation with a law enforcement museum on the first floor.

Askinosie Chocolate (514 E. Commercial St.) makes chocolate, white chocolate, and cocoa butter from scratch (cocoa beans!). The building itself dates from 1894, and previously saw action as a carriage factory. Tours of the factory are available for a small donation. Military memorabilia abounds at the **Air and Military Museum of the Ozarks** (2305 E. Kearney St.), including restored aircraft, a variety of military vehicles, dioramas, and flight simulators. You can even have your own personalized dog tags made.

Civil War buffs will want to visit **General Sweeney's Civil War Museum** (5228 S. State Highway ZZ). An official site of the Civil War Trust, it's the only museum to focus on the trans-Mississippi portion of the conflict, and houses more than 5,000 wartime artifacts.

FURTHER AFIELD

Just northwest of Springfield, you'll find **Fantastic Caverns** (4872 N. Farm Rd. 125). Acclaimed as "America's Only Drive-Thru Cave," the tour takes visitors along the path of an underground river in Jeeps, while the guides extol the considerable virtues of protecting the environment by powering the tour vehicles with propane. Furthermore, the cave was once owned by the Ku Klux Klan, which held meetings in one of the caverns here.

In contrast to the above, due north of Springfield via Highway H is **Crystal Cave** (7225 N. Crystal Cave Ln.). Here, the operators have endeavored to provide a cave experience in a more natural state. There are no vehicles; instead, visitors clamber about on narrow paths and must negotiate tight spaces. Unusual features include Rainbow Falls, the Cathedral, fossil crinoids, and numerous American Indian symbols.

The town of Marionville, southwest of Springfield on U.S. 60, has a reputation for **albino squirrels**. Keep your camera ready.

To the south of Springfield, via U.S. 65, is the town of Branson. Though considered a tad overblown by many, Branson does have at least one redeeming feature: the **Branson Scenic Railway** (206 E. Main St.). The restored *Ozark State Zephyr* plies the area and hearkens to the passenger service glory days of the 1940s and '50s.

To the northwest of Branson, via Highway 76, is a semi-Christian theme park called **Silver Dollar City** (399 Silver Dollar City Pkwy). The park sprang up due to the presence of nearby Marvel Cave, a subterranean attraction in the area since 1950. The

West of Springfield, Missouri. GPS: 32.21130,-93.48230

theme park was officially established in 1960, and then received some additional notoriety when a few episodes of the *Beverly Hillbillies* television series were filmed there in 1967.

 Head west out of Springfield on the Chestnut Expressway (Highway 266), which is Historic 66.

PLANO

In this vicinity is a **masonry building** (S. Farm Rd. 45) just a few feet from the edge of the highway that has been taken over by vines and other vegetation. The interior is completely gutted and roofless. Inside, many small trees

Former casket-making shop, near Plano, Missouri. GPS: 37.19282,-93.55078

are growing, reaching for the windows and the sky.

If you have a detailed map of this region, you can see that the later

version of Route 66 (present-day
Highway 266 from here to Paris
Springs, and Highway 96 from
Spencer to northeast of Carthage) were each plotted as nearly a straight line over the next
forty miles or so.

HALLTOWN

Established in 1833 and later
named after merchant George
Hall, Halltown is known for
its antique shops, the largest of
which is **Whitehall Mercantile**
(100 N. Park Dr.). Amazingly,

Halltown, Missouri. GPS: 37.19343,-93.62679

back in 1946, Jack Rittenhouse characterized Halltown by making mention of its antique shops.

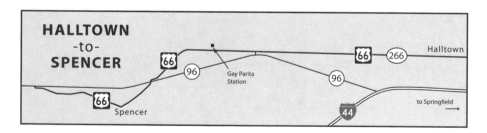

PARIS SPRINGS-SPENCER-
HEATONVILLE-ALBATROSS-PHELPS

Don't fail to stop at the **Gay Parita station** (21118 Historic Rte. 66) in
Paris Springs; it's pretty special.

Coming up is one of my favorite stretches of old Route 66. Ahead
of you now is a string of very small towns stretching between Halltown

Gay Parita station, Paris Springs, Missouri. GPS: 37.19430,-93.67919

and Carthage. Due to highway realignments, traffic was diverted south of here, pulling the lifelines from towns such as Albatross and Phelps. As a result, they became almost frozen in time.

As you pass through this section, I urge you to slow down considerably. Take your time exploring the communities of Paris Springs, Spencer, Heatonville, Albatross, and Phelps. You will see the **ruins of convenience stores, tourist courts, and other structures**, many of

Spencer, Missouri. GPS: 37.18444,-93.70272

This tiny station in Phelps, Missouri, has since been demolished. GPS: 37.19011,-93.90216

which look as though the owners left suddenly and never returned. You will also see some structures that have been assigned to new uses, such as a set of **tourist cabins** now being used as storage sheds.

RESCUE-PLEW-AVILLA

Between Rescue and Plew is a turnoff (YY North) to Red Oak. This reference will be more meaningful a short time later, when you encounter the turnoff for Red Oak II just outside of Carthage. Avilla has a deteriorating business district, but also some unexpected Route 66 spirit.

Avilla, Missouri. GPS: 37.19553,-94.12869

FURTHER AFIELD

You won't find this town on a road map, but here it is anyway, created by a local artist northeast of

Avilla, Missouri. GPS: 37.19555,-94.12978

Carthage. **Red Oak II** (County Loop 122) is a village—partly the original Red Oak—that was brought over from its original location more

Part of the art-inspired community of Red Oak II, Missouri. GPS: 37.21273,-94.27704

than twenty miles away and installed here, presumably to attract nostalgia-minded travelers—and it keeps growing. It features a multitude of vintage structures, including a blacksmith shop, diner, general store, church, a couple of filling stations, and several residences, both occupied and otherwise. There's even a mock cemetery.

CARTHAGE

 You can head into Carthage on current Highway 96 to Central Avenue, but there's an older alignment to the left (see the reference map) that wanders to the eastern side of Kellogg Lake and includes some old tourist courts. For a time, that alignment then proceeded west on Java Street before joining Garrison north of town.

The famed Carthage marble is quarried in this town, and more than a few Carthaginians have made their living in the field. Stop at the **Carthage Chamber of Commerce** (402 S. Garrison Ave.) for information about a home tour that begins and ends at the Jasper County Courthouse in the square and takes you on a drive to see the homes of several of Carthage's most prominent citizens. Constructed between 1870 and 1910, many of these residences were built by stone quarry and mine owners.

The **Jasper County Courthouse** (302 S. Main St.) itself was constructed in 1894–1895. There is a mural inside depicting the history of

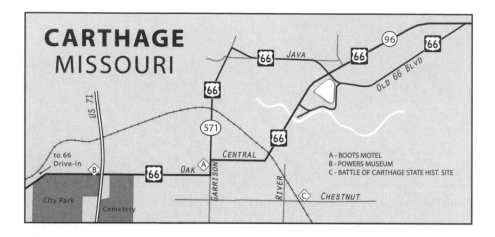

the area, painted by a local artist. In 2009, a Route 66 display was added that loosely resembles the former Boots Drive-In (see the reference map). The courthouse also features a wrought-iron, cage-style elevator that is still in operation. Take a stroll around the town square, which is lined with buildings dating from as early as the 1870s.

For a reminder of authentic Route 66, the **Boots Court Motel** (107 S. Garrison Ave.) is hard to beat. According to a local tourism brochure, Clark Gable once stayed at the Boots, in room 6. There used to be a Boots Drive-In & Gift Shop across the street in the streamlined building now housing a bank.

Boots Motel, Carthage, Missouri. GPS: 37.17844,-94.31403

CARTHAGE ATTRACTIONS

The **Battle of Carthage Civil War Museum** (205 Grant St.) features a mural, prints, historic relics, and souvenirs memorializing the battle and its participants. The Battle of Carthage was fought early in the war (1861) and was a victory for the Confederates, setting an early tone for the hostilities. Nearby is the **Battle of Carthage State Historic Site** (north side of E. Chestnut Rd., near S. River St.).

The historic **Phelps House** (1146 S. Grand Ave.) is a restored Victorian mansion that was built circa 1895. The house is built of local

stone, and some of the furniture and fixtures here are originals. It has ten fireplaces, each with different-colored tile, and a hand-operated elevator serving four floors. Tours are available.

Marlin Perkins, longtime host of the popular television series *Wild Kingdom*, grew up

Phelps House, Carthage, Missouri.
GPS: 37.16889,-94.30939

in Carthage, and there is a statue of him standing in the town's **Central Park** (S. Garrison Ave.). Belle Starr also grew up here, in her father's hotel downtown, prior to the Civil War.

Local history is the focus at the **Powers Museum** (1617 W. Oak St.), which has rotating exhibits with a variety of themes. The museum is on the former site of Taylor Tourist Park, later known as the Park Motor Court & Cafe. In 2005, the museum instituted what it calls its "Traveling Classroom Trunks" program for educators. The theme of one of these trunks is Jasper County highways, including Route 66 and other early auto trails.

On the western outskirts of town is the 1940s-era **66 Drive-In Theater** (17231 Old 66 Blvd.). This theater was restored in 1998, and

The 66 Drive-In is still in business on the west side of Carthage, Missouri. GPS: 37.17321,-94.36861

reopened exactly forty-nine years after its original grand opening in September of '49.

One of Carthage's most-visited attractions is the **Precious Moments Chapel & Gardens** (4321 S. Chapel Rd.). The compound includes a chapel, ornamental gardens, museum, gift shop, and snack bar.

Highway bridge just west of Carthage, Missouri. GPS: 37.17284,-94.40630

CARTERVILLE

Route 66 enters Carterville from the north along Pine Street. According to Rittenhouse, Carterville was already a virtual ghost town in 1946, with "boarded-up stores, empty buildings, and general air of desolation." Furthermore, it offered no facilities for motorists. My 1957 atlas, however, still affords it the status of a viable highway community.

Carterville, Missouri. GPS: 37.14919,-94.44251

WEBB CITY

Webb City is well worth some exploration. Named for a local farmer, John Webb, who discovered lead in the area, the town's fortunes were tied to mining in its early days. There seems to be an identity crisis of sorts, though, in Webb City: the water tower is emblazoned with "City of Flags," while a sign at a nearby park is marked "Zinc City." I haven't found anyone who can

**Downtown Webb City, Missouri.
GPS: 37.14560,-94.46310**

explain the "Flags" moniker. Since the town was established in 1876, I'm a little surprised they didn't call themselves the "Centennial City."

Webb City has a large neon arrow that points in the direction of its business district, which is slightly off today's main highway, MacArthur Drive. Adjacent to the business district are some very nice older homes

Among the many features of King Jack Park is this sculpture of praying hands on a hilltop. Webb City, Missouri. GPS: 37.14015,-94.46568

that are worth a walking tour. There are also some **murals**—one on the side of **Bruner Pharmacy** (101 W. Daugherty St.) and another inside **Mid-Missouri Bank** (100 N. Main St.). At Ball and MacArthur Streets is a 105-mm **howitzer named Jeannie**, said to have played a role in the liberation of France in World War II.

King Jack Park (555 S. Main St.) features a large sculpture of a miner with pick in hand that is named, fittingly, *Kneeling Miner Statue.* The park also features a tiny train depot, which was moved here after serving as part of an interurban commuting system that was shut down in the 1930s. The depot now houses the **Chamber of Commerce** (112 W. Broadway St.). There's even a streetcar here that runs on special occasions. Overlooking King Jack Park is the *Praying Hands Monument*, an enormous pair of praying hands created by sculptor Jack Dawson in the early 1970s. The body of water you see in the park is actually an old mining pit called **Sucker Flats.**

The **Clubhouse Museum** (115 N. Madison St.) makes its home in a building constructed in 1910, used as a "clubhouse" for the employees of the local commuter railway. The museum doesn't keep set hours, but you can call ahead for a tour or to arrange a rental for a special event: (417) 673-5866.

JOPLIN

 There are multiple Route 66 alignments going both to and through Joplin, some of which are shown on the reference map. Also, as you'd expect, 66 took a stair-step route through town in its earliest days, touching Zora, Euclid, and Broadway on its way west. Ultimately, Route 66 left Joplin via W. 7th Street.

There are multiple authentic routes through Joplin (see the reference map), primarily Rangeline Road, Main Street, and 7th Street. Exploration is the order of the day.

Pearl Brothers True Value Hardware (617 S. Main St.) sports a Route 66-themed mural on an outside wall. Downtown Joplin features

JOPLIN
MISSOURI
including
Carterville
& Webb City

A - KING JACK PARK
B - CLUBHOUSE MUSEUM
C - CITY HALL/T. HART BENTON MURAL

Wilder's Fine Foods (1216 S. Main St.), which has a terrific old neon sign.

Joplin is also the hometown of actor Dennis Weaver.

JOPLIN ATTRACTIONS

A mural inside Joplin City Hall (602 Main St.) named *Joplin at the Turn of the Century, 1896–1906* is the last signed large-scale work by Missourian artist Thomas Hart Benton. There are also sketches documenting the mural's progress.

Richardson's Candy House (454 Redings Mill Rd.) occupies the sixty-year-old Rock Tavern building and still does things the old-fashioned way. Watch hand-dipped chocolates and divinity being made. Somehow I'm reminded of an *I Love Lucy* episode . . .

Exhibits at Schifferdecker Park's **Dorothea**

Sign in downtown Joplin, Missouri.
GPS: 37.07776,-94.51381

Downtown Joplin. GPS: 37.08456,-94.51284

B. Hoover Historical Museum (504 S. Schifferdecker Ave.) recall the Joplin of the 1870s, with antique dolls, a miniature animated circus, and a replica of a nineteenth-century tavern. Also at Schifferdecker Park is the **Tri-State Mineral Museum**. The park is on the western outskirts of the city.

With a twenty-five-foot drop, **Grand Falls** (5685 Riverside Dr.) is Missouri's largest waterfall.

Downtown Joplin. GPS: 37.08475,-94.53737

FURTHER AFIELD

The **George Washington Carver National Monument** (5646 Carver Rd.), southeast of Joplin, marks George Washington Carver's birthplace. Carver was born into slavery, but through hard work became the director of agricultural research at the Tuskegee Institute. There, his experimentation led to the development of more than 400 new products made from peanuts, cotton, and soybeans.

Highway 66 leaves Joplin on W. 7th, heading due west, and it's only a few miles to the Kansas border. Look ahead to the Galena, Kansas, reference map so that you make your turn prior to the state line and don't miss anything. The **Hogs & Hot Rods Saloon**, formerly the State Line Bar & Grill will remind you that you are passing into the Sunflower State.

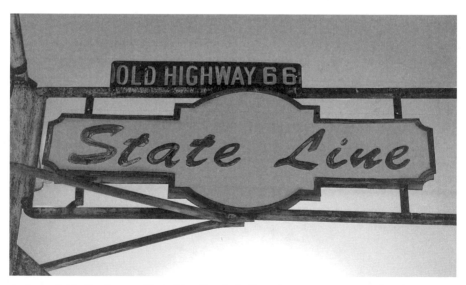

A sign outside the former State Line Bar & Grill, at the Missouri-Kansas border.
GPS: 37.08594,-94.61779

KANSAS

K ansas has a reputation, at least among some of us, for epitomizing the safety and security of home. The impressions we form at an early age are slow to change, and many of us in twentieth-century

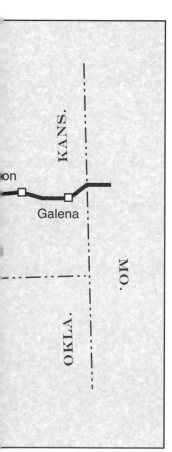

America have grown up with a picture of Kansas heavily influenced by the classic 1939 film *The Wizard of Oz*. Kansas was portrayed first as dull, then as a secure place to return to, but always—fundamentally—as Home. Perhaps this impression is reinforced by the fact that Kansas is so centrally located within the contiguous forty-eight states. The state of Kansas seems to be officially satisfied with this image, having adopted "Home on the Range" as its state song.

Even beyond that, stereotypes have a way of persisting. Someone who has never set foot in Kansas will tell you with great certainty that the state is made up of very flat, monotonous country, with nothing but wheat fields mile after mile after mile.

But in fact, Kansas is a place well worth getting to know. It's more diverse than most people realize, and it's far less a Home than it is a Crossroads. Numerous legendary trails traversed the state of Kansas en route to more remote objectives, such as California or Oregon, while others, like the Chisholm Trail, were laid out with Kansas as their destination.

A complete inventory of the historic tracks crisscrossing the state would be difficult to compile, but the list would have to include the Oregon

Trail, which took settlers to Oregon Territory by way of Topeka; the California Overland Trail, which followed the same route during its passage through Kansas; the Santa Fe Trail, a trade route to the ancient capital passing through the longest dimension of the state and exiting near Elkhart; the Pony Express Route, along which mail was carried between Missouri and California; and the Chisholm Trail, the path of countless cattle and cowboys between the ranches of southern Texas and the railheads at Abilene, Kansas.

Other trails in Kansas are less known, but served their purposes in their own time: the Parallel Road, the Ellsworth Trail, and the Pawnee Trail. U.S. Route 66 was one of many paths that touched upon Kansas only in order to reach someplace else.

Like so many of us, Route 66 never gave Kansas a chance, never got to know her well. The path of Route 66 barely took a nibble from the southeast corner of the state—a mere thirteen miles of road in a land of 82,000 square miles, 52 million acres, and 2.8 million people. To appreciate Kansas from so meager a sample is to emulate the blind man who tried to envision an elephant by touching only its tail.

The Kansas that you see from Route 66 isn't a lot like the stereotype you expect. No amber waves of grain shifting in the breeze here. Southeast Kansas is mining country, and mining districts are not often candidates for scenic postcard views. This is a different kind of bountiful earth, one that yields its rewards grudgingly and does not find its way easily into glossy tour guidebooks.

That's not to say this portion of Kansas is any less proud of what it is. Route 66 paid its respects here and departed; the people of Kansas have gotten used to this and have moved on with their lives.

As you head westward into Kansas, past the bar with the "State Line" sign overhead, you'll find your first stop in the Sunflower State: Galena.

 Just about four miles past Schifferdecker Park on the west edge of Joplin, turn right onto Front Street in order to enter Galena on the much preferred older alignment.

GALENA

Formerly two distinct towns, Galena and Empire, Galena annexed the latter in 1911. The town is named for lead-bearing ore, which is plentiful in the area.

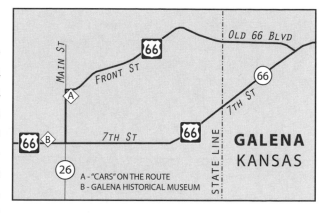

Surprisingly to this traveler, Galena is a very popular name for American towns. At least twenty-one other states have—or have had—a town so named.

Downtown Galena has a number of buildings with old advertising **murals** painted on the sides that are becoming visible again due to weathering.

GALENA ATTRACTIONS

Entering Galena from the east along Front Street, you'll make a left-hand turn onto Main. On the southeast corner is an old gasoline station now called **Cars on the Route** (119 N. Main St.). The owners serve today's

A popular stop in Galena, Kansas. GPS: 37.08051,-94.63916

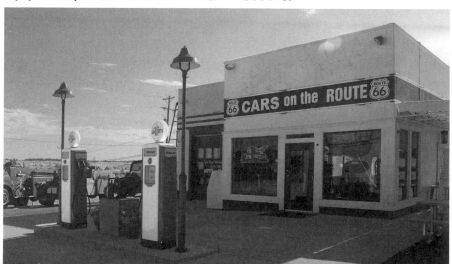

The old highway just east of Galena, Kansas. GPS: 37.08358,-94.63100

Mother Road adventurers with a combination welcome center, gift shop, and snack bar. Usually parked on the property is the tow truck that supplied the inspiration for the "Tow Mater" character in the movie *Cars*.

Also on Main Street in Galena is **Howard "Pappy" Litch Park** (S. Main St. and E. 5th St.), named for a local citizen and historian. The park contains one of the original 1952 Will Rogers Highway plaques—this one was brought from a site at the Missouri-Kansas border—and is located on a plot of land formerly occupied by a federal highway weigh station.

The old Katy railroad depot, which is right on Highway 66, now houses the **Galena Mining and Historical Museum** (319 W. 7th St.). Pappy Litch was one of the major forces in establishing this museum.

For a very short side trip, you can take Kansas Highway 26 south for two miles, from downtown Galena to **Schermerhorn Park** (3501 S. Main St.), which is in an area of the state called the Kansas Ozarks.

This retired M.K.T. Railroad depot now serves as the local history museum in Galena, Kansas. GPS: 37.07507,-94.64203

There, you'll find a great-looking WPA-constructed building and stone terraces from the 1930s. Formerly a Boy Scout meeting place, the structure has now been transformed into a nature center. Also in the park is a cave—Schermerhorn Cave—which, like Meramec Cavern in Missouri, is reputed to have been a hiding place of outlaw Jesse James.

 Depart Galena, heading west on 7th Street.

RIVERTON

This is truly the center of Route 66 in Kansas. **Nelson's Old Riverton Store** (7109 SE Highway 66), formerly the Eisler Brothers Store, built circa 1925, is the de facto headquarters of the Kansas Route 66 Association. It not only serves as a general store,

Riverton, Kansas. GPS: 37.07497,-94.70258

but also carries a wide array of roadie paraphernalia intended precisely for adventurers like you and me.

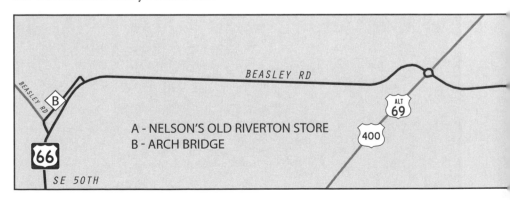

A - NELSON'S OLD RIVERTON STORE
B - ARCH BRIDGE

This bridge stands just west of Riverton, Kansas. GPS: 37.07327,-94.74101

Identifying plaque on the bridge near Riverton. GPS: 37.07327,-94.74101

FURTHER AFIELD

Northwest of Riverton is the town of Columbus. There is a **clock tower** (W. Maple St. and N. Pennsylvania Ave.) here featuring a 1919 Seth Thomas movement still in operation. The clock was built using public donations as a memorial to servicemen of the First World War (at that time known as the Great War).

The nearby **Columbus Museum** (100 S. Tennessee Ave.) includes memorabilia from the life of Merle Evans, a local boy who grew up to become a Ringling Brothers bandleader who toured with the circus for fifty years. Also at the museum is a giant ball of string that was featured on the *I've Got a Secret* television show in the 1950s.

A bit further north from Columbus is Scammon, home to the **Carona Depot & Railroad Museum** (6769 NW 20th St.), which houses an extensive collection of

Riverton

66

RIVERTON
KANSAS

memorabilia and equipment and includes two restored railroad depots.

North of Riverton via U.S. Highway 69/400 is the town of Pittsburg. Just north of Pittsburg on Highway 69 is **Mined Land Wildlife Area #1** (507 E. 560th Ave.), formerly a heavily mined area now converted for recreational uses, such as fishing. A resident buffalo herd is also kept there. Just to set your mind at ease, by "mined" they mean that ore excavation took place at one time—as far as we know, there are no undetonated explosive devices in the area.

While in Pittsburg, check out the **Crawford County Historical Museum** (651 S. Hwy 69) and the **Hotel Stilwell** (707 N. Broadway St.), which was built in 1880 and is listed on the historic register. Pittsburg also hosts the **Old Time Tractor and Gas Engine Show** in June.

The car parked nearby gives a clear indication of the enormous size of Big Brutus. West Mineral, Kansas. GPS: 37.27375,-94.94034

If you want to do even more exploring, turn west from U.S. 69 onto State Highway 102 to reach the town of West Mineral. Here stands **Big Brutus** (6509 NW 60th St.), the second-largest power shovel ever built. Sixteen stories high, Big Brutus has a shovel that could fill three railroad cars with one scoop. One look at this monster will erase any lingering doubts that this part of Kansas owes its livelihood to mining. Every June, the **Big Brutus Miners' Day Reunion** is held in West Mineral, where veteran miners reconvene to talk about old times. August gets even livelier, with the **Big Brutus Polka Fest** featuring dueling polka bands. The Big Brutus complex even includes RV and camping facilities.

 Back on 66: Just to the west of Riverton, the junction at U.S. 69/400 has been converted into a roundabout. Be sure to pass straight through it and exit onto Beasley Road. Further ahead is a restored arched bridge, sometimes referred to as the Rainbow Bridge, with a commemorative marker on a very short, one-way leg of the highway. Curve left onto SE 50th Street toward Baxter Springs.

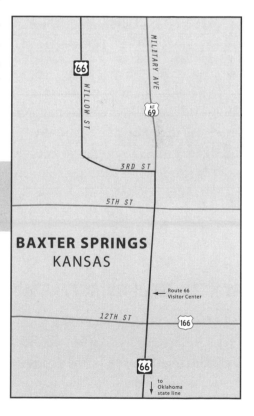

Enter Baxter Springs from the north on SE 50th Street, turn left on 3rd, and then turn right onto Military Avenue.

BAXTER SPRINGS

In 1863, at the height of the Civil War, Baxter Springs was the scene of a significant attack on Union forces by Quantrill's Raiders. The Bill Quantrill gang

On the grounds of the Baxter Springs Heritage Center, Baxter Springs, Kansas.
GPS: 37.02877,-94.73365

raided a U.S. Cavalry wagon train near here on October 6, and killed about 100 men. It became known as the Baxter Springs Massacre. The graves of many of those who died lie in the **Baxter Springs National Cemetery** on U.S. Highway 166, near Spring Valley Road.

Although some dispute the veracity of the tale, a **brick building** (1101 Military Ave.) in downtown was formerly a bank robbed by Jesse James in 1876. In the 1870s, Baxter Springs was widely considered the toughest town in Kansas.

BAXTER SPRINGS ATTRACTIONS

The **Baxter Springs Heritage Center & Museum** (740 East Ave.) features exhibits on the Buffalo Soldiers, the African American troops who were heavily involved in the resistance against Quantrill's Raiders. They got their nickname from the local Indians, who likened their coarse hair to that of the American bison. You can also pick up a numbered walking guide to the town, featuring such sites as a **log school building** dating from 1866; **John Baxter's inn and trading post**, from which the town eventually sprang; and a **replica of Fort Blair**, a Civil War-era army post. On the grounds of the museum is a small historical marker commemorating the **Black Dog Trail**.

The **Fort Blair Historic Site** (E. 6th St. and Military Ave.) was a campsite for Union troops in 1863. There is an information kiosk and a log structure at the site.

The **Johnston Public Library** (210 W. 10th) is housed in a building constructed in 1872 that was originally intended to be the county courthouse. Though it never served in that capacity, it has seen duty as a city hall, theater, and college. On the library's grounds is a monument erected by the Daughters of the American Revolution in 1931.

A 1930 cottage-style filling station now serves as the town's **Route 66 Visitor Center** (940 Military Ave.).

Route 66 Visitor Center, Baxter Springs. GPS: 37.02568,-94.73503

The former **Bilke's Western Museum** features a mural on its exterior depicting a longhorn cattle drive.

The **Little League Baseball Museum** (1408 Lincoln Ave.) features such stars as regional hero Mickey Mantle, who was from just across the border in Oklahoma. Mantle played a few years with the Baxter Springs Whiz Kids in the late 1940s. It was during this time that he hit a home run into the Spring River and was later approached by a scout for the New York Yankees. The rest, as they say, is history.

FURTHER AFIELD

A few miles outside of town is a small monument at the place where the states of Kansas, Oklahoma, and Missouri all come together at one point. This **Tri-State Marker** was constructed in 1938 by the Youth Work Administration. To find the marker, drive about six miles east of town on U.S. 166, then turn right just before the state line (Stateline Rd./SE 118th) and follow the road south. Note that this is a dead end.

A little west of Baxter Springs via U.S. 166 is the town of Chetopa, proud to call itself both the Catfish Capital and Pecan Capital of Kansas. The town holds an annual pecan festival the third Saturday in November. The **Chetopa Historical Museum** (419 Maple St.) includes a collection of buttons made at a nearby button-manufacturing plant and information about Osage Chief Che-to-pah, for whom the town was named.

Further west via U.S. 166 is the city of Coffeyville. The **Dalton Defenders Museum** (113 E. 8th St.) is dedicated to the memory of the local citizens who gave their lives to defend the town. In Coffeyville on October 5, 1892, the Dalton Gang tried to do what no one had ever done before: rob two banks simultaneously. The gang of five (some of whom were former residents of the town) split up and entered the Condon and First National Banks that morning. Some of the local citizens recognized them and went to the nearby Isham Hardware Store for weapons and ammunition. When the robbers emerged, they were met by armed citizens, and a shoot-out ensued. All but one of the gang were killed;

also killed were four of the eight town defenders. The museum also has exhibits pertaining to other local history, as well as mementos of Wendell Wilkie, who lived and taught school in Coffeyville. The **Condon Bank building** (807 S. Walnut St.) has been nicely restored and is now home to the Coffeyville Area Chamber of Commerce.

Just a mile south of the site of the shoot-out, you can visit the Daltons' graves in **Elmwood Cemetery** (4900 E. Truman Rd.). Emmett Dalton, the only survivor of the gang, returned to Coffeyville many years after the raid and placed a permanent marker over the graves.

Also in Coffeyville is the **Brown Mansion** (2109 Walnut St.). Completed in 1904 and incorporating some Tiffany-designed glasswork, the house is a three-story, sixteen-room residence built by one of the town's leading citizens, W. P. Brown, who made his money in the lumber and natural gas businesses. Guided tours are available (admission charged), and reservations can be made for private parties.

Located throughout Coffeyville are **murals** depicting facets of Coffeyville's history, including the Brown Mansion, the Perkins Building, Wholesale Grocery, Walter "Big Train" Johnson, and the Interurban.

At Pfister Park, housed in a 1930s-era hangar, is the **Aviation Heritage Museum** (2002 N. Buckeye St.). The hangar was constructed in 1933 as a Works Progress Administration project and was used until 1960, when the Big Hill Airport ceased operation. Vintage airplanes and memorabilia associated with the Coffeyville Air Base are on exhibit.

Route 66 travels under the guise of U.S. 69A as it moves south out of Baxter Springs. After sweeping across the Illinois prairie, crossing the mighty Mississippi, meandering through the Ozark region of Missouri, and then sampling the soil of Kansas, Route 66 is finally ready to enter that part of the country with which she is most intimately associated.

Prepare yourself. You are about to enter the Great American West.

OKLAHOMA

The pavement of Route 66 begins in Chicago, but the idea began here in Oklahoma. When the Joint Board of State and Federal Highway Officials was establishing the system of numbered

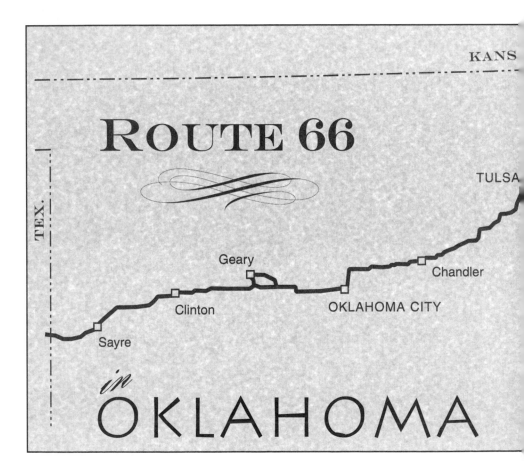

routes in the 1920s, Tulsa businessman Cyrus Avery envisioned a major artery passing right through the heart of his own state of Oklahoma. And he worked long and hard to make it a reality.

It is no accident that Route 66 cuts such a long, sweeping swath directly through the center of Oklahoma. If you look at a map of the United States and draw a more or less direct line from Chicago to Los Angeles, that path will miss the state of Oklahoma entirely. Even allowing for the curvature of the earth not apparent in such a map, the most logical path for such a highway would pass through very little of Missouri, none of Oklahoma, and directly through the heart of Kansas. Indeed, if the highway had been plotted along already-established trails

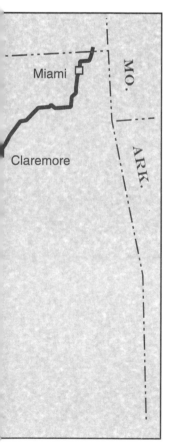

through Middle America, such as the Santa Fe Trail, that path, too, would have made Kansas (but not Oklahoma) a prominent part of the route.

However, U.S. 66 was deliberately calculated to take traveling Americans through Cy Avery's stomping grounds. He reasoned correctly that such a highway would put Oklahoma "on the map" and cause lots of travel-related dollars to be spent all across the state.

This placement of the highway became somewhat fortuitous when the Dust Bowl years of the 1930s imposed such a hardship on Oklahomans that many of them fled the region for California. Then, all of the surrounding roads became tributaries, adding their flow to the Mother Road and inspiring the dark *Grapes of Wrath* imagery, which the highway still evokes today.

One of the reasons Oklahoma needed to be put on the map, more so than some other states, has to do with its unique past. For many years, the area had been designated as Indian Territory and was home to tribes that had participated in the forced march, known as the Trail of Tears, to the region. It was only in 1907 that Oklahoma attained statehood; therefore, it had been a state for less than two decades by the time the interstate highway system was established in the '20s. By traveling through the state, however, Americans could see for themselves that Oklahoma was no longer a "territory," nor was it as primitive as that word implied. Route 66, then, would be Oklahoma's ticket to joining the twentieth century as a full partner.

If you've just traveled the old highway's short course through Kansas, you'll enter Oklahoma by moving south on U.S. 69. Like the small section of Kansas you've left behind, this part of Oklahoma is mining country, and there's very little to differentiate it at first. The changes, however, will appear soon.

Oklahoma is very 66-friendly, which fits its unofficial status as the birthplace of Route 66. By that, I mean you will have less difficulty following the old route here than you would probably have elsewhere. Official state maps, distributed free by the Oklahoma Department of Transportation, have for years now clearly marked the path of Historic Route 66. Not only that, but one of the later alignments of old 66, as it existed at the time of bypassing by the turnpikes, has been designated as Oklahoma 66. That means you can follow the double sixes almost continuously across the state. Keep in mind, of course, that the alignment marked as State Highway 66 is only one of many that the route followed over the years. As always, observation and exploration are your tickets to maximum enjoyment.

Less than five miles into Oklahoma, you'll come to the Route 66 community of . . .

QUAPAW

The village of Quapaw, about four miles from the Kansas state line, boasts a few buildings with **murals**—faded though they are—painted on them, which one of the locals told me were created in the 1970s. Keep alert as you cruise through town.

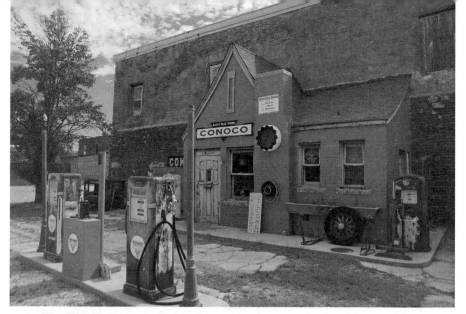

Commerce, Oklahoma. GPS: 36.93323,-94.87755

COMMERCE

Commerce is the boyhood home of baseball star Mickey Mantle, and gave him the nickname "Commerce Comet." The main drag (old 66 bypass) has been re-named Mickey Mantle Boulevard. At **Mickey Mantle's childhood home** (319 S. Quincy St.) is a metal-sided barn on the property full of dents where Mickey practiced his hitting. A few years ago, there was a plan to build a Mickey Mantle museum in town, but those plans have been abandoned. I spoke with someone involved in the project who told me it had been decided that such a museum would need to be located in a larger community (no decision as to where). On June 12, 2010, a large bronze statue of *The Commerce Comet* (420 D St.) was unveiled in front of Mickey Mantle Field

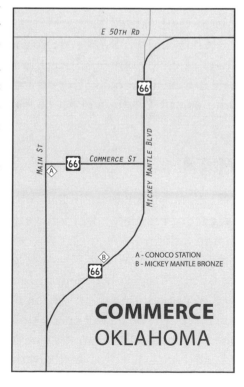

E 50TH RD

66

MAIN ST

MICKEY MANTLE BLVD

66 COMMERCE ST

A

B

66

A - CONOCO STATION
B - MICKEY MANTLE BRONZE

COMMERCE
OKLAHOMA

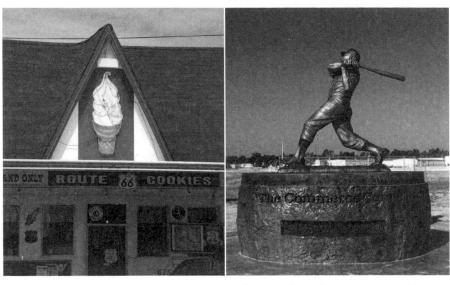

Commerce, Oklahoma.
GPS: 36.93323,-94.87755

Mickey Mantle Field, Commerce, Oklahoma.
GPS: 36.92480,-94.87191

on the south side of town.

Originally, Route 66 passed along the town's main business district on Commerce Street. Today, near the west end of Commerce Street, there is an old **cottage-style gasoline station** (101 S. Main St.) with a small collection of petroliana and such.

MIAMI

Named for an American Indian tribe and pronounced "my-AM-uh," this was at one time informally known as Jimtown, after four farmers named Jim in the area.

The jewel of Miami is by all accounts the **Coleman Theatre** (103 N. Main St.). Originally designed in Italianate style, during construction it was converted to Spanish Mission Revival, resulting in a unique piece of architecture. The theater opened in April of 1929, just six months before the beginning of the Great Depression. The Coleman was on the Orpheum Vaudeville circuit and saw the likes of Will Rogers, Tom Mix, the

Three Stooges, and Sally Rand as performers. Today, free guided tours are available.

MIAMI ATTRACTIONS

For regional history, visit the **Dobson Museum** (110 A St. SW), which includes American Indian artifacts, mining items, and other articles relating to the area's early settlement. There is also an extensive collection of Texaco-related materials.

A **Marathon Oil Gasoline Station** (331 S. Main St.) built in 1929 is thought to be one of the oldest of its kind still standing.

Also in Miami is **Route 66 Vintage Iron** (128 S. Main St.), a motorcycle museum with what they tout as one of the largest collections of Steve McQueen-owned gear.

In the spirit of the Mother Road, the citizens added a **reproduction of an early archway** over the road welcoming travelers to downtown Miami.

The Coleman opened its doors in 1929, at the threshold of the Great Depression. Miami, Oklahoma. GPS: 36.87648,-94.87755

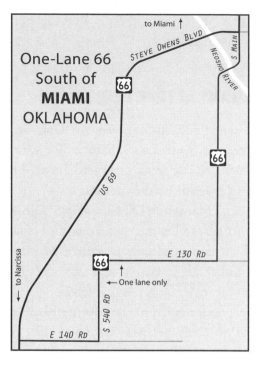

On the southern outskirts of Miami, you can still find some portions of old 66 that are even older than the route itself (pre-1926). In the vicinity are some one-lane-wide sections of concrete roadway that were paved in the early '20s. It's said that money was tight, and they only had half the amount needed to do the job completely. Rather than cover half the mileage, the decision was made to pave the full distance, but at half the normal width. This meant—and of course it still means today—that driving the road requires extreme caution, particularly where visibility is short. Just move your passenger-side wheels off onto the ample shoulder when necessary. To locate this section, just continue straight (on Main Street) past the Steve Owens Boulevard intersection, then turn right when you can no longer continue straight ahead. The one-lane section of 66 will demonstrate very clearly that early highway alignments were constructed with a considerable number of ninety-degree corners. The removal of such harsh turns by re-routing was a major thrust throughout the country during the 1930s.

NARCISSA-AFTON

Between Narcissa and Afton is another section of the one-lane 66. To access it, turn right onto a street called E. 200 Road. However, once you've explored this, you might want to backtrack a bit on the newer alignment, which passes the former site of **Buffalo Ranch** (21600 U.S. 69). Buffalo

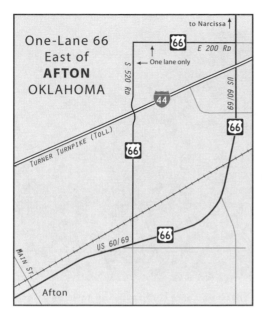

One-Lane 66
East of
AFTON
OKLAHOMA

to Narcissa ↑
66 E 200 RD
← One lane only
S 520 RD
44
US 60/69
66
66
66
TURNER TURNPIKE (TOLL)
US 60/69 66
MAIN ST
Afton

Ranch was a good old-fashioned "tourist trap" featuring trained animals (technically American bison), plus the requisite curio shop, etc. The ranch itself has been replaced by a modern truck stop/convenience store, but they do maintain a few bison in an adjacent field.

One of my favorite Mother Road artifacts is here in Afton: the sign for the **Rest Haven Motel**. I hope it's still there when you visit. A short distance away is the restored **Afton DX**

Afton, Oklahoma. GPS: 36.69496,-94.96099

This restored DX station serves as the de facto welcome center for the town of Afton, Oklahoma. GPS: 36.69444,-94.96211

Station and Packard showroom (12 SE 1st St.). The DX station is now an informal visitor center for Mother Roaders. Across the highway from the DX there used to be the World's Largest Matchbook Collection. Unfortunately for all of us, that building burned down in the summer of 2003—no irony intended.

Afton, Oklahoma. GPS: 36.68960,-94.97254

FURTHER AFIELD

Not far from Afton is Monkey Island, a peninsula community jutting into the Grand Lake o' the Cherokees, and home to **Darryl Starbird's National Rod & Custom Car Hall of Fame Museum** (55251 OK-85A). The collection features over forty street rods and other custom-built automobiles, as well as plenty of photographs and other memorabilia.

Just east of Afton you can take a side trip south on U.S. 59, across a portion of the Grand Lake o' the Cherokees, to the community of Grove. Perhaps the most popular destination in town is **Har-Ber Village** (4404 W. 20th Rd.), described as one of the largest antique displays in the country. It features a reconstructed turn-of-the-century village with over 100 buildings, as well as a walking trail, herb garden, and other exhibits.

The town of Grove is also host to the ***Cherokee Queen I and II***, a pair of paddlewheel riverboats that offer tourist excursions on the lake. In Grove's **Polson Cemetery** (E. 340 Rd.) is the gravesite of General Stand Watie—the last Civil War Confederate General to surrender, and a full-blooded American Indian.

VINITA-WHITE OAK-CATALE

 You'll enter Vinita on Illinois Avenue/U.S. 69. Just continue following 69, which will include a left turn onto Wilson Street. West of town, when State Highway 66 splits away, begin following 66.

One of the oldest settlements in Oklahoma and originally called Downingville, the town was later re-named for Vinnie Ream (1850–1914), the sculptress who fashioned the life-sized image of Abraham Lincoln in the nation's capitol. Vinita is also the birthplace of "Dr. Phil" McGraw of TV fame.

It was here in 1935 that Will Rogers had planned to attend the town's first-ever annual rodeo. He died, however, in a plane crash at Point Barrow, Alaska, just weeks beforehand. Nowadays, that rodeo is known as

When the Lewis Motel in Vinita, Oklahoma, was demolished, this sign was sold off and now stands on a ranch in California.

the **Will Rogers Memorial Rodeo**, and it is held each August.

Rogers somewhat facetiously called Vinita his "college town," having attended a secondary school here.

VINITA ATTRACTIONS

The town's self-guided Historic Homes Tour directs you to thirty-five turn-of-the-century houses built by the area's founding families. You can get a guide at the Eastern Trails Museum (below). General visitor information is available by calling (918) 256-7133, where you can also get directions to the **Barker Gang Gravesite** and the **Cabin Creek Civil War Battle Site**.

The **Eastern Trails Museum** (215 W. Illinois Ave.) has a re-created post office, general store, printing office, and doctor's office, as well as items representing American Indian history.

White Oak, Oklahoma. GPS: 36.61958,-95.26823

Clanton's (319 E. Illinois Ave.) is a longtime eatery with lots of old photos lining its walls. The **World's Largest Calf Fry Festival & Cook-Off** is held in Vinita each August, during which a full ton of the delicacies are consumed annually.

West of Vinita, you'll need to ignore the turnoff for U.S. 69 and continue straight ahead. Then begin following Oklahoma State Highway 66.

On the highway west of Vinita, Oklahoma. GPS: 36.62709,-95.19836

Just before you arrive at the town of Chelsea, on the left side of the highway, you can take a turn onto a very old alignment of 66 across the Pryor Creek Bridge. If you continue on this route, you'll pass through a few blocks of residences before being reunited with the more modern alignment, more or less in the central part of town, right beside what remains of the **Chelsea Motel** (N. Walnut Ave. and E. 1st St.), with its wonderful old sign.

CHELSEA

This community dates from 1882. The town includes an example of an **underground pedestrian tunnel** built to facilitate crossing the then-busy highway. A few miles to the south and west of Chelsea is the site of the **first oil well in Oklahoma**, which was established in 1889. Will Rogers's sister lived here, whom he is said to have visited frequently.

Here in Chelsea is an original Sears Roebuck pre-cut house, purchased

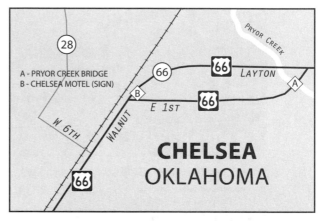

**This old bridge is on the east edge of Chelsea, Oklahoma.
GPS: 36.53809,-95.41545**

The modest Chelsea Motel had one of the nicest signs anywhere on Route 66. Chelsea, Oklahoma. GPS: 36.53777,-95.42652

in Chicago in 1913 for $16 and delivered by railroad car. The **Hogue House** (1001 S. Olive St.) is the only known example west of the Mississippi that is still owned by descendants of the original purchaser.

BUSHYHEAD-FOYIL

Modern Oklahoma 66 bypasses Foyil, so I recommend slowing down to take the old alignment through town along Andy Payne Boulevard.

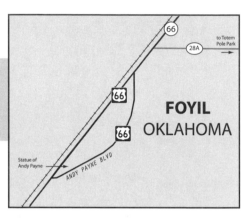

A Cherokee Indian chief lent his name to the community of Bushyhead.

Andy Payne, winner of the 1928 Bunion Derby—a cross-country footrace organized as a wildly extreme promotional stunt—was from the Foyil area. There is a **bronze statue of Andy Payne** on an old alignment of 66 (Andy Payne Boulevard) at the far western edge of town.

Foyil's claim to fame today is that it is the home of Ed Galloway's collection of concrete American-Indian-inspired structures, in what is commonly called **Totem Pole Park** (21300

Totem Pole Park, just outside Foyil, Oklahoma, is folk art at its very best.
GPS: 36.43773,-95.44924

Fiddle House, Totem Pole Park, near Foyil, Oklahoma.
GPS: 36.43773,-95.44924

Ed Galloway's Totem Pole Park, east of Foyil, Oklahoma.
GPS: 36.43773,-95.44924

E. Hwy 28A). This is truly a landmark, and a great old-fashioned roadside attraction to boot. Get there by leaving State Highway 66 and turning onto Highway 28A at the north edge of Foyil, and going about four miles east. The focal point of the collection is a ninety-foot-tall to-

Memorial to local hero Andy Payne, Foyil, Oklahoma.
GPS: 36.42690,-95.52758

tem pole made of brightly painted concrete. Ed Galloway created this collection of structures in the post-war years (the main totem pole in particular bears a date of 1948) as an expression of his own creative impulses.

SEQUOYAH

Established in 1871, the name of this settlement was changed to Beulah in 1909, after the postmaster's daughter. The name was changed back in 1913 to honor the famous Cherokee chief (also called George Guess) who developed the Cherokee alphabet. Remarkably, even the most advanced American Indian peoples had not developed written forms of their languages as late as the nineteenth century. Sequoyah, son of a Cherokee mother and a British trader named Nathaniel Gist, became convinced that the white men's superior power and influence derived from their written language. He began developing a system of writing for the Cherokee people, believing that this would help them maintain their independence from the whites. He developed his syllabary, a system of eighty-six symbols denoting all of the syllables of the Cherokee language, in about 1821. The system was easy to learn and use, and by 1828 it was being utilized for the *Cherokee Advocate* newspaper.

CLAREMORE

This is the county seat of Rogers County, which was named for Will Rogers's father, Clem Rogers. Claremore was known in years past as a place for "taking the waters." There was a well in town that produced a dark, malodorous substance called radium water (even though it contained no radium). This water was touted as being therapeutic for rheumatism and other ailments, and was a big selling point for staying at the **Hotel Will Rogers**

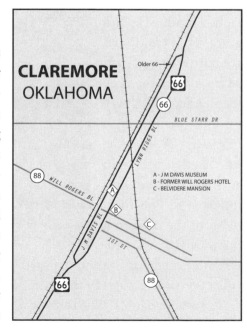

(940 S. Lynn Riggs Blvd.), which was known for its baths. Lately, the hotel has been undergoing redevelopment, with business space for lease on the ground level.

As you enter Claremore from the east, there is an older alignment of Route 66 off to your right (J. M. Davis Boulevard) that is pretty easy to recognize. Along that stretch, on the left-hand side, is an old motel court now serving duty as an apartment complex called the **Adobe Village** (402 N. J. M. Davis Blvd.). It appears to be from the 1930s and bears a resemblance to the Alamo Courts chain, which could once be found around this part of the country.

CLAREMORE ATTRACTIONS

The most important thing to see in Claremore is, of course, the **Will Rogers Memorial** (1720 W. Will Rogers Blvd.). The museum, mausoleum, and grounds are beautifully designed, and they offer far too much to even begin to list. Rogers's body was moved here in 1944, having been interred at Forest Lawn Cemetery in California from 1935 to 1944. Rogers had purchased the Claremore property with the intent of finally settling down permanently after his Hollywood career played itself out. Memorial services are held here annually on Rogers's birthday, November 4.

Rogers's most famous quote is: "I never met a man I didn't like." However, pithy statements were his stock-in-trade. There are thousands worth repeating, but he seemed to be speaking directly to people like you

A visit to the Will Rogers Memorial is well worth your time. Claremore, Oklahoma. GPS: 36.32085,-95.63217

and me when he wrote in 1930: "But if you want to have a good time, I don't care where you live, just load in your kids, and take some congenial friends, and just start out. You would be surprised what there is to see in this great Country within 200 miles of where any of us live. I don't care what State or what town."

The **J. M. Davis Arms & Historical Museum** (330 N. J. M. Davis Blvd.) is also a Claremore mainstay. Included in the thousands of fire-

arms on display are weapons owned by the likes of Pretty Boy Floyd, Cole Younger, Pancho Villa, and other outlaw types. This is the world's largest privately owned gun collection, with examples spanning six centuries of the gunsmith's craft. Besides the guns, there are trophy heads, swords, musical instruments, American Indian artifacts, World War I posters, and even John Wayne movie posters.

The **Claremore Museum of History** (121 N. Weenonah Ave.) includes the actual "surrey with the fringe on top" made famous in the musical *Oklahoma!*, which was based upon Lynn Riggs's play *Green Grow the Lilacs*. When the production premiered in the state in 1946, officials declared a state holiday.

On the campus of Rogers State

The Will Rogers Hotel still stands. GPS: 36.31279,-95.61588

University is Meyer Hall, which houses the **Oklahoma Military Academy Museum** (1701 W. Will Rogers Blvd.). The academy operated at this location from 1919 to 1971, when its functions were taken over by Claremore Junior College.

Several Claremore buildings are listed on the National Register of Historic Places, including the former **Will Rogers Hotel** (940 S. Lynn Riggs Blvd.), the **Belvidere Mansion** (121 N. Chickasaw Ave.), and Meyer Hall (see above). The Belvidere Mansion is a restored pre-statehood Victorian home offering tours by costumed docents. It has a ballroom that occupies the entire third floor of the house.

The **Swan Brothers Dairy Farm** (938 E. 5th St.), operated by three generations of the Swan family since 1923, offers a store and tours.

Claremore holds a **Bluegrass & Chili Festival** in September and a **Will Rogers birthday celebration** each November.

FURTHER AFIELD

Northwest of Claremore via Highway 88 is the town of Oologah, Oklahoma. Here, overlooking Oologah Lake, is Will Rogers's boyhood home, known as **Dog Iron Ranch** (9501 E. 380 Rd.). Access to the house, barn,

Belvidere Mansion, Claremore, Oklahoma. GPS: 36.31098,-95.60993

petting zoo, and vintage films and newsreels are provided for your enjoyment. Rogers was born in this log-walled house in 1879. Today, there are 400 acres and a herd of longhorn cattle on the property. The town itself also has a bronze statue called **The Cherokee Kid** (Maple St. and Cooweescoowee Ave.) of its favorite son on horseback.

Much of the town's turn-of-the-century downtown has been restored. The **Bank of Oologah** (Maple Street and Cooweescoowee Street), built circa 1906, boasts an authentic period interior and furnishings. Today, this bank is touted as having "closed during the Depression." I'm sure that, at the time, no one considered this to be much of a selling point.

On the same corner is the **Oologah Historical Museum** (202 Cooweescoowee Ave. W), with Will Rogers photos and a complete doctor's office on display. Miniatures of the *Cherokee Kid* statue in town (see above) are available in the museum's gift shop.

VERDIGRIS-CATOOSA

The Port of Catoosa is the nation's largest inland seaport, connecting Tulsa with the Mississippi River and the port of New Orleans. Here, the **Arkansas River Historical Society Museum** (5350 Cimarron Rd.) will educate you on the construction of the project. You might also want to visit the **Catoosa Historical Society Museum** (207 S. Cherokee St.), for a taste of the city's heritage. Look for the Frisco caboose parked outside.

At the **Cherokee Nation**

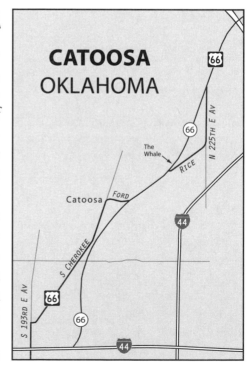

Roadside picnic area, Catoosa, Oklahoma. GPS: 36.19355,-95.73226

tourism bureau (777 W. Cherokee St.), you can get information about a plethora of significant sites across the state.

The **D. W. Correll Museum** (19934 E. Pine St.) houses a collection of rare and antique automobiles, rocks, gems, and other items in three separate buildings. Among the rare cars is a steam-powered Locomobile dating from 1898.

Near Catoosa is the **Catoosa Whale** (2600 Historic Rte. 66), an example of a small-scale mom-and-pop roadside attraction. Restored by volunteers in 2002, it is a large whale-shaped structure that is painted blue and sits in a small pond. In its heyday, visitors could enter the whale's mouth and then either slide down a chute, which exits behind the whale's ear, or dive off a small platform at the tail and into the surrounding swimming hole. Adjacent is a **wooden "ark"** that used to house a roadside menagerie. Just across the highway from them both is the former **Arrowood Trading Post** (2700 Historic Rte. 66).

Catoosa, Oklahoma. GPS: 36.19355,-95.73226

 Leave Catoosa on Cherokee Street. You'll then veer left (south) onto S. 193rd East Avenue, then make a right turn onto 11th Street.

LYNN LANE

This community appears east of Tulsa in my 1957 atlas, a little to the southwest of the current I-44/U.S. 412 junction, just inside Tulsa County. It has been swallowed by the expanding Tulsa city limits, which now run all the way out to the county line. The nearby **Lynn Lane Reservoir** (E. 21st St.) is a persistent reminder of the town's existence.

TULSA

Enter Tulsa on 11th Street, which runs for several miles to very near the town's center. A variation is to turn north at Mingo and go west on Admiral Place, which was the original alignment. That routing takes the traveler into the downtown area, just as all highways used to do. You would do well to explore downtown in either case.

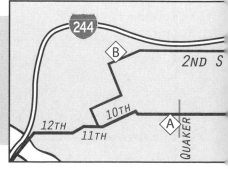

A city which owes much to the oil industry, Tulsa was also the home of Cyrus Avery, a man so instrumental not only in establishing Route 66, but also in routing it through his home state and town. Perhaps his strongest case was the presence of the 11th Street Bridge, now called the **Cyrus Avery Route 66 Memorial Bridge**, easily the best crossing of the Arkansas River at the time. Today that bridge has been converted to a Route 66 destination. The bridge itself is closed to traffic, and **Cyrus Avery Centennial Plaza** was added to its east end, including bronze sculptures.

Notorious outlaw Kate "Ma" Barker lived in Tulsa from 1930 to 1931. That was about the same time that Madison W. "Daddy" Cain bought a former garage and called it Cain's Dance Academy, later to become **Cain's Ballroom** (423 N. Main St.) and a thriving center for what later came to be called Western Swing.

In 1938, Tulsa gave birth to the Society for the Preservation and Encouragement of Barbershop Quartet Singing. Now headquartered in Kenosha, Wisconsin, as the Barbershop Harmony Society, the organization has thousands of chapters coast-to-coast and internationally. There are two quartets calling Tulsa home: the Tulsa Tones and Sound Decision.

Also in the 1930s, Meadow Gold Dairy, at that time a part of

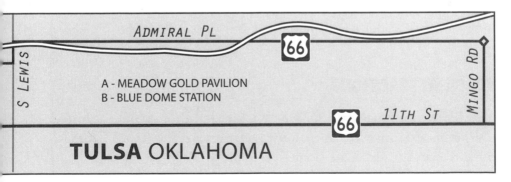

Beatrice Foods, erected a large rooftop sign on a single-story building on Route 66. In 2004, with the building about to be demolished, the iconic **Meadow Gold rooftop sign** (E. 11th St. and S. Quaker Ave.) was saved and restored. It now sits proudly on top of a purpose-made brick base a few blocks to the west. The Meadow Gold neon was ceremonially re-lit in May 2009.

In June of 1921, Tulsa was the scene of a race riot which took the lives of more than

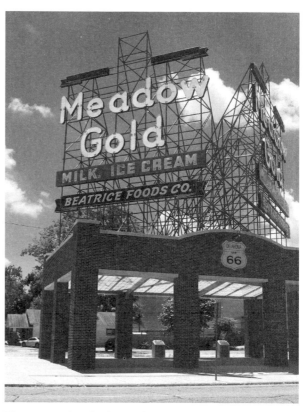

The restored and relocated Meadow Gold sign, Tulsa, Oklahoma. GPS: 36.14788,-95.97471

thirty people and left the city's African American district a burning ruin. Today, the **Greenwood Cultural Center** (322 N. Greenwood Ave.) and its **Mabel B. Little Heritage House** recall those dark days in the heart of Black Wall Street through photographs and memorabilia, while celebrating the neighborhood's resiliency.

TULSA ATTRACTIONS

The **Philbrook Museum** (2727 S. Rockford Rd.) combines a historical home, extensive art collections, and twenty-three acres of beautiful gardens. The Italianate home was built in 1927 by oil man Waite

Tulsa, Oklahoma.
GPS: 36.14788,-95.96821

East side of Tulsa, Oklahoma.
GPS: 36.14813,-95.87259

Phillips, and has been featured on the program *America's Castles*. Just a decade later, Phillips donated the estate to the city of Tulsa. Today, Philbrook is rated in the top sixty-five art museums in the country.

The **Gilcrease Museum** (1400 N. Gilcrease Museum Rd.) houses one of the world's most extensive collections of American Indian and Western art, and is surrounded by 475 acres of grounds with themed gardens.

The **Willard Elsing Museum** (7777 S. Lewis Ave.), on the campus of Oral Roberts University, features a four-foot jade sculpture among its sixty-year-old collection of gems, minerals, crystals, and other stones. Mr. Elsing at one time operated a rock and mineral shop on Route 66 at Joplin, Missouri. Enter at the giant *Praying Hands* sculpture, which is about sixty feet tall and weighs thirty tons—a rather arresting sight.

Lovers of Art Deco architecture have plenty to be thankful for here in

Blue Dome district, downtown Tulsa. GPS: 36.15581,-95.98694

Tulsa. A well-known example is the **Boston Avenue Methodist Church** (1301 S. Boston Ave.). Church tours are held every Sunday following the 11:00 AM service, or by appointment during the week. There are also a number of **Art Deco office buildings** in the downtown business district. You can take an Art Deco walking tour of the city by picking up a brochure at the **Tulsa Chamber of Commerce** (1 W. 3rd St.).

There is a **Frank Lloyd Wright creation** (3700 S. Birmingham Ave.) in a residential section of Tulsa. It's still a private residence, so no tours are available, but you can view two of its exterior facades by driving by.

Lovers of miniatures will want to see the **Ida Dennie Willis Museum of Miniatures, Dolls, and Toys** (628 N. Country Club Dr.). The collection includes an ever-changing array of trains, planes, robots, and dolls, all housed in a 1910 Tudor mansion. One of many interesting exhibits is the Gates collection of ethnic and advertising dolls.

The **Tulsa Air and Space Museum & Planetarium** (3624 N. 74th E. Ave.), which is on the grounds of the Tulsa International Airport, has lots of aircraft on display, including an F-14 Tomcat (same as the one used in Top Gun) and a Lear 24D corporate jet. For those addicted to hands-on experiences, flight simulators are also on hand.

The **Tulsa Historical Society Museum** (2445 S. Peoria Ave.), located in a 1919 mansion, is the official repository of the city's history, including official documents, vintage photographs, and other artifacts.

A drive-in movie theater, the **Admiral Twin Drive-In** (7355 E. Easton St.), still operates in the northeastern sector of town. Starting out with a single screen in 1951 and called the Modern Aire, the name was changed a short time later when the second screen was added. The theater is featured as a hangout for characters in 1983's feature film *The Outsiders*, directed by Francis Ford Coppola.

At **Creek Council Oak Park** (1750 S. Cheyenne Ave.), a 170-year-old oak tree marks the spot where the Creek Indians arrived in the 1830s after traversing the Trail of Tears, thus establishing the site which would later become Tulsey-town.

There's a seventy-six-foot-tall oil worker sculpture, known as the **Golden Driller**, standing outside Tulsa Expo Center (4145 E. 21st St.). The center is said to contain the world's largest unobstructed interior volume. The

Tulsa is oil country.
GPS: 36.13334,-95.93080

roof is suspended by a system of booms and cables, which allows adequate room inside for over-sized equipment shows. In fact, the original Golden Driller (he was upgraded in the 1970s) was put on display inside the building for a while prior to his outdoor placement in 1966.

Tulsa, Oklahoma. GPS: 36.14452,-96.00306

In downtown Tulsa you'll find the **Center of the Universe** (1 S. Boston Ave.), a sort of acoustical mystery location. Stand in this spot, recite some words, and you'll hear your voice strongly reverberating back to you. The effect is quite striking. The location is marked by a circular design in the Boston Avenue pedestrian walkway.

Just yards away from the Center of the Universe is the **Oklahoma Jazz Hall of Fame** (5 S. Boston Ave.), which is housed in the Art Deco-inspired former Tulsa Union Railroad Depot, as well as a seventy-two-foot sculpture titled *Artificial Cloud,* created in the early 1990s for the city's Mayfest celebration.

In downtown Tulsa, on a very early alignment of Route 66, stands the **Blue Dome** (S. Elgin Ave. and E. 2nd St.). A distinctively shaped former gasoline station, the restored Blue Dome is now the de facto centerpiece of a thriving new entertainment district.

FURTHER AFIELD

About forty-seven miles north of Tulsa is the city of Bartlesville. The city's historic district includes nearly fifty buildings from the oil boom period of 1900 to 1920. Bartlesville is also home to the **Inn at Price Tower** (510 S. Dewey Ave.), a Frank Lloyd Wright creation from 1956 said to have been designed based on the structure of a tree. It's now a hotel and museum with twenty-one architecturally fascinating guest rooms, some of which are two-story suites. The inn also has its own restaurant and bar.

The **Bartlesville Community Center** (300 SE Adams Blvd.) was designed by a student of Wright's (Wesley Peters) and features the world's largest cloisonné mural.

The **Frank Phillips Home** (1107 SE Cherokee Ave.) is a twenty-six-room Neoclassical mansion completed in 1909. Phillips was the founder of the Phillips Petroleum Company, the firm that branded their gasoline with a highway shield emblazoned with the number "66." You can find out more about Phillips and and his business at the **Phillips Petroleum Company Museum** (410 S. Keeler Ave.).

Frank Phillips's country home and guest ranch, which he named **Woolaroc** (1925 Woolaroc Ranch Rd.), is just outside Bartlesville. The ranch was designed as a sort of Old West preserve, and attracted the likes of presidents, tycoons, and other celebrities of the day as guests. The 3,700-acre compound, established in 1925, features a museum of Western art, a collection of Phillips Petroleum memorabilia, a lodge house, picnic areas, nature trails, a petting barn, roaming bison, and the Phillips family mausoleum.

The **Bartlesville Area History Museum** (401 S. Johnstone Ave.) is on the fifth floor of the City Center, formerly known as the Hotel Maire and later named the Burlingame. Of course, the museum has many things on exhibit, but at the core of it all is a collection of photographs taken by Frank Griggs, who moved to the area in 1908 and began recording daily life through about 200,000 photographic negatives.

Discovery 1 Park (200 N. Cherokee Ave.), formerly called Johnstone Park, contains a replica of the first commercial oil well in Oklahoma, named the Nellie Johnstone No. 1.

Bartlesville also holds an annual **Bi-Plane Expo** the first weekend of June.

Not far from Bartlesville is the town of Dewey, home to the **Tom Mix Museum** (721 N. Delaware St.). Before he became a movie star, Mix served as marshal in Dewey from 1911 to 1912. Three of his five wives were from this town. Mix's film career came to include more than

300 films, some of which are available for viewing in the museum's small auditorium.

The **Dewey Hotel** (801 N. Delaware St.) in downtown Dewey was built in 1900 and now serves as a museum.

A few miles east of Dewey on Durham Road is **Prairie Song Indian Territory** (402621 W. 1600 Rd.), a replica nineteenth-century village of twenty or so hand-hewn log buildings.

Leave Tulsa on Southwest Boulevard. Follow Southwest, which becomes Frankoma Road, en route to Sapulpa via the communities of Red Fork and Oakhurst (see the reference map).

RED FORK-OAKHURST

Recently added at Red Fork is the **Route 66 Village** (3770 Southwest Blvd.), consisting of some rail cars and an oil derrick.

Route 66 Village is a railroad-dominated roadside display in the Red Fork area (west Tulsa).
GPS: 36.10798,-96.01614

SAPULPA

Entering Sapulpa, Old Sapulpa Road and New Sapulpa Road merge to form N. Mission Street. Route 66 then turns west on Dewey Avenue through the downtown district. West of downtown, keep alert for the old alignment that crosses Rock Creek on a brick-paved bridge.

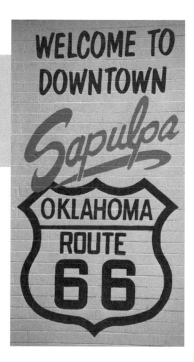

The former **Liberty Glass Company** (1000 N. Mission St.) was established here in the early 1900s by George F. Collins. The idea for the name seems to have come from the fact that 1886—the year Sapulpa was established—was the same year that France gave the gift of the Statue of Liberty to the United States. In *A Guide Book to Highway 66*, Jack Rittenhouse mentions Liberty Glass when describing his journey through Sapulpa in 1946.

Downtown Sapulpa includes a number of reproductions of **antique advertising murals**. These appear on the sides of several buildings along old Route 66.

Be sure to explore Sapulpa thoroughly, because an older alignment

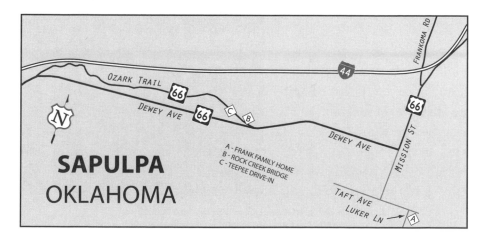

at the far end of town takes you over a brick-paved iron truss bridge called **Rock Creek Bridge** and past the **Tepee Drive-In** theater (13166 W. Ozark Trail). This alignment will take you back in time for a bit and well away from the roar of traffic.

On an old alignment of 66, Sapulpa, Oklahoma.
GPS: 35.99471,-96.13969

SAPULPA ATTRACTIONS

Although the well-known Frankoma Pottery Company has closed, the **Frank family home** (1300 Luker Ln.) is now open for tours, conducted by John Frank's daughters, Joniece and Donna. The home was designed in the mid-1950s by Bruce Goff, and incorporates brickwork and tiling in the traditional Frankoma Pottery styles and colors. Tours may be scheduled by calling (918) 224-6566.

Housed in a circa-1910 building that was formerly the home of the YWCA, the **Sapulpa Historical Museum** (100 E. Lee Ave.) features an 1890s-era kitchen and schoolroom, a telephone exhibit, and items pertaining to the Frisco Railroad.

The **Sapulpa Fire Museum**

Local boosterism brochure.

Now-extinct roadside stand near Kellyville, Oklahoma.

(124 E. Lee Ave.) includes historic photos, vehicles, and other artifacts.

The **Waite Phillips Filling Station Museum** (26 E. Lee Ave.) is a beautifully restored 1923 structure that includes several period automobiles.

KELLYVILLE

On my earlier trips through here, there was an old store west of Kellyville with a plywood American Indian sign out front. The Indian's arm was extended, as if pointing, and lettering on his outstretched arm promised: SOUVENIRS. Long closed, it was a treat for the Route 66 traveler to stumble upon. The sign has since been removed, however, and the remaining structures are nondescript. This is one of many disappearances reminding me to photograph, photograph, photograph.

The road is easy to follow west of Kellyville, and you'll cross over I-44 along the way and approach Bristow from the north (see the reference map).

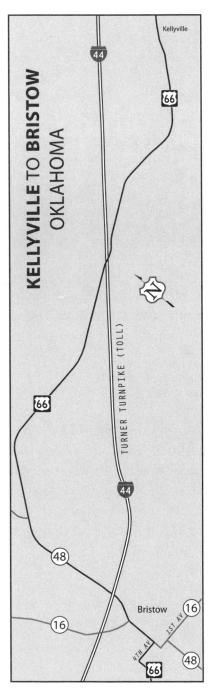

KELLYVILLE TO BRISTOW
OKLAHOMA

BRISTOW

According to the local chamber of commerce, Bristow's 6th Avenue was at one time known as "Silk Stocking Row," due to the fact that there were more millionaires living here than in any other place in Oklahoma.

BRISTOW ATTRACTIONS

The **Bristow Historical Museum** (1 Railroad Pl.) is located in a restored 1923 railroad depot and features rotating exhibits pertaining to the area's history, from its time as Indian Territory to the present.

As you pass through Bristow, keep your eye out for a sign pointing to the **Wake Island Memorial** (Veteran's Memorial Dr.) in the western part of town. The city has commemorated those veterans who served in the Battle of Wake Island in the Second World War, and there are some nice pedestrian-friendly walking paths in the vicinity.

You can't see it, but along the stretch of road between Bristow and Stroud, there is an enormous **underground storage cavity**—a depleted gas field—which is used to store natural gas during periods of surplus.

What you can see is that there are at least three cemeteries along Route 66 between Bristow and Depew, and then there are two more west of Depew, where 66 approaches the Turner Turnpike (I-44).

DEPEW

The village of Depew is rather isolated. The Mother Road cut off the somewhat circuitous route through Depew early on. Take at least a few extra minutes to drive through this town, though. You'll see evidence that it was once a much busier place.

Bristow, Oklahoma. GPS: 35.83581,-96.38823

Downtown Depew, Oklahoma. GPS: 35.80296,-96.50752

OZARK TRAIL MARKERS

The Ozark Trail marker near Stroud is one of several which once stood in the area. There is a similar one—a replica—in the town of Stratford, Oklahoma, erected in the summer of 1997. That reproduction includes an inscription that is instructive for today's explorer:

OZARK TRAIL PYRAMID

By 1916, plans were underway to promote a network of roads through Oklahoma called the "Ozark Trail." The trails were planned by the Ozark Trail Association. Its mission was to promote a system of better roads connecting the surrounding states. These were the first roads to be classed as public supported highways.

Early plans were "grandiose." Originally the Ozark Trail was to be a link from ocean to ocean. The route was to be marked with impressive pyramids and concrete mileage posts. These roads were intended to be "above high water, hardsurfaced, and later oiled." Routes increased rapidly as towns competed to be included on the Trail.

The Ozark Trail Pyramid was one of many marking the trail for travelers in the early 1920s. Oklahoma trails crossed the state, east to west and north to south. They have either become U.S. Highways or follow the same course, such as U.S. 60, U.S. 62, OK 9, the famous "Route 66," and the current Turner Turnpike. This pyramid was one of several placed on the trail from Tulsa to Dallas. Chandler, Meeker, Shawnee, and Sulphur also had identical pyramids marking the trail along this particular route.

Work began on the Stratford Pyramid in December 1921. The buried base was six feet square, the next section was four feet square, the top tapered and stood twenty-two feet high. The original pyramid stood in the center of Main and Hyden Streets, which is only ½ block to the east. Due to traffic and safety reasons, this replica pyramid could not be in the original location. It was constructed as close to the original site as possible. "Ozark Trail" appeared on all four sides of the upper part of the pyramid and each side listed the mileage for the next towns along the route. In April 1923, the pyramid was wired and lighted. In the early 1940s, it was pushed over and buried where it stood. In the early 1970s, its pieces were exhumed, partially restored, and now stands on a private ranch near Stratford. One other "original" pyramid, which is presumed to be the Chandler pyramid, is located west of Stroud off Highway 66.

This replica was erected in the summer of 1997.

STROUD

Stroud was established in 1892. Henry "Bear-Cat" Starr and his gang robbed two banks here in 1915. Starr was the nephew of the famed Belle Starr.

The focal point of Stroud is the **Rock Café** (114 W. Main St.), which is built of stones that were unearthed

A stop at the Rock Café is a longstanding Route 66 tradition. Stroud, Oklahoma. GPS: 35.74891,-96.65428

during the construction of Route 66 in the area. The café features a nice sign that fans of neon will appreciate. The Rock Café suffered a devastating fire in May 2008, and there were a lot of doubters who thought it was lost to us. However, through a lot of hard work and the sheer determination of the café's owner, Dawn Welch, "The Rock" reopened one year later, nearly to the day. Dawn, by the way, also happens to be a big part of the inspiration behind the character of Sally the Porsche in the 2006 movie *Cars*.

Also in Stroud is the **Skyliner Motel** (717 W. Main St.), which also has a good-looking neon sign. Look for it near the west end of town.

STROUD ATTRACTIONS

The **Stroud Library** (301 W. 7th St.) is an example of 1929 Art Deco architecture, and was originally built by Bell Telephone.

This part of Oklahoma considers itself wine country, and there are indeed several wineries nearby if that's your thing. As an example, just a mile or so west of downtown Stroud is **StableRidge Vineyards and Winery** (2016 OK-66). Their tasting room

Stroud, Oklahoma. GPS: 35.74918,-96.66220

is in a former Catholic Church that was built from 1898 to 1902.

Stroud is home to the **International Brick & Rolling Pin Competition and Festival**. The competition pits a handful of cities named Stroud against one another in games of skill. The other Strouds are in Canada, Australia, and the U.K.

West of Stroud, there is a left turn you can take (at N. 3540 Rd.) that follows the old Ozark Trail Highway. This early 66 alignment features an **Ozark Trail monument** (a tall obelisk) at one of its intersections. This old path of the highway is more easily spotted when facing east, because the later Route 66 alignment curves to your left, and straight ahead is an obviously older alignment that will take you directly to the marker—that's the way I was first able to find it.

DAVENPORT

Watch for high water in this vicinity. The first time I took Route 66 through Oklahoma, I had to skip Davenport altogether due to the closure of several roads at the time. There is an old **Texaco station** (Broadway Ave. and 7th St.) in town that has an ever-changing array of vintage vehicles parked on its lot. Painted on the side of one of the buildings in the tiny downtown district is artwork known as the **Land Run Mural** (Broadway Ave. and Main St.).

Downtown Davenport, Oklahoma. GPS: 35.70531,-96.76531

Davenport, Oklahoma. GPS: 35.71058,-96.76574

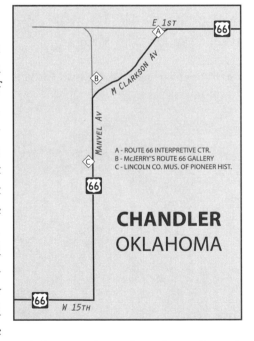
(marginal convertible icon) Be on the lookout for the **Lincoln Motel** (740 E. 1st St.) as you reach the eastern outskirts of Chandler. Built in 1939, and very much a product of the 66 era, the motel is still in business. Our friend Rittenhouse made mention of it way back in 1946.

CHANDLER

Chandler, the seat of Lincoln County, was established with a land run in 1891, and calls itself the Pecan Capital of the World. The town of Cromwell, southeast of here in Seminole County, is reputed to be the site of the last Old West-style gunfight. That was in 1924, and it took the life of Bill Tilghman, former U.S. marshal at Dodge City and sheriff of Lincoln County, Oklahoma. Poor Bill—he was seventy years old and had been retired for quite a few years when he was called upon that one last time. Tilghman is buried in the **Oak Park Cemetery** on the west side of Chandler.

The former National Guard Armory is now a Route 66 must-stop in Chandler, Oklahoma. GPS: 35.70967,-96.87630

CHANDLER ATTRACTIONS

The **Route 66 Interpretive Center** (400 E. Rte. 66) opened in 2007 in what was once the National Guard Armory. It's located right where 66 takes a sweeping left turn, transitioning from east–west 1st Street to north–south Manvel Avenue. Aside from the Mother Road exhibits, the building also houses offices for the Oklahoma Route 66 Association and the local chamber of commerce.

While in Chandler, consider paying a visit to Jerry McClanahan's art gallery, **McJerry's Route 66 Gallery** (306 Manvel Ave.), in the north part of town. Jerry's Route 66 artwork is well-known, and he was honored with the prestigious Will Rogers Award in June 2010. Hours are irregular (after all, he's an artist), so be sure to call ahead: (903) 467-6384.

Further to the south on Manvel Avenue is an old cottage-style **Phillips 66 station**. It has gradually been receiving

The heart of Chandler, Oklahoma. GPS: 35.70371,-96.88090

restorative work. For example, it had been modified
from its original form by
the addition of two garage
bays, probably during the
1950s, but those additions
have now been removed.

The **Lincoln County
Museum of Pioneer His-
tory** (717 Manvel Ave.)
showcases Chandler's col-
orful early history, with an
emphasis on their legend-
ary sheriff, Bill Tilghman.

Chandler, Oklahoma. GPS: 35.69547,-96.88080

It also hosts Miss Faye's Touring Historical Marionette Theater and rare
films by cinematographer Benny Kent.

Between Chandler and Warwick there is a **Meramec Cav-
erns barn**. However, you won't notice it heading west, as the painted side
of it faces eastbound travelers in hopes of enticing them to stop at the cave
many miles ahead of them in Missouri.

Motorcycle Museum, Warwick, Oklahoma. GPS: 35.68637,-97.00004

Near Warwick, Oklahoma. GPS: 35.69556,-96.94547

WARWICK

In the loosely defined community of Warwick, you'll come upon the **Seaba Station Motorcycle Museum** (336992 OK-66). This museum has been restored by its newest owners to its circa-1920s state, and their passion for motorcycles is on full display. The building was formerly an engine-rebuilding shop and gasoline station. Take a look in back for the stone outhouse, still standing after so many years.

WELLSTON-LUTHER

Wellston was cut off from the main route in the 1930s, but there is a loop through town that is marked as 66B that follows the older, more circu-

itous alignment. At the junction of 66B on the east side of town is the site once occupied by Pioneer Camp, a tourist campground; a pair of masonry bases that once supported an

Business district of Luther, Oklahoma.
GPS: 35.66179,-97.19589

This old station is slowly decaying between Luther and Arcadia, Oklahoma.
GPS: 35.66012,-97.27373

archway over the entrance to the camp are still visible here. You'll also find the **Butcher Barbeque Stand** (3402 W. Rte. 66) here.

Luther has a small downtown just south of the highway with several **vacant storefronts**.

West of Luther, you can access a dead-end remnant of an **older 66 alignment**. There is a large sign at the entrance marked "Private Historical Site."

Further west of Luther and just east of Arcadia are the remains of a **stone gasoline station** (circa 1920s) reputed to have been the scene of a counterfeit ring. It's small, but it's also one of my favorite ruins on the route, one that I photograph each and every time I pass through here. With each visit, I find that these ruins have deteriorated a bit more.

ARCADIA

There is a **historical marker** on the eastern outskirts of town designating the eastern boundary of the infamous 1889 Land Run.

ARCADIA ATTRACTIONS

Arcadia has a literary connection. Washington Irving, well-known as the author of the popular tale "Rip Van Winkle," camped here in 1832. He wrote about his travels in this area in *A Tour of the Prairies*, which was

The Round Barn has stood in Arcadia, Oklahoma, for well over 100 years.
GPS: 35.66216,-97.32583

published in 1835. Look for the marker east of the **Round Barn** (107 Oklahoma 66). Mr. Irving is considered by some to be the United States' earliest professional author, having written *A History of New York* in 1809 under the pseudonym Diedrich Knickerbocker. Like Shakespeare, Irving is credited with putting some phrases of his own invention into the vernacular. He is credited with the expression "almighty dollar," referring to "that great object of universal devotion throughout our land." He also is credited with the expression "happy hunting ground" to refer to the American Indians' life in the hereafter. If that's not enough, then consider that his pen name of Knickerbocker has been synonymous with New York and New Yorkers since shortly after the publication of his *A History of New York* at the tender age of twenty-six.

The Round Barn, a world-famous Route 66 landmark, was constructed in 1898. The barn, which was restored in the 1990s and now houses a small gift shop, is filled with photographs and other memorabilia having to do with unusual barns around the world. These include circular and octagonal barns, as well as other unconventional configurations. The upper level, above the gift shop, is available for rental for special events.

Also on the National Register is the **Tuton Drug Store** (201 N. Main St.), which is now the office of Chesrow-Brown Real Estate.

Keep your sleuthing eyes open in Arcadia for a very old alignment of Route 66 that deviates from the main pavement for a short distance, and includes the **home of author and publisher Jim Ross** (13100 E. Old

Hwy 66). Ross took his inspiration for the house's design from the ever-popular cottage-style Phillips 66 stations.

The western outskirts of Arcadia are dominated by the monumental **POPS** (660 Oklahoma 66), a new Route 66 attraction that reaches out and grabs your attention like classic tourist traps of the past. You certainly can't miss a sixty-six-foot-tall illuminated pop bottle standing a few yards from the roadway. Inside, POPS has countless brands and flavors of soft drinks to choose from, as well as a snack bar and internal combustion

One of the newer roadside attractions on the route is this sixty-six-foot-tall lighted pop bottle. Arcadia, Oklahoma. GPS: 35.65879,-97.33554

fuel for your iron horse. This decidedly over-the-top concept was brought to life by Rand Elliott, the same architect who designed the Oklahoma Route 66 Museum in Clinton, Oklahoma, in the 1990s.

ELMER McCURDY

For those of you interested in strange stories, this has to be one of the strangest. I have read four or five slightly different accounts of the Elmer McCurdy saga, and each one is as bizarre as the next.

In 1976, a film crew shooting an episode of *The Six Million Dollar Man* was on location at a Los Angeles-area fun house. One of the crew members moved what was thought to be a dummy hanging from the ceiling, but the "dummy's" arm fell off. Inside were what appeared to be the bones and joints of a real human being. That man was soon identified as Elmer McCurdy.

McCurdy was an outlaw who died in a shoot-out at the hands of authorities in 1911. His body was taken to a mortuary in Pawhuska, Oklahoma, where the undertaker, not knowing how long he might need to hang on to the body before it was claimed, added arsenic to the usual embalming fluid and thereby mummified McCurdy's remains. Months passed, and the body still had not been claimed. By this time, McCurdy's corpse had become something of a local attraction, and people came by and paid a nickel apiece to look at it.

Many years later, the funeral home had changed hands, the principals in the whole affair were deceased, and no one knew any more that the dried-up "dummy" in town was a real human body. A carnival passed through and offered to take the "dummy" off the current owner's hands for a small price. A deal was struck, and Elmer McCurdy entered show business posthumously.

No one knows for sure just how many places McCurdy's mummified body had been displayed before he was discovered at the fun house that day in 1976. No relatives ever presented themselves to claim the body. Finally, a historical group arranged for McCurdy's body to be returned to Oklahoma for burial. The Warren Monument company of Guthrie furnished a tombstone bearing the inscription:

ELMER MCCURDY

SHOT BY SHERIFF'S POSSE IN OSAGE HILLS ON OCT 7, 1911
RETURNED TO GUTHRIE, OKLAHOMA FROM LOS ANGELES COUNTY,
CALIFORNIA FOR BURIAL, APR 22, 1977

McCurdy was then laid to rest in Summit View Cemetery in Guthrie, Oklahoma. To ensure that the body would remain interred and not be trotted out again as a curiosity, the state medical examiner ordered that two cubic yards of concrete be poured over the coffin before the grave was closed.

FURTHER AFIELD

A real treat awaits you just a short trip north of old 66. Just a few miles east of downtown Edmond, take either 12th Street or U.S. 77 north for twenty miles or so to the very historic town of Guthrie, Oklahoma. On the outskirts of the town, you'll see a still-working drive-in theater. In business since 1951, the **Beacon Drive-In** (2404 S. Division St.) had an appearance in the movie Twister.

For some twenty years, beginning in 1890, Guthrie was the capital of Oklahoma (or Indian Territory, as it was known at the time). Virtually all of the city's downtown was constructed during that period, and today, Guthrie boasts the largest contiguous urban historical district on the National Register, consisting of 2,169 structures in 400 blocks on 1,400 acres, including fourteen city blocks of Victoriana. The territory achieved statehood in 1907, and the capital was moved to Oklahoma City a few years later in 1910. The National Trust for Historic Preservation honored Guthrie as one of its "Dozen Distinctive Destinations" in 2004.

Tom Mix used to tend bar here at the still-hopping **Blue Belle Saloon** (224 W. Harrison Ave.). Just outside the Blue Belle, staged gunfights are held in the street for much of the year.

The **Scottish Rite Temple** (900 E. Oklahoma Ave.) is among the largest of its kind in the world, with an enormous number of stained-glass artworks. Guided tours are available.

The **Gaffney Building** (214 W. Oklahoma Ave.) houses both the Chamber of Commerce and the Oklahoma Frontier Drug Store Museum. The folks at the C of C will answer any questions you may have, and the drug store is well worth touring. Not only will you see all the tools of the trade from a circa-1890 pharmacy, but the attendant on duty when we were there was extremely knowledgeable, having been a practicing druggist himself for many years. In 2006, an apothecary garden was added to cultivate and study medicinal plants.

Physically connected to one of the 1,946 public libraries endowed by the Carnegie Foundation in this country, the **Oklahoma Territorial Museum** (406 E. Oklahoma Ave.) presents a history of Oklahoma during its earliest days, including the Land Run of 1889 and the subsequent influx of settlers. There is even some information about the infamous case of Elmer McCurdy.

Back on Route 66 heading west out of Arcadia, past POPS, there is little Route 66 flavor evident between here and the town of Edmond; however, the stretch is rather rural in character and therefore relaxing.

This schoolhouse dates from pre-statehood days. Edmond, Oklahoma. GPS: 35.65288,-97.47884

EDMOND

Following Route 66 through Edmond means turning left (south) at Broadway. A right at that corner takes you into the smallish business district.

EDMOND ATTRACTIONS

In Edmond you'll find the **1889 Territorial School** (124 E. 2nd St.), the first public school established in Oklahoma Territory. It later housed a camera shop beginning in 1950, but in 2007 it was rededicated in keeping with its historical past.

The **Edmond Historical Society Museum** (431 South Blvd.), housed in an armory building constructed by the WPA in 1936, displays photos, documents, and artifacts relating to the town's development. There are also traveling exhibits, which change throughout the year. In the 1950s, this building was used to house and train dancing bears for the local circus.

The **Arcadian Inn** (328 E. 1st St.), a bed and breakfast, was originally a one-story private residence built in 1908. Twenty years later, the owner decided to convert it to two stories by lifting up the original house and constructing a new first story and basement underneath. How's that for doing things the hard way?

Edmond is proud to be a supporter of public art. **Stone and bronze sculptures**, as well as a number of **murals**, can be seen throughout the city. A guide published by the city's convention and visitors bureau lists 115 works of art, including a WPA-era **etched glass mural** inside the city hall (101 E. 1st St.).

If you like unusual architecture, you can check out the **Hopewell Baptist Church** (5801 NW 178th St.), designed by Bruce Goff in the 1940s. It's been nicknamed the TeePee Church, since that's what it was built to resemble. It is conical in shape, about eighty feet tall, and was constructed using "tent poles," which are actually surplus oilfield pipes donated by an oil drilling company.

 Between Edmond and Oklahoma City is **Memorial Park Cemetery** (13313 N. Kelley Ave.). This is the burial place of Wiley Post. Although Post is more widely known these days as the friend of Will Rogers who was piloting the plane in which they both perished in 1935, he was actually very accomplished in his own right. He first attained prominence in 1930 by winning the National Air Race Derby, a race from Los Angeles to Chicago (ring a bell?) in a plane named the *Winnie Mae*. He made the first successful solo flight around the world in 1933, and also designed the first pressurized flight suit. The aviator's likeness and biography are carved in a large stone over the burial plot.

Between Edmond and Oklahoma City, leave U.S. 77/Broadway at Kelley Avenue and continue south. From there, you have a couple of choices, including a "beltway" route that skirted downtown but took in the village of Britton, where the Owl Courts tourist complex still stands. The primary route went all the way to the capitol before turning west.

OWL COURTS

BRITTON, OKLA., 4 MILES NORTH OF
OKLAHOMA CITY

ON HIGHWAY 66 BY-PASS (LOOP)

OWL COURTS

PRIVATE BATH

MR. AND MRS. W. E. SILKWOOD, OWNERS AND MANAGERS
BRITTON, OKLAHOMA

The Owl Courts in much better days.

OKLAHOMA CITY

Oklahoma City successfully ousted Guthrie as the state capital in 1910. For many years, the **capitol building** (2300 N. Lincoln Blvd.) here was unusual for this country, because it didn't have a dome. A dome was indeed a part of the original design, but it was omitted for reasons of economy. In 2002, the citizens of Oklahoma decided to finally top their capitol with a dome, so the one you see today is a modern add-on. Oil was struck here in 1928, and before the boom was over, there were twenty-four oil wells pumping on the actual grounds of the Oklahoma state capitol.

The Owl Courts complex is on the bypass portion of Route 66 in the community of Britton. Oklahoma City, Oklahoma. GPS: 35.56548,-97.52711

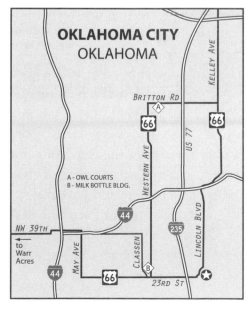

Route 66 took many different paths through Oklahoma City over the years, so you would do well to explore extensively if you can tolerate the traffic. The best-known route traced present-day Broadway out of Edmond (which becomes Kelley) straight toward the capitol, where it turned west on 23rd, north on May, and west again on NW 39th Street Expressway. Alternatively, a turn from Kelley onto Britton Avenue and then a left on Western Avenue takes you through the village of Britton along a more obscure "beltline" route. Also, be sure to cruise Classen Avenue, where you'll see a great example of symbolic architecture when you pass a little **triangular building with a giant milk bottle on top**.

Here's what the state capitol looked like until the dome was finally added in the twenty-first century.

This old postcard depicts a dome that was designed, but not actually built.

The **first automatic parking meter** was invented and installed in Oklahoma City by brothers Carlton and Gerald Hale on July 16, 1935. Initially, the meters were placed on only one side of the downtown street. Within three days, the merchants from the other side of the street petitioned to have their side metered also. They liked the constant and rapid turnover that the meters engendered. Two years later, on June 4, 1937, Sylman Goldman introduced the **first shopping cart** here.

On July 22, 1933, Machine Gun Kelly kidnapped millionaire Charles Urscher from his **home** (327 NW 18th St.). Kelly was the gangster who coined the phrase "G-Man."

Oklahoma City, Oklahoma. GPS: 35.49411,-97.53212

OKLAHOMA CITY ATTRACTIONS

Oklahoma City has known tragedy. The worst-ever act of terrorism on American soil—up until that time—occurred here April 19, 1995, at the Alfred P. Murrah Federal Building. Be sure to visit the **Oklahoma City National Memorial** (620 N. Harvey Ave.).

In the heart of Oklahoma City is the **Myriad Botanical Gardens and Crystal Bridge Tropical Conservatory** (301 W. Reno Ave.). Truly an oasis, the gardens cover a seventeen-acre tract and include rolling hills surrounding a sunken lake. The focal point of the gardens is the seven-story, 224-foot-long Crystal Bridge Tropical Conservatory, a greenhouse providing a habitat for an extensive collection of palms, orchids, cacti, and exotics from around the world.

Be sure to pay a visit to the **National Cowboy & Western Heritage Museum** (1700 NE 63rd St.)—formerly the National Cowboy Hall of Fame. This is a

Oklahoma City, Oklahoma.
GPS: 35.49318,-97.53469

large, first-rate com-
plex that includes
major exhibition
galleries, a replica
turn-of-the-century
Western town, and
several heroic-sized
works of sculpture,
including a rendering
of James Earle Fraser's

world-famous *End of*   **Route 66/Western Avenue, Oklahoma City.**
the Trail, which won   **GPS: 35.56255,-97.53102**

a gold medal at the 1915 Pan-Pacific International Exposition in San
Francisco. Fraser also designed the Indian Head (or Buffalo) nickel,
which began production in 1913. Also contained within the museum is
the Hall of Fame of Western Film, which includes video clips and other
memorabilia associated with the likes of Gene Autry, Gary Cooper, Tom
Mix, and Slim Pickens, among many others. There is also a research archive that includes photographs, papers, and the personal effects of actor
Walter Brennan and several other Western notables.

Just down the street from this museum is **Gabriella's Italian Grill**
(1226 NE 63rd St.). In the 1930s, this place was a speakeasy known as
the Kentucky Club, and was frequented by Pretty Boy Floyd. The building reportedly has features such as trap doors to facilitate escape in the
event of a police raid.

The **Science Museum Oklahoma** (2100 NE 52nd St.) is actually a
collection of museums. Included are the Hands-On Science Museum,
the Kirkpatrick Planetarium, and the Air Space Museum. With all of
these attractions essentially under one roof, it's a near-overdose for the
mind.

Built in 1958, the **Gold Dome** (1112 NW 23rd St.) was constructed
using R. Buckminster Fuller's geodesic dome principles, and includes a
gold-anodized aluminum roof. The Dome originally housed a bank, but
has recently been rehabilitated for retail and office space.

The **Paseo Arts District**, centered at NW 30th and Dewey, is a historically rich neighborhood that has been taken over by the city's art community. Several artists have studios and galleries in this area, and the district hosts an annual art festival each Memorial Day weekend.

Bricktown is a former warehouse district that has been turned into an entertainment hot spot with bars, restaurants, and music clubs. Recently added are some canals, which are plied by water taxis. The loading area for the narrated taxi rides is across from the **Chickasaw Bricktown Ballpark** (2 S. Mickey Mantle Dr.), home of the minor-league Oklahoma City Dodgers. The **American Banjo Museum** (9 E. Sheridan Ave.), which claims to have the largest collection of banjos in the world, relocated to Bricktown in 2009 after having been in the town of Guthrie for years.

The **Oklahoma Country & Western Music Hall of Fame** (3925 SE 29th St.) consists of more than 10,000 square feet of items dedicated to country-and-western music performers.

The **45th Infantry Division Museum** (2145 NE 36th St.) is a highly regarded military museum and has something of interest for everyone. Oklahoma's role in

Evidence of the Mother Road spirit in Oklahoma City, Oklahoma. GPS: 35.51117,-97.59312

At Ann's Chicken, Oklahoma City. GPS: 35.51117,-97.59312

the Civil War and American Indian Wars is represented here, but displays also include items from Hitler's bunker that were captured by the 45th in 1945. There are over 200 original "Willie and Joe" cartoons by artist Bill Mauldin, and outside are dozens of military vehicles, aircraft, and artillery.

On the grounds of the Will Rogers World Airport is the **99s Museum of Women Pilots** (4300 Amelia Earhart Ln.). Amelia Earhart is prominently represented here—as well as other early female aviators—and there are materials on display pertaining to women in the space program.

The **Oklahoma State Firefighters Museum** (2716 NE 50th St.) has helmets on display worn by Ben Franklin, John Hancock, and Paul Revere. Also on display is Oklahoma's first fire station (established in 1864) as well as 100-year-old fire equipment that was actually used in Oklahoma communities.

The **National Softball Hall of Fame and Museum** (2801 NE 50th St.) covers all variants of the game, including fast, slow, and modified-pitch versions. The museum is housed in the Amateur Softball Association (ASA) headquarters. The ASA stadium hosts national and world class competitions in the sport.

The **Jim Thorpe Association and Oklahoma Sports Hall of Fame** (4040 N. Lincoln Blvd.) honors excellence in athletics, with a variety of awards and scholarships that they bestow annually.

The **Henry Overholser Mansion** (405 NW 15th St.) was built, naturally, by Henry Overholser. This 1903 Victorian-style home contains ninety percent of the original family furnishings and is notable for its hand-painted, canvas-covered walls.

Built in 1928, the **Governor's Mansion** (820 NE 23rd St.) offers guided tours every Wednesday. The house is said to be haunted by the ghost of Oklahoma's Depression-era governor, William H. "Alfalfa Bill" Murray. On the grounds is a swimming pool shaped like the state's boundaries.

The **Oklahoma History Center** (800 Nazih Zuhdi Dr.) has over 200,000 square feet devoted to the state's heritage, organized by themes such as aviation, commerce, and geology, to name just a few.

The **Harn Homestead & 1889er Museum** (1721 N. Lincoln Blvd.) is a complex of structures not far from the state capitol building. This homestead was claimed in the Land Run of 1889, and includes a stone-and-cedar barn, three houses, and the former Stoney Point School, a

Oklahoma City, Oklahoma. GPS: 35.51493,-97.52986

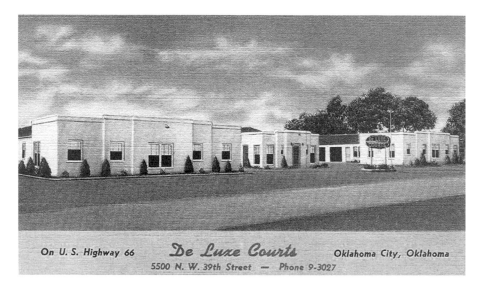

On U. S. Highway 66   *De Luxe Courts*   Oklahoma City, Oklahoma
5500 N. W. 39th Street — Phone 9-3027

one-room schoolhouse dating from 1897. The school was in regular use until 1947, and was moved here in 1988.

Does pigeon racing tickle your fancy? The **American Pigeon Museum and Library** (2300 NE 63rd St.) has dedicated itself to the heritage of the pigeon. A project of the American Homing Pigeon Institute, there is a small museum housed in a 1930s brick house on ten acres of land. There are educational exhibits, pigeon lofts, and cultivated gardens. Pigeon races are held in the fall. White pigeons are also available here for release at weddings and other special events.

The **World Organization of China Painters Museum** (2700 N. Portland) houses a large collection of hand-painted China, along with a gift shop, research library, and classrooms.

The **Classen High School Museum** (1901 N. Ellison St.) and the **Central High School Museum** (815 N. Robinson St.) are in competition to see who has the best school spirit. Classen has the country's largest high school alumni organization and boasts Admiral William Crowe as one of its constituents. Central High's building (circa 1910) was designed by the architect of the state capitol and is on the National Register of Historic Places.

Evolved from an organization called the Oklahoma Hall of Fame, the **Gaylord-Pickens Oklahoma Heritage Museum** (1400 Classen Dr.) opened its high-tech doors in 2007, and has received several accolades. The museum seeks to tell the story of Oklahoma through its most distinguished citizens, and you can search the database of more than 600 hall of fame inductees going all the way back to 1928.

The **Oklahoma Museum of Telephone History** (111 Dean A. McGee Ave.) covers more than a century's worth of history in the form of vintage telephones and telephone company memorabilia.

The **Oklahoma Railway Museum** (3400 NE Grand Blvd.) is an open-air museum with a family-friendly vibe. You can even ride a train!

Oklahoma City still has an operating drive-in movie theater, the **Winchester Drive-In** (6930 S. Western Ave.), built in 1968. It's located on the south side of town, away from the Mother Road.

 You'll leave Oklahoma City headed west on 39th Street Expressway.

WARR ACRES-BETHANY

Warr Acres was named for a real estate developer named Clyde B. Warr. The town of Bethany was established in 1906 by members of the Nazarene Church. Today, both cities seem to be embedded in Greater Oklahoma City. The **Bethany Historical Society Museum** (6700 NW 36th St.) is located inside city hall.

Route 66 is a multilane, divided thoroughfare in these parts. Just west of Bethany, it crosses a corner of **Lake Overholser**. Named for OKC mayor Ed Overholser, the lake at the time of Rittenhouse was a recreational area with speedboat rides. Prior to World War II, plans were laid to make Lake Overholser a layover center for seaplane excursions. This, of course, is a mode of travel that never really caught on well. Today, Alaskans use seaplanes very commonly, but they are short on roads up there.

**This old bridge is at the edge of Lake Overholser, west of Bethany, Oklahoma.
GPS: 35.51463,-97.66275**

A few years ago, I would have strongly encouraged you to take the old 66 alignment that crosses the vintage (1924) **Lake Overholser Bridge** and then hugs the lake's northern shoreline (N. Overholser Drive). It meets up with the later Route 66 alignment at Yukon. However, that stretch of road has undergone such build-up and modernization lately that there's little of the Route 66 flavor left, so there isn't much to recommend it anymore. Don't feel bad if you skip it by staying on the later alignment.

YUKON

Singer Garth Brooks and actor Dale Robertson both hail from Yukon, and there is a sign at the edge of town proudly proclaiming Brooks as its native son. Pay a visit to the **Garth Brooks Water Tower** (I-40 and Garth Brooks Blvd.).

YUKON ATTRACTIONS

You are in **Chisholm Trail** country now. Some sources say that
9th Street through Yukon closely approximates the route of the
Chisholm Trail. Other sources say
that U.S. 81, which runs through
El Reno farther west, is more authentic. In truth, being a cattle
trail, the Chisholm was of course
never paved, so the precise route
varied considerably. It was subject
to the vagaries of such things as
water availability, prevailing weather, and individual whim. What we

Yukon, Oklahoma's biggest landmark.
GPS: 35.50784,-97.74666

can be more certain of is that the trail ran from southern Texas, through
central Oklahoma, and on to the cattle markets in Abilene, Kansas. The
trail was named for Jesse Chisholm, who was among the first to make
regular use of the trail and to advocate its use by others. Yukon holds a
Chisholm Trail Festival every year, as do many of the towns and cities
through which the trail once passed.

The **Yukon Community Center** (2200 S. Holly Ave.) has a Chisholm
Trail monument and also contains a "Bank Shot" setup. This is a sort
of cross between basketball and miniature golf, consisting of bizarrely
shaped backboards on which you can test your skill and patience in sink-
ing your "free throws." I've never seen one of them anywhere else.

A major landmark here in Yukon is the **Yukon's Best Flour mural**,
which is emblazoned prominently on the side of a grain storage facility
on the south side of the highway in town, right at the railroad tracks.

Yukon's Best Railroad Museum (328–346 Cedar Ave.) is a static
display of a caboose and other rail cars across the boulevard from the
Yukon's Best Flour mural. Full tours of the rail cars can be scheduled by
calling (405) 354-5079.

The **Yukon Historical Society Museum** (601 Oak St.) is housed in a 1910 school building and includes a doctor's office, Czech history room, and other local history.

About five miles north of town is **Express Clydesdales** (12701 W. Wilshire Blvd.). Rare black-and-white Clydesdale horses make their home here in a 1936 barn restored by Amish specialists from Indiana. There is also a gift shop and visitor center.

EL RENO

El Reno sits at the junction of two famous highways of very different kinds: U.S. 66 and the Chisholm Trail (roughly at U.S. 81). The town, which is the seat of Canadian County, was reportedly named for a Civil War general, Jesse L. Reno, who was killed in action in 1862.

Look for **VFW Post 382** (1515 S. Rock Island Ave.) as you pass through town. There is

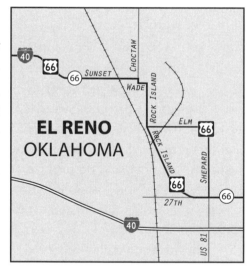

a retired airplane displayed out front that saw action in World War II.

EL RENO ATTRACTIONS

The **Canadian County Historical Museum** (300 S. Grand Ave.) has the old Rock Island depot as its core, but also has extensive grounds featuring a jail house, a hotel, a one-room school, an 1889 Land Run marker, and other items of historical and cultural interest, including the nation's first Red Cross canteen. Recently established is the Heritage Trolley, which originates at the CCHM and takes riders downtown to restaurants and shopping destinations.

In El Reno is a **Benevolent and Protective Order of Elks Lodge** (415 S. Rock Island Ave.) that was part of an exhibit at the 1904 St. Louis World's Fair. The structure was pulled apart and transported here, where it was re-assembled. That 1904 fair was where the first hamburger on a bun was introduced.

El Reno, Oklahoma. GPS: 5.52234,-97.95031

On the first Saturday in May, the town of El Reno grills a **750-pound onion burger**, and you can get a free bite of the "Big One" for as long as it lasts. El Reno is widely considered the home of the onion burger, with several small restaurants specializing in them, including Johnnie's, Sid's, and Robert's.

El Reno, Oklahoma. GPS: 35.51443,-97.94837

FURTHER AFIELD

Travel a little to the north of El Reno via U.S. 81, and you'll be approximating the path of the Chisholm Trail. The town of Kingfisher is proud of its Chisholm Trail heritage, but a

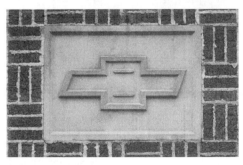

El Reno, Oklahoma. GPS: 35.53148,-97.95309

little less proud of its gridiron record. Between 1905 and 1919, Oklahoma University beat the Kingfisher football team by scores of 55–0, 32–0, 51–0, 46–5, 66–0, 104–0, 40–0, 74–0, 67–0, 67–0 (again), 96–0,

Canadian County Historical Museum, El Reno, Oklahoma. GPS: 35.53065,-97.95833

179–0, and 157–0. In thirteen games, Kingfisher was outscored by a whopping 1,034–5.

Kingfisher was the birthplace of an outlaw named John King Fisher. He was reputed to be a major-league rustler in the 1870s, and is said to have admitted to killing seven men, "not counting Mexicans."

Another outlaw clan, the Daltons, grew up on a farm in the vicinity. Buried in the **Kingfisher Cemetery** (OK 3 and N2830 Rd.) are Adeline Lee Younger Dalton—mother of the Dalton boys and cousin of Cole Younger—and her son, Emmett Dalton. Kingfisher is also where W. C. Coleman, of Coleman Lantern fame, first began selling lamps door to door in the 1890s.

More information about the Chisholm Trail can be found both north and south of El Reno, at the **Chisholm Trail Museum** in Kingfisher (605 Zellers Ave.) and the **Chisholm Trail Heritage Center** in Duncan (1000 Chisholm Trail Pkwy). There are still visible trail ruts at **Monument Hill** near Duncan.

Stop by the information center for the nearby **Fort Reno** (7107 W. Cheyenne St.), which you'll encounter in a few miles as you head west along the Mother Road. Established in 1875, Fort Reno was an

El Reno, Oklahoma.
GPS: 35.53407,-97.95232

important post for keeping the Cheyenne and Arapaho tribes at bay during the territorial struggles of the time, and later achieved a reputation for raising a large proportion of the U.S. Army's horses during the pre-mechanized era. It was here that Black Jack, the riderless horse in President Kennedy's funeral procession, was raised. The cemetery here contains the grave of one Ben Clark, an accomplished scout and sometime Pony Express rider. During the Second World War, the fort functioned as a prisoner-of-war camp for German and Italian captives, some of whom were also laid to rest in the cemetery.

 Back on 66, about four miles west of El Reno and just north of the highway is Fort Reno (see above). Although much of it

The chapel at Fort Reno. GPS: 35.56286,-98.03416

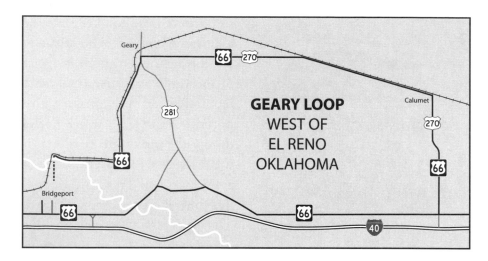

remains, today it looks like many a ghost town.

Though Route 66 was eventually straightened, for a time it veered north and passed through the town of Calumet. You can take this older course by turning north on U.S. 270. The description that immediately follows refers to this older route through Geary. If you choose to take the later route straight ahead, you can pick up that thread in the town of Hydro.

CALUMET

Prior to the nineteenth century, "calumet" was the name given to what is now commonly called the "peace pipe." It is said to have come from the French *chalumeau*, meaning "reed."

GEARY

The **Canadian River Historical Society Museum** (100 E. Main St.) includes the area's first log jail, as well as a train caboose and a furnished 1901 home.

North of Geary, near the banks of the Canadian River, at the rather isolated **Left Hand Spring Camp**, is the grave of Jesse Chisholm, the man for whom the trail we crossed a little earlier was named. There are granite monuments marking Chisholm's grave and that of Chief Left Hand, an Arapaho Indian.

   Heading south out of Geary, U.S. 281/OK 8 will return you to the "through" alignment of Route 66. If you're feeling adventurous, there is a partially paved road you can veer onto at the edge of town that parallels the railroad tracks. This was at one time the main highway. After about four miles or so, a right will take you toward Bridgeport and the old river crossing which gave the town its name. You can no longer make the crossing there, however. The other direction takes you back to a rendezvous with the newer 66 alignment, near the convergence of the Canadian, Blaine, and Caddo county lines.

Where U.S. 281 and OK 8 turn south and leave us is what is known as **Hinton Junction**. There is a ruin of a café there, which I'm told was also a bus station at one time.

Former café at the Hinton Junction, east of Hydro, Oklahoma.
GPS: 35.53633,-98.34660

BRIDGEPORT

Bridgeport was bypassed by Route 66 as the crossing of this branch of the Canadian River was moved further downstream. What remains of this town is quiet indeed. The last time I patrolled these streets, there was a skunk doing the same thing who acted as if he owned the place.

FURTHER AFIELD

South of Bridgeport via U.S. 281 is the town of Hinton. The **Hinton Historical Museum & Parker House** (801 S. Broadway Ave.) contains one of the state's largest collections of buggies and carriages, as well as nineteenth-century farm machinery, bicycles, and several antique cars. One of the buggies is said to be "Oklahoma's Largest."

Just outside Hinton is the **Red Rock Canyon State Park** (116 Red Rock Canyon Rd.), reputed to be the haven of horse rustlers and cattle thieves in days gone by. A covered-wagon migratory trail (California Road) once passed through the park, and today one of the many hiking trails will take you to some of the remaining wagon ruts from those days.

Both before and after Hydro, you'll pass over a stretch of the route that is truly classic. The roadway is segmented concrete, and it rises and falls with the gentle hills in this area. Even though the interstate is only yards away on your left, you get a true taste of what cross-country auto travel was like decades ago. Savor it, and remember it after you've returned home.

South of this Bridgeport-Hydro stretch of highway, there are some features called **Steen's Buttes** or **Caddo Mounds**. They were reported by army explorers as early as 1840, and were subsequently used as landmarks for 49ers en route to California during the Gold Rush years. On some maps, one of the mounds is designated as "Dead Woman's Mound."

Lucille's famous station, near Hydro, Oklahoma. GPS: 35.53695,-98.58833

HYDRO

The highway passes just south of the town of Hydro. At a crossroads called Provine, you'll see **Lucille's**, a fixture on Route 66 since 1941, when Lucille Hamons and her husband began operating a gas station and tourist court here. Lucille passed away in 2000, but not before earning the nickname "Mother of the Mother Road." For years, she spent time with each and every traveler who came through here, passing along stories of the road gleaned from her many years at its shoulder.

If you take the short detour north into Hydro's downtown, **Nutopia Nuts 'N More** (206 W. Main St.)—formerly Johnson's Peanut Company—offers seasonal tours, and the gift shop is open all year.

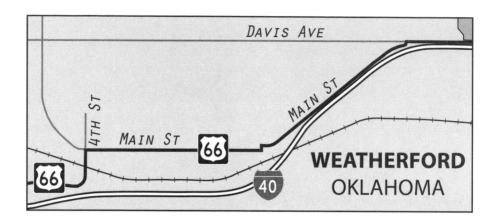

WEATHERFORD

Enter Weatherford on E. Main, which clings closely to I-40 at first, then stops at a "T" intersection. Turn left, then make a quick right to continue on Main.

Weatherford is home to **Southwestern Oklahoma State University** (100 E. Campus Dr.), which holds an annual **Jazz Festival** every February.

WEATHERFORD ATTRACTIONS

Being the birthplace of an astronaut has its responsibilities. Approaching Weatherford from the east, you'll pass the entrance to the **General Thomas P. Stafford Air & Space Museum Airport** (3000 E. Logan Rd., Bldg. 2). It features moon rocks, space suits,

Weatherford, Oklahoma. GPS: 35.53842,-98.65933

At the turnoff for the General Thomas P. Stafford Air & Space Museum Airport, Weatherford, Oklahoma. GPS: 35.53686,-98.66974

Weatherford, Oklahoma.
GPS: 35.52971,-98.68614

rocket boosters, and other memorabilia. You can even walk through a space shuttle fuel pod.

Also on the eastern outskirts of town is a modern-day restaurant named **Lucille's Roadhouse** (1301 N. Airport Rd.), which honors the memory of Lucille Hamons (see the Hydro section, above). They've gone to some lengths to conjure the general shape and form of the original Lucille's, and retro-style gasoline pumps at the entrance complete the effect.

Check out the **Heartland of America Museum** (1600 S. Frontage Rd.), which opened its doors in 2007. On display are a portable jail, a one-room school, and a diner that once stood on Route 66 where Elvis Presley is said to have stopped in at least three times.

To the south of Weatherford is **Fort Sill** (435 Quanah Rd.), where numerous American Indian chiefs were imprisoned. Some of them, notably Geronimo, are interred here.

 Leaving Weatherford, turn left onto 4th Street, which soon curves west.

CLINTON

There are multiple Route 66 alignments through town. I suggest you sample all of them; they are all attractive in their own way. The modern "bypass" route boasts the first-rate Oklahoma Route 66 Museum, which every true-blue 66-er needs to visit.

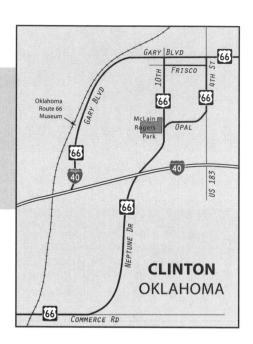

This town was named for Judge Clinton Irwin. For years, the U.S. 66 Highway Association, an early booster organization for the highway, was run here in Clinton by Jack and Ruth Cuthbert, who became known as "Mr. and Mrs. 66."

CLINTON ATTRACTIONS

On the east side of town is the **Mohawk Lodge Indian Store & Trading Post** (22702 Route 66 N), first established in 1892 and occupying this location since 1940. The original sales counter was brought over in the move

Clinton, Oklahoma. GPS: 35.51411,-98.94016

The Oklahoma Route 66 Museum in Clinton is a must-stop for every Mother Road adventurer. GPS: 35.50648,-98.98671

and is still in use. The owners say it's as much a museum as it is a store.

McLain Rogers Park, on Historic 66 (S. 10th St.), has a classic enamel-and-neon sign dating from 1936, and a WPA-constructed outdoor theater.

This tiny restored diner is on the grounds of the Oklahoma Route 66 Museum in Clinton. GPS: 35.50648,-98.98671

The **Oklahoma Route 66 Museum** (2229 W. Gary Blvd.) opened here in 1995 on a later bypass route around town. The building itself is uniquely Route 66-themed, and was designed by the same architect who later gave us POPS in Arcadia. All of the museum's exhibits are very professionally done, por-traying the highway's changing roles in society through the various de-cades of the twentieth century. More recently, a tiny restored Valentine diner, which once served Route 66 travelers in Texas, was placed on the museum grounds. The restoration work on the diner earned Virgil Smith the Cyrus Avery Preserva-tion Award the following year.

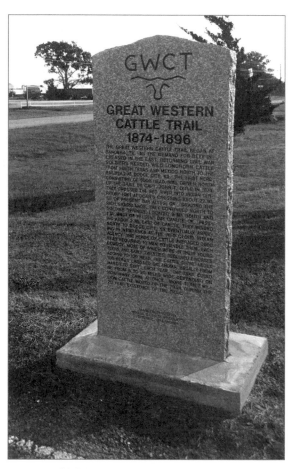

Canute, Oklahoma. GPS: 35.42178,-99.27152

FOSS-CANUTE

There is a ruin of an old roadside establish-ment here at Foss with red, peeling paint, called **Kobel's Place** (OK 44 and OK 66). A little to the north on Highway 44, just past the railroad tracks, is the actual town. Also north of town via Highway 44 is **Foss State Park** (10252 Oklahoma 44). Further west, Canute is notable for its **Catholic cemetery** on the east side of town, which includes a stone grotto dating from around 1930. A church dating from 1926 is now the

The former Cotton Boll Motel, Canute, Oklahoma. GPS: 35.42202,-99.27849

Canute Heritage Center (N2080 Rd.). Also in Canute is the **Cotton Boll Motel** (Historic Rte. 66 and 6th St.), which is now being used as a private residence. The big neon sign, however, remains.

ELK CITY

This town was originally called Crowe, but the townspeople attempted to persuade Adolphus Busch to put a brewery here by renaming the town Busch. When that plan failed, the name Elk City was adopted, after the nearby Elk Creek. The Dodge City (Kansas)

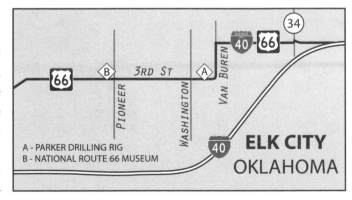

Cattle Trail is said to have passed through here in the nineteenth century; the town was established in 1901. According to Jack Rittenhouse, Elk City was the site of an early experiment in collective health care in the 1940s (could this have been the first HMO?). Also in the '40s—August 15, 1946, to be precise—song composer extraordinaire Jimmy Webb was born right here in Elk City.

ELK CITY ATTRACTIONS

In 1998, Elk City introduced the **National Route 66 Museum** (2717 W. Hwy 66). This museum covers the route in all eight states through which it passed. It's becoming more impossible to miss all the time—the exterior now includes perhaps the most enormous Route 66 shield ever built. The large kachina figures outside once stood at the Queenan Trading Post, an old-school curio shop on Route 66 that closed long ago. The muse-

National Route 66 Museum, Elk City, Oklahoma. GPS: 35.41186,-99.43701

Part of the Old Town Museum Complex, Elk City, Oklahoma. GPS: 35.41186,-99.43701

um is part of an ever-expanding collection of buildings known as the **Old Town Museum Complex** (2717 W. 3rd St.), which includes both historical and painstakingly reproduced buildings, railroad cars, and other

Elk City, Oklahoma. GPS: 35.41186,-99.43701

features of interest. The family of museums now includes a transportation museum and a farm and ranch museum, and all of this is within the same city block.

A brief oil boom period in the area is recalled by a huge oil derrick, **Parker Drilling Rig No. 114**, which stands about seventeen stories tall. It's located right next to the old Casa Grande Hotel, which hosted a Route 66 conference way back in 1931 and now houses the **Anadarko Basin Museum of Natural History** (204 N. Main St.). A few blocks west, at the corner of Washington, is an expanse of lawn on the south side of the highway with a **bronze elk sculpture** on display.

SAYRE

There are what appear to be **storm cellar entrances** (4th St. and Elm Ave.) on either side of Route 66 as it passes through town. These actually lead to an underground pedestrian walkway, which allowed the once-busy thoroughfare to be crossed safely. They are of course no longer needed, but there are many other towns along the route whose citizens would have appreciated this same innovation in the days when traffic was incessant.

SAYRE ATTRACTIONS

The **Beckham County Courthouse** (302 E. Main St. #101), which is in the town square, made a cameo in the film version of *The Grapes of*

This courthouse in Sayre, Oklahoma, made a cameo appearance in the film *The Grapes of Wrath*. GPS: 35.29128,-99.63766

Wrath. The post office (201 N. 4th St.) is decorated with a **Depression-era mural** depicting the Oklahoma Land Run. **Owl Drug**, (4th St. and Main St.), which has opened and closed numerous times over the years, has the state's largest antique soda fountain.

The **Short Grass Country Museum** (106 E. Poplar Ave), which is in the old Rock Island depot, features changing exhibits pertaining to early day life in Beckham County and western Oklahoma's shortgrass country in general.

Model railroaders should see the **RS&K Railroad Museum** (411 N. 6th St.), which features hundreds of model trains, including working layouts, as well as railroad memorabilia.

Evidence of the Route 66 spirit in Sayre, Oklahoma. GPS: 35.30819,-99.63742

FURTHER AFIELD

North of Sayre via U.S. 283 is the town of Cheyenne, where you can find the **Washita Battlefield National Historic Site** (18555 Hwy 47A) and the **Black Kettle Museum** (101 L L Males Blvd.). These sites center around a surprise cavalry attack on a Cheyenne village headed by Chief Black Kettle in 1868. The U.S. troops of the 7th Cavalry were commanded at that time by Lieutenant Colonel George A. Custer. There

Sayre, Oklahoma. GPS: 35.30883,-99.63572

is also a sculpture on the grounds of Cheyenne's **Roger Mills County Courthouse** (503 Broadway) commemorating the events.

 The Sayre-Hext-Erick stretch of old 66 is an open book for you to read. As you drive this corridor, you will see that there are two older, unused lanes of highway to your right. Those indicate the original alignment of 66 through here, right beside the railroad track. The pair of lanes you are driving on were added later, as eastbound lanes separated from the other lanes by a median, in the days when Route 66 was a major thoroughfare in this area. Later, as I-40 was completed to the south, traffic diminished significantly on 66 and two of its lanes were retired.

What remains of the small community of Hext is between old 66 and I-40, just north of exit #14.

Abandoned highway lanes near Hext, Oklahoma. GPS: 35.25837,-99.73860

Downtown Erick, Oklahoma. GPS: 35.21376,-99.86671

ERICK

The main street through town (Route 66) has been named Roger Miller Boulevard, in honor of Erick's favorite son, who in turn is most noted for his rendition of the song "King of the Road." The town now has a **Roger Miller Museum** (101 S. Sheb Wooley Ave.), and holds an annual **Roger Miller Festival** in his honor.

Also hailing from near

Erick, Oklahoma.
GPS: 35.21376,-99.86671

Erick, Oklahoma. GPS: 35.21493,-99.87379

Erick is performer Sheb Wooley. Sheb was a country music performer in the late 1940s, then went to Los Angeles and took acting lessons to pursue a film career. He got the break he was looking for when he was cast in an Errol Flynn film in 1950. He became better known, though, for his extended role in the television series *Rawhide*.

Open sporadically or by appointment, the **100th Meridian Museum** (101 S. Sheb Wooley Ave.) presents information relating to the oft-disputed boundary line between Oklahoma and the Republic of Texas. At one time, the area you are entering here was claimed by the Lone Star State.

Attached to the rear of the 100th Meridian Museum is what the town of Erick likes to call the **Bonebrake Hardware Museum** (102 S. Sheb Wooley Blvd.). You can't go in; you just have to shade your eyes and peer into the windows. The story goes that the Bonebrake family, who owned and ran the hardware store, simply closed the door and walked away sometime in the 1960s, and everything inside is still just as they left it.

A block south of Route 66 is **Crow's Resale** (201 S. Sheb Wooley Blvd.)—formerly SandHills Curiosity Shop—located in an old meat

market. The exterior is festooned with countless vintage signs: oil companies,
soft drinks, Greyhound,
and even S & H Green
Stamps.

TEXOLA

This town was named for
the fact that it rests nearly
astride the Oklahoma-Tex-
as border (the more obvi-
ous name, "Texhoma," was
already taken by another
town in the state; there's

One-cell jailhouse, Texola, Oklahoma.
GPS: 35.22010,-99.98885

also a Lake Texoma on the border). Texola can rightly be called a ghost
town, having only a tiny fraction of its residences and commercial buildings inhabited. There is a **tiny jail** (one cell, actually) just a block or so
off of Route 66.

Texola is Oklahoma's quiet farewell to the Mother Road.

This seasoned road warrior has since vanished without a trace. Texola, Oklahoma.

TEXAS

Texas, proud as it is to be the largest state in the contiguous for-ty-eight and prouder still of its heritage as a former independent republic, ranks next-to-last in the mileage it can claim along

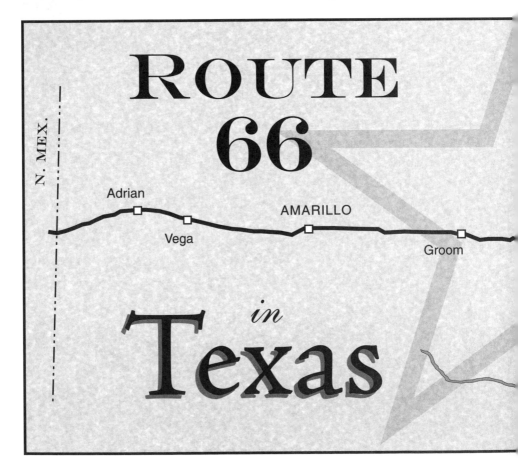

the path of Route 66. That's because the Mother Road crosses the state through what is known as the Texas Panhandle. That panhandle, the northernmost extension of the state, is but an eroded stump compared to what might have been.

If you took time to stop at the 100th Meridian Museum back in Erick (see page 270), then you know at least a part of the story. You know that if the Texas-Oklahoma border had been decided differently, the westbound Route 66 traveler of today would have entered the great state of Texas at what is now Erick, Oklahoma. What you might not know is that, if some other political decisions had been made a bit differently, that same traveler would not be leaving Texas until he'd passed through what is now Albuquerque, New Mexico, and crossed over the Rio Grande some 400 miles to the west.

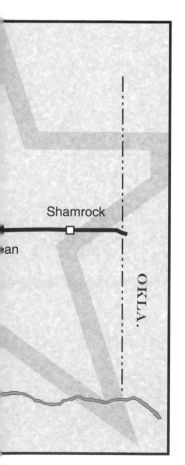

During Texas's early days of statehood (1845–1849), it laid claim to territory almost fifty percent larger than its current boundaries, including portions of present-day Oklahoma, New Mexico, Kansas, Colorado, and Wyoming. Since some of this territory was contested by other factions within the U.S., emotions ran high on the subject. At the same time, the former Republic of Texas (1836–1845) had incurred significant debts in its struggle for independence. Texas therefore ceded about one-third of its territory in exchange for $10 million in an agreement known as the Compromise of 1850. Much of the territory given up in 1850 makes up the portion of present-day New Mexico east of the Rio Grande.

Texas, as someone once said, is a State of Mind. And fittingly, there's very little to indicate that, just moments after leaving Texola, one has entered the Lone Star State. Your first signal, other than the official state line sign erected by the highway department, is the character of the pavement itself. This early stretch of Texas highway is made up of the classic segmented concrete, which imparts that rhythmic thump, ka-thump, ka-thump to your pneumatic-tired journey. You'll also note that the road tends to rise and fall with the general lay of the land. If you can succeed in ignoring the raging interstate just a few yards to your right, the rhythm of the road will provide you with that elusive taste of what long-distance highway travel was like decades ago.

Just west of the state line, and right about where old 66 sidles up to the edge of Interstate 40, is the community of Benonine.

BENONINE

My 1957 atlas sees fit to depict Benonine just west of the Oklahoma-Texas state line, but you won't see much from the highway today.

SHAMROCK

Route 66 is part of a distant past, but life goes on in Shamrock, albeit at a different pace than in the Mother Road era. As befits a town with such a name, Shamrock puts its all into the annual St. Patrick's Day celebration. Men grow beards in preparation for the big day—not only is there a prize for best beard, there is even a price on the head of any adult male failing to sport one.

Midway through town is the junction with U.S. 83, a major north-south highway. Before the interstates came along, the crossing of U.S. Routes 66 and 83 in the center of town was a very happening place, and this intersection was, and still is, dominated by the U-Drop Inn.

The **U-Drop Inn** (1242 N. Main St.), known for a time as Nunn's Café, is an Art Deco masterpiece made all the more impressive by its placement on the Texas plain. The structure, dating from 1936, thrusts two steeple-like projections heavenward. The story goes that, when first constructed, there was a contest to come up with the name for the new

U-Drop Inn, Shamrock, Texas. GPS: 35.22660,-100.24876

enterprise. The winner was a youngster who suggested the U-Drop Inn name and collected the cash prize. Fortunately for today's traveler, the building recently underwent a thorough restoration, right down to every last piece of neon tubing. Neon outlines many of the structure's exterior design features, which makes it quite an amazing sight at dusk and later. The local chamber of commerce now has its offices here. Viewers of the 2006 movie *Cars* might also recognize the U-Drop as inspiration for part of Radiator Springs. A thoroughly modern touch has now been added: the parking lot now features several Tesla charging stations.

SHAMROCK ATTRACTIONS

The **Pioneer West Museum** (204 N. Madden St.) is housed in the former Reynolds Hotel, which dates from the 1920s. The museum has twenty or so rooms filled with a variety of exhibits, with subjects ranging from Plains Indian culture to NASA moon-mission articles. There are rooms outfitted as doctor and dentist offices, a general store, and a pioneer-era schoolroom. Next to the museum is a restored **Magnolia fuel station**.

Shamrock, Texas. GPS: 35.21547,-100.24773

There's a **fragment of the true Blarney Stone** on display at Elmore Park (400 E. 2nd Street). The Blarney Stone itself is in County Cork, Ireland, and is reputed to confer eloquence on those who kiss it. Legend has it that the original Lord Blarney was rather accomplished in stretching the truth.

The town has recently taken an interest in its **water tower** (101 S. Main St.), said to be the tallest of its type in the state. There is now a small park at the foot of the tower that offers some information on its construction and general history.

LELA

These days, Lela is little more than the crossing of I-40 with Farm Road 1547.

Just west of Lela, and on the way to McLean, you can see some trees in the median which are the remnants of the windbreaks referred to by Jack Rittenhouse as he came through here in 1946. It's clear from the shape of these trees that there's a prevailing wind in these parts. It was near here on one of my own Texas 66 forays that I nearly ran over a five-foot snake trying to cross the road.

You might notice during your time in the Texas panhandle that peo-ple are rather "neighborly" around here. That is, if you make eye contact with passing drivers, you'll find them giving you "The Wave." The hand that's on top of the steering wheel will suddenly have its fingers springing upward into a sort of peacock spread that means "howdy." Please learn to duplicate this maneuver so as not to appear out of place.

MCLEAN

Upon entering the town of McLean, Route 66 splits into eastbound and westbound segments separated by a city block, with two lanes running in each direction.

McLean has been quite tena-cious about refusing to roll over and die. There are a number of re-born highway businesses here, some of which have gone through multiple incarnations attempting to find fa-vor—and a future—with today's motoring public.

McLean, Texas. GPS: 35.23058,-100.59211

MCLEAN ATTRACTIONS

This is an excellent town in which to get out onto the sidewalk and do some exploring on foot. McLean is home to the **Texas Route 66 Museum** (100 Kingsley St.), which shares an address with the **Devil's Rope Museum**. Both are worth stopping into. You certainly can't help but be impressed with the enormous balls of barbed wire on display out front. This building formerly housed a brassiere factory known as Marie Foundations. The Route 66 Museum exhibits include a mock 1950s-era diner and a large snake sculpture that once graced the property of the former Regal Reptile Ranch in Alanreed, just several miles west of here. Although I'm not knowledgeable on the subject of barbed wire ("devil's rope," that is), I have it on good authority that the Devil's Rope Museum houses one of the finest collections of the wire in the world. Believe me, there are people that take this stuff very seriously, indeed—almost as seriously as you and I take old Route 66, for example.

A restored **Phillips 66 station** (1st St. and Gray St.) is right on the highway (west-bound), and is an irresistible photo opportunity. It's the tiny, classic, cottage-style variety of Phillips station, much like the one you saw earlier in Chandler, Oklahoma. This one was restored by the Texas Route 66 Association (circa 1991).

This tiny station dates from the 1920s. McLean, Texas. GPS: 35.23281,-100.60183

The **McLean-Alanreed Area Museum** (116 N. Main St.) houses panhandle history exhibits as well as artifacts relating to the World War II prisoner-of-war camp located near here. If you're traveling east to west, you'll need to backtrack in order to get to the old POW camp site. To reach the historical marker, take I-40 exit #146 and then go north on County Line Road for about a mile or so. Part of the McLean/Gray County Airport is on the site of the camp.

McLean is also home to a surprisingly good lunch place, the **Red River Steakhouse** (101 W. Hwy 66).

ALANREED

Alanreed has been known by several names over the years, including Prairie Dog Town and Spring Tank. But Gouge Eye is by far the most colorful, and was obtained in connection with a barroom brawl.

At one time, there was a community to the north of Alanreed called Eldridge (or Elderidge). That town was established prior to Alanreed, and even had a post office. However, when the railroad came through a few miles to the south, the lure of those steel rails and the promise of commerce made the citizens of Eldridge pack up their belongings (and their post office) and relocate to the Alanreed townsite. You can still see a remnant of

Alanreed, Texas. GPS: 35.21236,-100.73442

the community of Eldridge by going north on Highway 291. About five miles north of I-40, turn west on a dead end called County Road X. After a short distance, you'll come to a small **cemetery** that once served the town. There are few marked graves there, and fewer still with actual names. One of them marks what is thought to be the grave of a twelve-year-old girl who died from a rattlesnake bite.

While in Alanreed, be sure to travel along the older highway alignment that takes you right through the heart of the village of Alanreed (3rd Avenue). There are some very old **café ruins** here, as well as a restored gas station—the **66 Super Service Station** (Hwy 271 and Main St.). The station bears a plaque: "Built by Bradley Kiser 1930—then in downtown

Alanreed." When one peers around Alanreed today, it's a little difficult to think of it as ever having what one would call a "downtown" district, but if you're at Mr. Kiser's old station, you're standing in the middle of it, with the ruined **Magnolia Café** only a few yards away.

At the site of the former Regal Reptile Ranch, Alanreed, Texas. GPS: 35.21483,-100.73200

North of the "old" alignment, and right alongside the interstate, there is a newer, bypass-style Route 66 alignment that now acts as a sort of frontage road. It was there that the **Regal Reptile Ranch** once lured families out of their iron chariots with the promise of a close-up look at rattlesnakes, Mexican beaded lizards, and other natural curiosities of the American Southwest. The ranch is now gone, a victim of time and the bulldozer. Several years ago, there were still a few ruined buildings and quite a bit of fencing with some of the original lettering visible.

On the west side of Alanreed, there used to be some ruins of motel courts that have since been completely removed, leaving only an empty lot. I bring this up as a reminder to you that what you see today may be gone tomorrow, so keep your camera handy and use it—not only for the enrichment of your own experience, but perhaps for the sake of posterity as well.

FURTHER AFIELD

West of Alanreed, the Highway 2477 North exit will take you on a side trip to Lake McClellan, an old stopover with WPA-era structures, now designated as the **Lake McClellan Creek National Grassland**.

Also at the above exit, you can get turned around in order to visit the eastbound I-40 rest area. It's Route 66-themed, and the stylized architecture pays homage to the 66 Courts that used to stand in Groom until recently—in Mother Road years, that is.

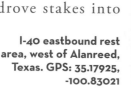 You'll notice, once you've left Alanreed heading west, that the Texas landscape begins to change as the lower plains of the eastern panhandle give way to the **Caprock**, an elevated plateau from which the rest of Texas slopes noticeably downward toward the southeast and the Gulf of Mexico. As you climb, the landscape seems to open up to ever more impressive views of the surrounding countryside.

Also in this vicinity, you might initially be confused by some signs along the road first announcing Donley County, then Gray County, and then Donley again. It's not that the shape of those counties is so irregular; rather, the highway wanders back and forth across a political boundary that was designed by a man with a ruler in his hand. The highway's path, on the other hand, makes some allowances for the lay of the land.

Once atop the Caprock, you are on the Llano Estacado, or **Staked Plain**. There are multiple theories about how the area got its name, but the one given the most credence comes from the days of Francisco Coronado. When Coronado's entourage began crossing the region, they drove stakes into

I-40 eastbound rest area, west of Alanreed, Texas. GPS: 35.17925, -100.83021

the ground as a substitute for natural features (trees, boulders), which in this area are rare-to-nonexistent. This was done to prevent them from needlessly retracing their steps. The Staked Plain begins roughly at the Caprock escarpment and continues to just east of the Pecos River Valley in New Mexico.

JERICHO

At Texas Highway 70 South, about the only remaining thing to be seen is a ruined **motel court** and a **cemetery** nearby. The cemetery has some unique features and is worth a look. The area around Jericho, however, earned an ugly reputation during the days of Route 66 travel as being something of a quagmire. There was an unpaved section, or gap in the pavement, that could be difficult to navigate under some conditions. Travelers were advised to take extra care in the vicinity of Jericho Gap, lest they become another ledger entry for the folks making a living towing stranded vehicles out of the mess.

Jericho, Texas. GPS: 35.16572,-100.92145

Long-disused tourist accommodations, Jericho, Texas.

BOYDSTON

Little is left of this community other than an interstate exit for Boydston Road. However, my 1957 road atlas portrays it as on par in size with other neighboring communities, such as Alanreed or Groom, and about two miles west of the Highway 70 North junction. There is still a tiny **cemetery** in this vicinity, about two miles south of I-40.

GROOM

Exit Interstate 40 at the first Groom exit—the one with the **leaning water tower**. I wish I had a nickel for every time I've heard someone describe this water tower as having "one leg shorter than the others." To the careful observer, this is pure hokum. Look carefully and you'll notice that the water tower has five appendages—four legs and one central water conduit. The end of that

Distinctive landmark on the edge of Groom, Texas.
GPS: 35.19778,-101.08238

water pipe was intend- ed to be beneath the surface of the ground, so it is in fact longer than the four true legs, which is why the tow- er sits at such an angle. The legs are actually all the same length, just as they should be. The owners of the Britten

Downtown Groom, Texas. GPS: 35.20045,-101.10674

Truck Stop that once operated here thought that the spectacle of the leaning tower made for a good gimmick; besides, it would've been un- necessarily expensive to install the thing properly.

Make a left turn under the interstate here to enter the town of Groom. The road will soon take you to the right, and you'll be surrounded by the spirit of old Route 66. Groom has that lonely and delicious air about it of a town that was robbed of its life by the bypassing of the old highway. The road is very wide through town and the traffic is very light, so take your time. There was a pair of more or less identical motels in town that were called **Golden Spread**, but their signs have long since been re- moved and the premises converted to other uses—one of them has been transformed into a mini-warehouse rental facility. "Golden Spread" is an old term referring to the relatively rich resources to be found here in the High Plains region of the country, including rich soil, mineral deposits, and plentiful subterranean water for irrigation.

My favorite Groom landmark—now demolished—was what remains of the **66 Courts**, just across the road from the grain elevators. It was at one time a combination motel court and Magnolia gasoline station. For years, there was an Edsel parked beneath the 66 Courts sign that made for a great photo opportunity, and there were several other retired road warriors scattered on the property. It was the 66 Courts that provided the inspiration for the vaguely Art Deco-flavored design of the eastbound I-40 rest area west of Alanreed.

GROOM ATTRACTIONS

A modern addition to the community of Groom is a **giant cross** (I-40) that can be seen from quite a distance. It's said to be the largest in the western hemisphere, reaching 190 feet tall. The complex surrounding the cross includes sculptures depicting the various Stations of the Cross. The whole thing is lit up at night.

CONWAY

If you're on I-40 as you approach Conway, make sure to exit at Highway 207. As you enter Conway, on your right you'll see some buildings surrounded by chain-link fencing. A little further on, you'll come to a crossroads with what was at one time a **mom-and-pop-style gas station** or convenience store. A right turn here quickly returns you to the interstate. Continue straight ahead (Highway 2161) so as not to join the mad rush any sooner than necessary.

Conway, Texas. GPS: 35.20760,-101.37827

Conway, Texas. GPS: 35.20763,-101.38259

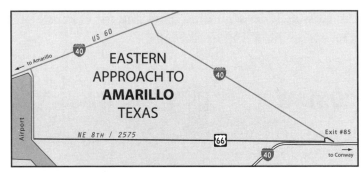 Highway 2161 will eventually veer north toward I-40, where you will have at least two route options to choose from (see the reference map). Both entail joining the interstate (at exit #89) and taking it as far as exit #85 (Business Loop 40/Route 66). One choice is to follow BL-40/66 north-west, where it joins up with U.S. 60 and then veers southwest into Amarillo. The second choice, from exit #85, is to look immediately for a left turn onto Highway 2575. This will take you on an earlier alignment that had to change when the airport here on the west side of town was conceived. You can take 2575/NE 8th Avenue all the way to the edge of the airport, turn north on B Avenue, and then be forced to join BL-40/U.S. 60 (see the main Amarillo reference map).

AMARILLO

As was the case with most cities of significant size, the path of Route 66 through Amarillo varied over the years. The easiest alignment to follow is one of the later incarnations, which more or less bypassed the core of the city via what is now Amarillo Boulevard. This version of the route takes a northerly detour around the city, and this alignment still retains plenty of evidence of its having been a major thoroughfare in the pre-interstate era. Most of this part of Amarillo has been neither maintained nor restored over the intervening years, and gives the traveler a genuine taste of the seedier side of the highway life-cycle. The majority of the motels that remain accommodate a longer-term clientele, and most of the other buildings have been recycled many times over and enlisted in lines of

Nice-looking graphics at the Silver Spur Motel, Amarillo, Texas. GPS: 35.22212,-101.78950

work that their original owners and designers neither envisioned nor intended.

An earlier alignment of the highway went directly through the heart of the city, during the years when that was common practice. A section of 6th Street, roughly between Georgia and Western Streets, has recently seen some revitalization work in order to make the most of its Mother Road heritage. This has resulted in some modest gentrification of the neighborhood, with a collection of antique shops, cafés, and boutiques now lining this stretch of the route. This neighborhood is sometimes referred to as "Old San Jacinto."

Amarillo was first settled as a buffalo-hide tent camp in the 1880s and named for the nearby Amarillo Creek, which was in turn named for the yellowish soil and wildflowers that were prevalent in the area. Curiously, Amarillo is closer to four other state capitals (Santa Fe, Denver, Topeka, and Oklahoma City) than it is to that of its own (Austin). This undoubtedly contributes to the region's independent-mindedness.

The city is considered the Helium Capital of the World, producing about ninety percent of the world's supply of the unique element. There

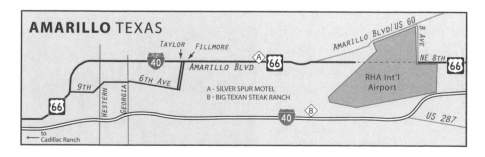

is a **six-story structure** (1200 Streit Dr.) that commemorates the centennial of the discovery of helium in the area. When it was first erected in 1968, articles were collected to create four time capsules, the last of which is not slated to be opened until the year 2968—nearly 1,000 years after its interment! Included in the capsule is a $10 passbook savings account at a local bank, which will then be worth at least $1 quadrillion, assuming the bank—and money, for that matter—still exists.

Amarillo is one of the quirkiest towns on Route 66, if not in the entire country. A disproportionate amount of that quirkiness seems to be attributable to one man, the late Stanley Marsh 3 (starting with that Arabic numeral in his name). He's the man behind something collectively referred to as the **Dynamite Museum**, a series of mock road signs scattered throughout the city and proclaiming odd bits of philosophy, poetry, or just plain nonsense. Conceived by Mr. Marsh and erected by his merry band of part-time college students aspiring to be artists, they appear in front of small businesses, in residential neighborhoods, and in places that might aptly be described as no place in particular. Stanley Marsh 3 is even better known for having commissioned *Cadillac Ranch* (see the Amarillo Attractions section below) and *Floating Mesa* (see the Further Afield section below), a sort of topographic illusion about eleven miles out of town.

AMARILLO ATTRACTIONS

In terms of its significance in Route 66 lore, the only thing in Amarillo that's in the same league with *Cadillac Ranch* would be the **Big Texan Steak Ranch** (7701 I-40 Access Rd.).

Amarillo, Texas.
GPS: 35.19305,-101.75430

After serving steaks to Mother Road travelers for many years, the Big Texan Steak Ranch responded to the shift in American travel habits by relocating to the shoulder of Interstate 40 in 1968. There, they continue their long-standing tradition of serving a seventy-two-ounce steak at no charge, provided the person ordering it can consume it (and all of its accoutrements) in less than an hour. There is a sort of Hall of Fame on the premises where you can read the names of those patrons who have been successful in meeting that challenge over the years. As the sign outside says, "The Public Is Invited Come One Come All."

Included in the Big Texan restaurant and motel complex is a gift shop which has a display case featuring live rattlesnakes, a latter-day nod to the reptile ranch traditions of the glory days of 66. And just to make sure you notice the place, there is usually an enormous model of a beef steer on a small trailer parked out front. The steer features a painted-on saddle blanket emblazoned with "Big Texan Steak Ranch Motel."

Created in 1974, **Cadillac Ranch** (I-40 Frontage Rd.) has become a sort of mecca for Route 66 pilgrims. Ironically, the construct, which was assembled by an art co-op calling themselves the Ant Farm, came

Big Texan Steak Ranch, Amarillo, Texas. GPS: 35.19305,-101.75430

along too late to be contemporary with Route 66 in the region. Instead, it was placed in a field beside I-40, the highway which had supplanted U.S. 66. That said, no trip through the Texas panhandle is complete without taking a walk out into that field

The world-famous *Cadillac Ranch* art installation, Amarillo, Texas. GPS: 35.18911,-101.98739

to absorb some of the energy contained in those upended Cadillacs, which are said to be positioned at the same angle as the sides of the Great Pyramids of Egypt. Encroaching suburbia led to the relocation of the ranch in 1997. It now sits in a field on the west side of town, between I-40 exits #60 and #62.

This 1970s-era postcard shows *Cadillac Ranch* in the early years of its existence.

For those of you who never visited it at its original location, it must seem improbable that such an installation would literally be picked up and moved after twenty-odd years, but that's exactly what happened.

The **American Quarter Horse Association Heritage Center and Museum** (2601 I-40 East) is a world-class facility dedicated to the history and continued appreciation of the American Quarter Horse. The AQHA is the world's largest horse breed registry, and has had its headquarters (right next door to the museum) in the panhandle town of Amarillo since the 1940s. There is even a research library and archive for the serious enthusiast.

Harrington House (1600 S. Polk St.) is a Neoclassical mansion built in 1914 that was later owned by one of Amarillo's most prominent and philanthropic families. The home contains the Harringtons' extensive collection of fine and decorative arts accumulated over decades of world travel. The house is in the midst of a two-block section of Polk Street featuring some of the city's most prestigious older homes—the Polk Street Historic District. Tours of the Harrington House are conducted Tuesdays and Thursdays by prior arrangement; call (806) 374-5490.

Former restaurant on Amarillo Blvd.
GPS: 35.22205,-101.80943

The **Carey-McDuff Gallery of Contemporary Art** (508 S. Bowie St.) displays the work of artist Lightnin' McDuff. He prefers to work with metal, and there is a veritable menagerie of creatures here made from scrap iron, old farm implements, and so forth. He is also the creator of what has been dubbed the *Ozymandias* sculpture outside of town (see the Further Afield section).

If you like buildings that don't really want to look like buildings, check out the **Beef Burger Barrel** (3102 Plains Blvd.). This barrel-shaped walk-up started life as an A&W Root Beer stand, and over the years has had several names, menus, owners, and even varied locations.

Railroad buffs might want to see the **Madame Queen** (S. Lincoln St. and SE 2nd Ave.), one of only five "Texas Type" Baldwin locomotives. This one is the original prototype of the 2-10-4 configuration dating from 1930. It moved to this location after spending more than forty years at its previous Santa Fe depot location. The name comes from a fictional character from the *Amos 'n' Andy* radio series.

FURTHER AFIELD

Northwest of town, about ten miles past Amarillo Boulevard, is **Floating Mesa** (Ranch Rd. 1061). It's an art installation that creates an illusion of a natural mesa that has been sliced horizontally, so that its top hovers above the base with no visible means of support. For the best effect, start looking for it around seven miles from the Amarillo Boulevard junction. As you get closer, you'll see it more clearly and the illusion will become less effective.

The Beef Burger Barrel, Amarillo, Texas. GPS: 35.20406,-101.87142

A Route 66-era relic on Amarillo Blvd. GPS: 35.22214,-101.77901

Just south of Amarillo, near the town of Canyon, is the **Palo Duro Canyon** (11450 State Hwy Park Rd. 5). The first time you lay eyes on it, you're guaranteed to be surprised and impressed. The bright red cliffs are stunning. Cut by the Prairie Dog Town Fork of the Red River, the Palo Duro Canyon runs for many miles and is hundreds of feet deep. The drive through it is around sixteen miles, but also available are horseback excursions, hiking trails of varying levels of strenuousness, and even a scenic railroad.

The city of Canyon is home to the **Panhandle-Plains Historical Museum** (2503 4th Ave.), the largest history museum in Texas. Housed in a WPA-era building, this museum is truly first-rate, with sections dedicated to art, Western heritage, petroleum, transportation, and paleontology. Included are several dinosaur fossils, a wood-bodied Model A Ford (serial no. 28), and a replica Pioneer Town.

Canyon was also once the stomping grounds of artist Georgia O'Keeffe, who taught art classes at the local college for a time.

On U.S. 60 on the outskirts of Canyon, Texas, is a giant cowboy statue at the site of the former Cowboy Café. **"Tex Randall"** (N. 3rd Ave. and N. 14th St.) was built in 1959 as a promotion for Wheeler's Western Store, which has long been closed. Tex is said to measure forty-seven feet in height and seven tons in weight. His future as a panhandle landmark is uncertain, so much so that the Society for Commercial Archeology included him in their "Falling By the Wayside List" in 2009.

Commissioned by Stanley Marsh 3 and inspired by the timeless Shelley poem is the ***Ozymandias* sculpture** (I-27 and Sundown Ln.), a piece by artist Lightnin' McDuff. True to its poetic inspiration, it's a pair of torso-less legs recalling the temporary nature of man's works. There's even a tongue-in-cheek (but very official-looking) historical marker at the site advising that this was the actual ruin which inspired Shelley's poem, and that the face of the statue had been removed and placed in the Amarillo Natural History Museum—which is, of course, nonexistent.

Northeast of Amarillo, near the shore of Lake Meredith, is the **Alibates Flint Quarries National Monument** (Canadian River Breaks). Here, thousands of years before the Egyptians constructed the Great Pyramids, ancient Americans were quarrying a distinctive type of flint from which they made tools and weapons, which they subsequently traded with their neighbors throughout much of North America. These quarries were used continuously from about 10,000 B.C. to A.D. 1800. Contained on the grounds are pueblo ruins and petroglyphs (rock art). Free guided walking tours (about 1.5 miles) are available.

When you're ready to leave Amarillo, use BL-40 on the north side of I-40. When it tries to put you on the interstate, drive straight ahead on Indian Hill Road. Take Indian Hill as far as you can, then turn left and quickly right onto the north service road. Continue all the way to Vega.

BUSHLAND-WILDORADO

There is little to note in the neighboring communities of Bushland and Wildorado. Bushland took its name from one W. H. Bush, who owned the land on which the town site was founded. Wildorado is marked by some cattle feed lots on the eastern approach to town.

VEGA

Opinions differ as to the midpoint of Route 66—for every person who claims it's in Vega, there's another who says it's actually in Adrian, a few miles farther west. What seems certain is that the halfway point of Route 66, as it wends its way from Lake Michigan to the Pacific Ocean, lies somewhere here in the Texas Panhandle.

Unraveling this disagreement is not as simple as it might appear on the surface. While you will see some rather exacting figures published for the total mile-

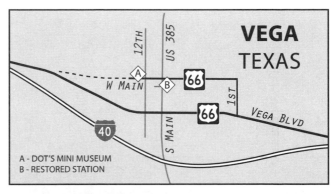

Old filling station, Vega, Texas. GPS: 35.24607,-102.42881

age of Route 66—2,448 being one of the most popular—that "precision" is more smoke than substance. The route itself, and the total mileage that comprised it, was always in a state of flux. While in one town the road might add some miles in order to bypass the downtown area, at the same time hundreds of miles away in another state, the highway department would be rounding off some corners, replacing them with curves, and thereby shortening the overall length. Such changes occurred again and again, all along the route, and continued over the course of decades. In fact, even though U.S. 66 officially no longer exists, the roadway you drive today continues to undergo some of those same processes in its

Small-town museum, Vega, Texas. GPS: 35.24589,-102.42834

current role as a collection of secondary roads.

The town of Vega was established in 1900 by the Chicago, Rock Island, and Gulf Railroad, and is the Oldham County seat, a post it took over from the nearby town of Tascosa in 1915. South of the courthouse is a 1920s-era **Magnolia gasoline station** (222 N. Main St.) that has been restored, partly through funding from the Route 66 Corridor Preservation Program.

Stretch your legs awhile in Vega by popping into **Dot's Mini Museum** (105 N. 12th St.). Dot amassed an extensive collection of artifacts over a lifetime on Route 66. Dot herself is now deceased, but her family has chosen to continue making the collection available to the public.

A newer addition to Vega is the **Milburn-Price Cultural Museum** (1005 Coke St.), run by Greg and Karen Cull.

FURTHER AFIELD

About forty miles north of Vega on U.S. 385 is **Old Tascosa**, a Western-

Vega, Texas. GPS: 35.24730,-102.43092

style ghost town. In the 1870s, Tascosa was a lively place, and functioned as a supply depot for some large area ranches, such as the XIT and the LIT. It was the seat of Oldham County, was heralded as the Cowboy Capital of the Plains, and boasted its own newspaper, the *Tascosa Pioneer*. Such famous characters as Kit Carson and Billy the Kid were known to walk its streets. Billy the Kid was eventually killed by Pat Garrett, the sometime-sheriff of Oldham County (you can visit Billy's grave later on, at Fort Sumner, New Mexico). Tascosa's decline came when it was bypassed by the railroad in 1887. The county seat was moved south to Vega in 1915; it's said that, at the time of the balloting, there were only fifteen residents of Tascosa left. The last of those residents, Mrs. Mickey McCormick and her dog, finally departed around 1940.

It was around this time that Cal Farley, champion wrestler and successful Amarillo businessman, entered the picture. In 1938, he founded his Boys Ranch; the old townsite is now on the ranch grounds. Its center was at the old Oldham County Courthouse, now the **Julian L. Bivins Museum** (U.S. 385). Mr. Bivins donated the first acreage around the old town, on which a home for wayward and homeless boys was built. The compound has since expanded to include over 10,000 acres and cares for about 300 to 400 boys and girls annually. Visitors to the ranch are welcome daily. In September, the youngsters (ranging from four to eighteen years of age) participate in an annual Labor Day rodeo.

Before leaving Tascosa/Boys Ranch, be sure to visit the classic Old West cemetery, aptly named **Boot Hill**, which is maintained by Boys Ranch residents.

Getting back on Route 66, stay on the I-40 north service road all the way to Adrian. In about seven miles, you'll come to the interchange for Landergin. It was never really a town, but rather a railroad siding, a location given a name by railroaders for their own convenience. Landergin was the site of the "Run to the Heartland" celebration in 1996, the first of many national Route 66 celebrations to come. With both Vega and Adrian laying claim to the Midpoint of the Route, Landergin made an ideal compromise, situated as it is between the two rivals for the title. That celebration was the scene of the first presentation of the John Steinbeck Award, with Michael Wallis being the first honoree. Not much has been happening at this place the last several years, however.

Adrian, Texas. GPS: 5.27089,-102.67285

ADRIAN

Here in Adrian, we are still at the midpoint of Route 66. Fittingly—and in a battle of one-upsmanship—the **Midpoint Café** (305 W. Rte. 66), formerly Zella's Café (circa 1928), has a slogan to match: "When You're Here, You're Halfway There." There is a small monument to that effect across the street from the café, and many travelers find it to be an irresistible photo

op. The city of Adri-
an has even painted
their water tower to
proclaim it the mid-
point of Route 66.

While in Adrian,
keep on the lookout
for the former **Bent
Door Café** (301 W.
Rte. 66). Years ago,
someone used parts
from an airport
control tower in the

**The former Bent Door Café, Adrian, Texas.
GPS: 35.27096,-102.66814**

construction of this roadside business. As in so many other cases, there
has been talk for some years of returning the place to its former glory. I
have seen a postcard of this place from the 1960s, at which time it was
operating as Tommy's Café, with a yellow-and-red sign similar to the one
in front of the Midpoint Café today.

In Adrian there has been an outbreak of the same fever so prevalent
in Amarillo—various installations of the **Dynamite Museum** (see page
288) now abound here. Among them is my personal favorite: "Art is
what you can get away with."

Adrian, Texas. GPS: 35.27096,-102.66814

Leaving Adrian, stay on the north service road again for a few miles, until you reach Highway 18 (at exit #18), where you'll need to enter I-40. Then exit at #0 for Glenrio.

GLENRIO

Glenrio can rightly be called a ghost town. Each time I have ventured here it has been deathly quiet, except for the barking of the junkyard dogs that commences a few moments after my arrival. Barking dogs, with no

In the border town of Glenrio, Texas.
GPS: 35.17917,-103.03942

human owners in evidence, do not make for pleasant exploring. Today, Glenrio consists of a few ruinous buildings of unknown identity, and the equally ruinous "Last Motel in Texas" whose sign is no longer legible from either direction. Back in the day, if you approached from the west, that side of the sign read "First Motel in Texas."

Route 66, Glenrio. GPS: 35.17939,-103.03669

Old motel near the Texas-New Mexico state line, Glenrio. GPS: 35.17886,-103.04194

Glenrio, Texas. GPS: 35.17867,-103.04352

All in all, Glenrio is a somewhat spooky locale, which makes it all the more startling to learn that in the 1940s this was a thriving, bustling place. A current resident of Fort Worth tells me that he worked for the Texas Highway Department in Glenrio at an official welcome station from 1941 to '42. He witnessed firsthand the so-called "Okies" traveling westward with all of their earthly possessions tied to the roofs of their automobiles. At that time, they were headed for work at the shipyards and defense plants of California.

Glenrio was founded in 1903, shortly after a railroad line was established in the vicinity. Many have observed that the name is formed from the English "glen" (for "valley") and the Spanish *rio* (for "river"), even though the actual town site is located neither in a valley nor along a river.

According to a former resident of Glenrio, a film crew spent about three weeks in the town filming portions of *The Grapes of Wrath* in 1938. At the time, full-time residents of the town numbered about thirty.

Somewhere in the middle of Glenrio is the New Mexico border, but the Llano Estacado continues as far as the eye can see, having no respect for political boundaries.

NEW MEXICO

New Mexico—Land of Enchantment. The name is fitting, in that the place, its people, and its traditions have a way of winning the hearts of all those who visit. Those of us fortunate enough

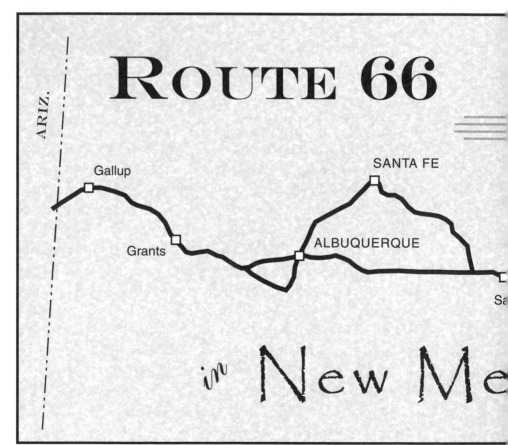

to spend time in New Mexico invariably speak again and again of our experiences here, and perhaps even talk of making it our permanent home.

The land itself is beautiful, with its spreading plains, purple mountains, and colorful, overarching, cloud-filled skies. These features in themselves are alluring, but beyond that there is the profound sense of respect one feels for the centuries of history and tradition that permeate the land. Perhaps nowhere is there a more successful commingling of disparate cultures to form a unique whole than there is here in New Mexico. Tread softly, for you are on hallowed ground.

The Llano Estacado continues to the Pecos River Valley. This land was formerly a part of Texas, the part that was ceded to appease jealous rivals who worried over the enormous influence a full-sized Texas might wield as a state.

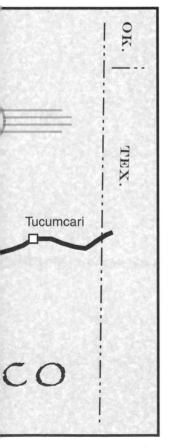

The land has seen and been inhabited by every walk of mankind: farmer, rancher, miner; American Indian, Spaniard, Anglo; the base, the virtuous, and the merely foolish. All have left their marks, and those marks are here for you to see.

Here in the West, scars on the earth are slow to heal. New Mexico is a treasure chest of archaeological discoveries, some uncovered long ago, others waiting to be revealed. Here in New Mexico are the stone ruins of centuries-old civilizations and the still-visible wagon ruts of trade routes rendered obsolete by the iron horse. Also to be seen are the scars left by abandoned stretches of Route 66.

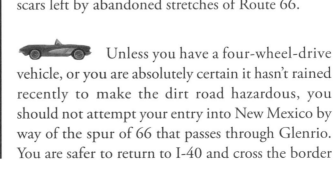 Unless you have a four-wheel-drive vehicle, or you are absolutely certain it hasn't rained recently to make the dirt road hazardous, you should not attempt your entry into New Mexico by way of the spur of 66 that passes through Glenrio. You are safer to return to I-40 and cross the border

that way. You'll see
a sign advising you
that you are entering
Mountain Time, a
very real-world indi-
cation that you are
now starting a new
chapter in your Route
66 adventure.

Part of that new
chapter involves cuisine. In this part of the country, virtually every restaurant has a "Mexican" or "New Mexican" section of the menu. This can
make for some strange bedfellows, such as the Chinese buffet that offers
tacos, or the sandwich shop that has refried beans as a side order. And
be prepared for the first time you are asked the Official State Question:
"Red or Green?" The choice of either red or green chili sauce with your
Southwestern meal is such a profound—and yet ordinary—question in
these parts that the state of New Mexico passed a bill in 1999 adding
the question to the list of other officially recognized items such as the
state flower, state bird, and so forth. (Incidentally, if you have difficulty
choosing, you may want to answer "Christmas," ensuring that you get
some of each.)

ENDEE

The name of this community
was most likely adopted from
the name of the **N D Ranch**,
which was established in the area
in the 1880s. If you took the
unpaved road out of Glenrio,
you'll come upon Endee about
five miles west. If you had to use

There aren't many motorists passing through Endee, New Mexico these days. GPS: 35.13835,-103.10677

the interstate, you can exit at NM 93 and turn south to visit Endee.

The old route from Endee to San Jon is also unpaved. Depending on conditions, you may need to go north and pick up I-40 for the ride into San Jon. If so, don't feel bad; my 1957 atlas shows Endee as having already been bypassed at that time in favor of a newer alignment to the north, where today's I-40 roadbed is.

BARD

Although Bard usually shows up on older (1930s–1940s) maps of the area, there is not much for today's traveler to see. I've been unable to find out much of anything about it in my own research. Try some exploring south of I-40 at exit #361, which is about four or five miles east of San Jon. Today, there are a few ruinous buildings on the north side of I-40, but of course our highway was to the south.

SAN JON

There are still several abandoned motels on the old route through town, among them the **Western**

San Jon, New Mexico.
GPS: 35.10614,-103.32738

San Jon, New Mexico. GPS: 35.10622,-103.33218

Motel. There has been an early '60s Plymouth sedan sitting in the parking lot of the Western for years now.

 You can avoid the interstate and take old 66 all the way into Tucumcari from San Jon (on the south frontage road).

TUCUMCARI

This is the town that changed my life by starting me on a quest to see all of Route 66—more on that in a moment.

Formerly called Six-Shooter Siding, there are at least two stories circulating as to how Tucumcari (pronounced "two-come-carry") got its

Route 66 east of Tucumcari, New Mexico. GPS: 35.16811,-103.67314

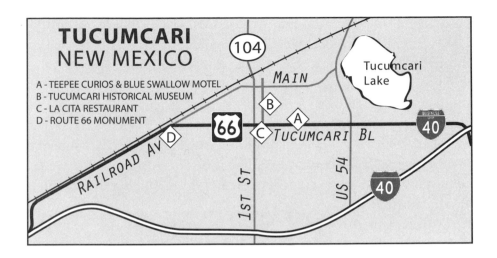

TUCUMCARI
NEW MEXICO

A - TEEPEE CURIOS & BLUE SWALLOW MOTEL
B - TUCUMCARI HISTORICAL MUSEUM
C - LA CITA RESTAURANT
D - ROUTE 66 MONUMENT

modern name—one romantic, and one less so. Legend states that an American Indian maiden named Kari was so devastated by the death of her lover, Tocom, that she took her own life. Her father, upon discovering the tragedy, exclaimed, "Tocom! Kari!" A wonderful fable, with shades of *Romeo and Juliet*, but sober heads inform us that the name actually comes from a Comanche word, *tukamukaru*, meaning to lie in wait, as in an ambush.

Near Tucumcari, New Mexico.
GPS: 35.15442,-103.46263

Near Tucumcari, New Mexico.
GPS: 35.16815,-103.48155

Speaking of sober heads, I lost mine permanently in 1992 on a trip through here on my way to Fort Worth, Texas, from Greeley, Colorado. My wife and I were on the stretch of I-40 west of Tucumcari, heading east, when we started seeing billboards shouting "TUCUMCARI TONITE!" and "ON HISTORIC ROUTE 66!" Since it was around nightfall, we decided on the spur of the moment to stay the night in Tucumcari, a long-standing tradition for Route 66-ers that we were unaware of at the time. Pulling off the interstate and prowling through Tucumcari absolutely floored me. We saw a souvenir stand in the shape of an American Indian teepee, and then we came across a restaurant shaped like a Mexican sombrero. I thought: "I can't believe there are still places like this! This is amazing!" I've been coming back to Route 66 year after year ever since. And it still amazes me.

Tucumcari has lots of Route 66 spots that folks around the globe recognize. There's **Teepee Curios** (924 Historic Rte. 66), of course, which in the 1940s was actually a gasoline station. The Mexican restaurant we ate at that night was **La Cita** (820 S. 1st St.), and it has since been painted to make it even more dazzling to the eye. The real cornerstone of Tucumcari highway businesses, though, has got to be the **Blue Swallow**

Tucumcari, New Mexico. GPS: 35.17167,-103.71490

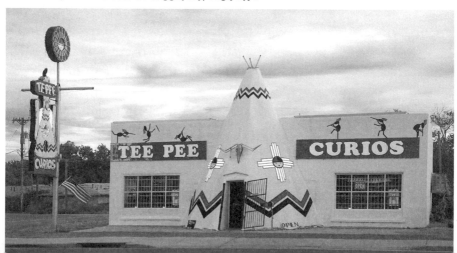

Motel (815 E. Rte. 66 Blvd.). Built in the 1940s from surplus WWII cabins, the motel was later presented as an engagement present to Lillian Redman, the proprietess for many years, by her husband-to-be, Floyd. That was in 1958. Lillian kept things going for many years and only recently (in Mother Road terms) has it fallen into other capable hands.

Tucumcari truly has a wealth of vintage roadside businesses, far beyond the short description in this book. You could spend hours just exploring, not only along the old route with its dozens of classic neon signs,

Longstanding roadside eatery in Tucumcari, New Mexico. GPS: 35.17144,-103.72473

but also downtown, where you'll find the still-running, Depression-era **Odeon Theatre** (123 S. 2nd St.) and a large, recently restored **railroad depot** (103 W. Railroad Ave.). As if Tucumcari didn't have enough going for it already, in recent years they've added several **murals** scattered throughout downtown, including a Mother Road-themed one on the side of Lowe's grocery.

South of town you'll see **Tucumcari Mountain**, tattooed with a big letter "T." The **Tucumcari Mountain Cheese Factory** (823 E. Main St.) is a few blocks north of

Blue Swallow Motel, Tucumcari.
GPS: 35.17197,-103.71660

66, housed in an old Coca-Cola Bottling Plant building that dates from 1951.

Also in town is the **Mesalands Dinosaur Museum and Natural Sciences Laboratory** (222 E. Laughlin Ave.), run by Mesa Technical College. Notable is the fact that the dinosaur models on display are cast in bronze (rather than the more fragile plaster or resin that is more common), and visitors are invited to touch. These bronze castings are made right here at the college by students and volunteers.

The **Tucumcari Historical Museum** (416 S. Adams St.), which of course includes an exhibit on Route 66 through the area, is housed in a 1903 schoolhouse.

Tucumcari, New Mexico. GPS: 35.17190,-103.72033

Mesalands Dinosaur Museum, Tucumcari.
GPS: 35.17360,-103.72394

Tucumcari, New Mexico.
GPS: 35.17189,-103.73774

As you're passing the convention center on the west end of town, pause to admire the **Route 66 monument** (1500 W. Rte. 66 Blvd.) by artist Thomas Coffin. The piece was installed in 1997, and incorporates a '50s-style automotive tail fin, a mock-adobe base, and, of course, the double sixes.

Tucumcari now has an official **Route 66 Museum** (15th Street). Look for it behind the convention center at the extreme western end of town.

You will have to enter I-40 for a while at the west end of Tucumcari, but be sure to leave it at exit #321 for the run into Montoya.

Western outskirts of Tucumcari, New Mexico. GPS: 35.16933,-103.74947

MONTOYA-NEWKIRK

Route 66 crosses a fair number of other routes of significance in its course. For example, we crossed the Chisholm Trail back in Oklahoma, which was used primarily for the transport of cattle. Another cattle trail is at hand now. The **Goodnight-Loving Trail** crosses our path somewhere between the communities of Montoya and Newkirk. One of the best maps I've seen places it very close to Newkirk, so Highway 129, which stretches northward out of Newkirk, must be the closest thing we have

West of Tucumcari. GPS: 35.16346,-103.76165

Montoya, New Mexico. GPS: 35.09709,-104.06100

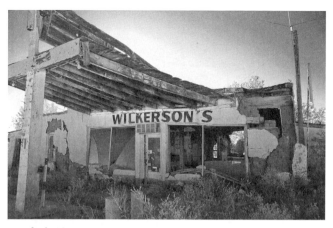

Newkirk, New Mexico. GPS: 35.06865,-104.264690

to an actual road that follows that course. The Goodnight-Loving Trail passes through Fort Sumner to the south of us before going on to the markets in Denver and Cheyenne to the north. Very little remains of Montoya, but Newkirk actually has a crumbling business district right beside the highway.

CUERVO

Cuervo has been what can only be called a ghost town for many years. Although there are still some inhabitants, large tracts of the town are now deserted, with broken windows and gaping doors.

The ghost town of Cuervo, New Mexico. GPS: 35.03070,-104.40900

 At Cuervo, you'll need to join I-40 to continue west. Leave I-40 at exit #277 for the town of Santa Rosa.

SANTA ROSA

In Santa Rosa, the I-40 Business Loop works fine, since it's very straightforward and will enable you to see just about everything you may have heard of in town. If you're feeling more adventurous, there is an older, non-continuous alignment that entered a little to the south along what is now Blue Hole Road and the nearby airport. However, keep in mind that much of it is inaccessible and/or privately owned.

While New Mexico is generally an arid place, Santa Rosa is the exception. Thanks to a collection of artesian springs in the area, it's a veritable garden spot, nicknamed the City of Natural Lakes. The most famous of the springs here is the **Blue Hole** (1085 Blue Hole Rd.), which attracts scuba divers from far and wide to ply their trade. The Blue Hole is more than eighty feet deep and sixty feet wide, with water temperatures hovering around

Near the Blue Hole, Santa Rosa, New Mexico. GPS: 34.94637,-104.65869

sixty-four degrees Fahrenheit. Another favorite with scuba divers is **Perch Lake** (585 Lake Dr.), which has a twin-engine plane submerged below for exploration.

The Blue Hole, U. S. Fish Hatchery, Santa Rosa, N. M.

Santa Rosa, New Mexico.

If you're into classic cars, check out the **Route 66 Auto Museum** (2866 Will Rogers Dr.). Look for the yellow car atop a pole outside the place.

Here at Santa Rosa, Route 66 crosses the Pecos, a river prominent in the lore of the American West. This is reportedly the place where Coronado made the crossing, too, in 1541. From the Pecos River crossing, the highway begins climbing toward the continental divide, more than 200 miles to the west. In the movie *The Grapes of Wrath*, there's a brief scene showing a steam-powered train crossing a long bridge over a river. That

Route 66 Auto Museum, Santa Rosa. GPS: 34.94662,-104.65446

scene was shot right here, where the railway crosses the Pecos River, a little to the north of the automobile bridge.

FURTHER AFIELD

About ten miles south of Santa Rosa via State Route 91 is **Puerto de Luna**, an abandoned Spanish settlement. Along the way, the road follows

Santa Rosa, New Mexico. GPS: 34.94635,-104.65891

the Pecos River Valley, and there is some very attractive canyon country here.

About forty-five miles southeast of Santa Rosa via U.S. 84 is **Fort Sumner** (Billy the Kid Dr. and Old Fort Park Rd.), both a military post and a town of the same name. It was here in 1881 that Billy the Kid was shot and killed by Pat Garrett. His gravesite is here at Fort Sumner—or at least we think it is (more on that in a moment). Billy the Kid (or William Bonney) was a hired gun in the range wars of Lincoln County, New Mexico, and in that capacity he killed a man for every year of his life "not counting Indians and Mexicans," by his own account.

Fort Sumner was constructed in 1862, and was a major stop on the Goodnight-Loving cattle trail, which ran from Texas to Wyoming. In 1869, the land the fort stood on was sold to Lucien B. Maxwell, who converted the officers' quarters to a private residence. This was where Billy was killed by Garrett years later. Judging from conditions in Fort Sumner today, if anyone could get their hands on Billy's corpse now, it would be torn into at least two pieces. An explanation is in order.

Billy the Kid Museum in the town of Fort Sumner, New Mexico. GPS: 34.46651, -104.22937

In downtown Fort Sumner is the **Billy the Kid Museum** (1435 E. Sumner Ave.). This museum originated in the 1950s, and it shows its age. There are disintegrating mannequins of Billy the Kid and Pat Garrett, a stuffed two-headed calf, old farm implements, and antique typewriters—the flotsam and jetsam that a down-to-earth museum curator accumulates over the decades. Outside is a graveyard with markers for Billy and two of his cohorts, surrounded by a chain link fence. Fastened to the fence, however, and located so that it appears in virtually every snapshot taken of the gravesite, is a small sign that states: "REPLICA." What gives? According to the lady at the museum, the replica had to be created because the real grave is in such a very poor state.

So where is the real grave? To get to it, drive about seven miles southeast of the town of Fort Sumner (U.S. 84 East to NM 212 South) to the **Old Fort Sumner Museum** (3501 Billy the Kid Rd.), established in 1932. This museum also has Billy the Kid artifacts, such as Billy's letters to the governor asking for amnesty. Outside is what is billed as "The Real Grave of Billy the Kid." This grave is completely covered with a metal cage to prevent vandalism. It seems that the original headstone was stolen in 1950 (remember the lady at the replica grave saying the real one was in bad shape?) and wasn't recovered until twenty-six years later. Then it was stolen again in 1981, and recovered once again. Now they take no chances. The ground over the grave has even been encased in concrete, just to make sure there won't be any more funny business.

Adjacent to the Real Billy the Kid Grave and the Old Fort Sumner Museum is the **Fort Sumner**

Billy the Kid's gravesite at the Old Fort Sumner Museum. GPS: 34.40379, -104.19344

State Monument. This is the site of Navajo and Apache confinement at the hands of the U.S. military in the 1860s.

 Back on the road: Leaving Santa Rosa, the old highway we love so much has pretty much been buried by the interstate, so join I-40 on the west side of town. How long you stay on the interstate will depend on which of two versions of Route 66 you decide to take.

Several miles west of Santa Rosa, you'll come to a crossroads. Not so much in the physical sense, as in the spiritual sense. What you do encounter physically is the junction where U.S. 84 splits off and heads north. That northerly route more or less follows the older Route 66 alignment, which for several years wandered up through Santa Fe. Straight ahead is the alignment born in the 1930s, when a straighter course was carved through the countryside, shaving significant miles and time from the passage through New Mexico. The two alternate paths will meet again in Albuquerque.

The narrative immediately following takes you along the older route through Santa Fe. If you choose to take the later route straight to Albuquerque, you can pick up the account for that segment below, at the Flying C Ranch.

ROMEROVILLE

In order to take the older alignment—the Santa Fe Loop—leave I-40 at exit #256 (U.S. 84 North).

The town of Romeroville was named for Don Trinidad Romero, who entertained President Rutherford B. Hayes at his home, and whose father founded the Romero Mercantile Company, a firm which became one of the leading wholesalers of the region.

From Romeroville onward, Route 66 closely approximates the track of the **Santa Fe Trail**. The trail originated in central Missouri (at Old Franklin) and took a northerly tack through Kansas and Colorado. It was a very significant trade route for several decades of the nineteenth century, connecting the ancient city in newly independent Mexico with the western United States.

FURTHER AFIELD

Founded in 1835, Las Vegas, New Mexico, is a very special place indeed. Over the past four centuries, the area has been inhabited by American Indians, Spanish conquerors, Anglo settlers, desperadoes, robber barons, and dance-hall girls, all of whom have wielded their respective influences. Doc Holliday and his girlfriend, Kate Elder, moved here in 1879 and opened a saloon; they were followed a few months later by their friend, Wyatt Earp. Butch Cassidy once worked in town as a bartender. Bob Ford, a Las Vegas saloon keeper, was the man who later became known for killing Jesse James. In 1915, Tom Mix made several of his Westerns here. And filmmaking in the town didn't stop there. The town fire station appears in a scene from *Easy Rider*, where Jack Nicholson's character makes the decision to hit the road with Peter Fonda and Dennis Hopper. Scenes from *Charlie Siringo* and *Red Dawn* were also made here.

Las Vegas boasts more than 900 buildings (that's right, 900!) on the National Register of Historic Places. Two of the most notable are the **La Castaneda Hotel** (524 Railroad Ave.), an example of the Harvey House collection of fine railroad-era hotels, and **El Fidel Hotel** (500 Douglas Ave.). Walking tour information is available at the local chamber of

La Castaneda is the former Harvey House in Las Vegas, New Mexico.
GPS: 35.59414,-105.21152

commerce office (727 Grand Ave.).

Sharing the same address with the chamber of commerce is the **City of Las Vegas Museum and Rough Rider Memorial Collection** (727 Grand Ave.). The collection commemorates Teddy Roosevelt's famous Rough Riders, who distinguished themselves in the Spanish-American War in Cuba, and also exhibits American Indian artifacts and items pertaining to the local history of Las Vegas. The museum is housed in a WPA-era structure that was originally built as the city hall. When the Rough Riders were originally formed, the largest contingent from any one state or territory came from New Mexico; later, in 1899, Las Vegas hosted the group's first reunion. Over the years, many attendees of those reunions donated various mementos of the campaign, and so established the collection now held here at the museum.

The **Bridge Street Historic District** offers an impressive array of architectural styles, including Victorian, Italianate, and nineteenth-century commercial structures.

A series of several **acequías**, or early irrigation channels, are preserved here in Las Vegas. There is also an operating **drive-in theater** (Hwy 518) north of town.

Five miles northwest of Las Vegas stands **Montezuma Castle** (Hwy 65), an opulent resort hotel from the 1880s on the grounds of the Armand Hammer United World College of the American West.

About twenty-eight miles or so to the northeast of Las Vegas is **Fort Union National Monument** (NM 161), a significant stop on the old Santa Fe Trail. Fort Union was the chief quartermaster depot for nearly fifty other western forts during the late 1800s, and its troops stood guard here to protect the settlers in the region and the travelers on the Santa Fe Trail, the two major branches of which—the Mountain Branch and the Cimarron Cutoff—converged in this vicinity. Just outside the fort is the largest network of visible **Santa Fe Trail wagon ruts** still remaining. Fort Union was also the intended objective of Confederate forces in the Battle of Glorieta Pass, which occurred west of here and is sometimes called the "Gettysburg of the West." There is a 1.25-mile tour trail that

Some of the many ruins at Fort Union, northeast of Las Vegas, New Mexico. GPS: 35.90484,-105.01131

explores not only ruins of the fort, but also adobe villages nearby. You will also find a visitor center there, along with a museum.

Back on Route 66, go southwest out of Romeroville. The modern highway (I-25/U.S. 84) closely adheres to the path of the old Santa Fe Trail. Cross to the opposite side of the interstate, turn left, and use the frontage road for several miles (marked Frontage Road 2116).

TECOLOTE-BERNAL-SAN JOSE-SERAFINA-SANDS

This is a string of very small rural villages. At Sands (exit #319), cross to the south side of the interstate and continue on Frontage Road 2116.

ROWE

At the village of Rowe (exit #307), cross the interstate again and join NM 63 heading north.

Colonial-era mission at Pecos, New Mexico. GPS: 35.55015,-105.68618

PECOS

Here you'll find the very old **Pecos Pueblo**, which once held over 2,000 residents. It was abandoned circa 1838, at which time its remaining inhabitants reportedly headed to Jemez. There is also a **Benedictine Monastery** located on the northern edge of the pueblo.

Prior to reaching the Pecos Pueblo, you'll pass the entrance to **Pecos National Historical Park**, which includes the ruins of two Spanish colonial missions, as well as ancient pueblo features. Unlike most pueblo ruins, the kivas here are accessible to the public. The ruins are very scenic, and there is an easy self-guided trail sprinkled with interpretive plaques to explain all of the features. The park also now includes the Glorieta Battlefield a few miles to the north.

 Leave Pecos heading westward on NM 50 toward Glorieta.

GLORIETA

Just prior to reaching the village of Glorieta, you'll find a historical marker by the side of the highway. It was here, at a Santa Fe Trail stopover called **Pigeon's Ranch**, that the Battle of Glorieta Pass occurred in March of 1862, during the American Civil War. There is still one adobe structure remaining from the eighteen-room stage station complex, hard up against the roadside. The battlefield is a National Historic Landmark.

In Glorieta, join I-40 (exit #299) in order to get through Glorieta Pass, the passage through the mountains that made this circuitous route to Santa Fe a necessity in the days of the old trail.

 Leave I-40 at exit #294, stay on the north side of the freeway, and follow Old Las Vegas Highway for several miles. Leave Old Las Vegas Highway near exit #284 and begin following NM 466/Old Pecos Trail.

SANTA FE

Route 66 through Santa Fe was short-lived, so there aren't many routes to choose from, as you'll find with many of the larger cities. What makes Santa Fe difficult is that many of the downtown streets have been converted to one-way, so you can't drive the city the way you'd like—the way motorists traveled it in the highway's early days. The current traffic patterns are more conducive to eastbound travel. The gist of it is this: Route 66 entered from the southeast along Old Pecos Trail, which then merges with Old Santa Fe Trail, which comes to an end at the central plaza. Route 66 then left town for Albuquerque, heading southwest along Cerrillos Road. Take your time and explore Santa Fe, but make sure you heed the one-way signs.

Santa Fe is the oldest capital city in the U.S., having been designated as such in 1610, when the plaza was laid out and the Palace of the Governors was established. It is also the focal point of the

famous Santa Fe Trail, a primarily trade-oriented route that was at its most important from about 1821 until 1880, when railroad transport effectively supplanted it.

Your entry into town is along the same path as the old trail, and the modern-day street is so named: **Old Santa Fe Trail**. A monument to mark the end of that trail was placed at the southeastern corner of the central plaza by the Daughters of the American Revolution in 1911. It was

not until a year later, in 1912, that New Mexico attained statehood. Today, the **La Fonda Hotel** (100 E. San Francisco St.) occupies the site of the old 1920 inn that marked the end of the trail and served as a mass meeting place for those who had made the arduous journey. It is said that Billy the Kid washed dishes at the inn for a time.

Oddly, the Sangre de Christo Mountains near Santa Fe were the set for the filming of the "Oh, What a Beautiful Morning" scene from the movie *Oklahoma!*

SANTA FE ATTRACTIONS

Santa Fe's Museum Hill is a collection of museums: the **Museum of Spanish Colonial Art** (750 Camino Lejo), the **Museum of International Folk Art** (706 Camino Lejo), the **Museum of Indian Arts and Culture** (710 Camino Lejo), and the **Wheelwright Museum of the American Indian** (704 Camino Lejo). Also part of the Museum Hill family are **five historical monuments** that are located across the state.

The **Georgia O'Keeffe Museum** (217 Johnson St.) is housed in a renovated adobe mission church. O'Keeffe is one of only a very few widely disparate American artists with memorial museums: Norman Rockwell, Frederic Remington, and Andy Warhol are among them.

Canyon Road, said to have originated as an American Indian foot trail, is Santa Fe's gallery district, lined on both sides with upper-echelon art galleries, coffee houses, and so forth.

An interesting tale awaits you at the **Santa Fe National Cemetery** (501 N. Guadalupe St.). Among the thousands of simple, identical headstones in these hallowed grounds stands a lifelike statue of Private Dennis O'Leary. The statue depicts the young O'Leary in his army uniform, leaning against a tree. Legend states that he was a lonely and unhappy soldier stationed at Fort Wingate, and that he carved the likeness himself in his free time. According to the story, he wrote a suicide note describing the location of the statue and asking that it be placed over his grave. He then shot himself with his own pistol. Army records, however, list his death as having been a result of tuberculosis. When Fort Wingate was decommissioned in 1911, Private O'Leary and several others were re-interred here.

While you're here, take the **Santa Fe Southern Railway** on a day trip. The thirty-six-mile, four-hour round trip runs from the historic depot (410 S. Guadalupe St.) to the nearby town of Lamy. The old Santa Fe depot, established in 1880, has been an inspiration to artists and photographers for generations.

The **Miraculous Staircase** is located in the Loretto Chapel (207 Old Santa Fe Trail). There is a very interesting story involving a "mysterious carpenter" who constructed the unusual staircase in the latter part of the 1870s. He appeared with a donkey and a toolbox, constructed the staircase over the course of several months, and then abruptly vanished without pay or thanks. The staircase was innovative for its time, incorporating two full turns (720 degrees) and showing no obvious means of support. The Miraculous Staircase has been the subject of an episode of *Unsolved Mysteries* as well as numerous articles over the years.

The **Chapel of San Miguel por Barrio de Analco** (401 Old Santa Fe Trail), constructed from 1626 to 1628, is referred to as the oldest continuously occupied church. At the same site is the **Mission of San Miguel**

Ambiance at the El Rey Inn, Santa Fe, New Mexico. GPS: 35.66445,-105.97371

of Santa Fe, which was constructed in 1610. The mission displays a bell that was cast in Spain in 1356 and then brought here by oxcart in the early 1800s.

Nearby is the **Oldest House** (215 E. De Vargas St.), which dates from approximately A.D. 1200.

Established in the 1930s, the **El Rey Inn** (1862 Cerrillos Rd.) is a terrific place to stay the night in Santa Fe. It's utterly unique, and it's right on old 66.

FURTHER AFIELD

Fans of Georgia O'Keeffe may want to know that about forty-five miles or so north of Santa Fe is the **Georgia O'Keeffe National Historic Site**, at Abiquiu. The 5,000-square-foot adobe structure here at Ghost Ranch was the artist's home and studio for more than forty years.

Further north from Santa Fe, and certainly more than just a side trip, is the very historic and distinctly artsy Taos County, which includes the **Taos Pueblo** and **Ranchos de Taos**. The **San Francisco de Asis Mission Church** (60 St. Francis Plaza) is one of the most painted and photographed buildings in the United States. Note that the Taos Pueblo charges a fee for admission, parking, and photography, and that the pueblo has no modern conveniences such as electricity and plumbing.

LA BAJADA HILL, BETWEEN SANTA FE AND ALBUQUERQUE, NEW MEXICO

Nearby is the **Kit Carson Home & Historical Museum** (113 Kit Carson Rd.), where the famous frontiersman kept his residence from 1843 to 1868. Carson and his wife are both buried nearby. Also visit the **Ernest L. Blumenschein House** (222 Ledoux St.), home to the artist and co-founder of the original Taos Society of Artists.

Narrated trolley tours of Taos are available, as are walking tours of Taos Pueblo. The Taos area is also a hub for skiing in winter and river rafting in summer.

To the north of Taos, at Arroyo Hondo, is the **D. H. Lawrence Ranch & Memorial** (506 D. H. Lawrence Ranch Rd.). The Lawrences spent about two years here in the 1920s, and the surroundings are said to have been significant influences on a number of his books. When Lawrence died in 1930, his wife scattered his ashes here at the ranch. The ranch is a sprawling 160 acres nestled in the Sangre de Christo Mountains.

Leave Santa Fe via Cerrillos Road/NM 14. Join I-25 at the interchange at exit #278, then leave the interstate at exit #248. Turn south on NM 313.

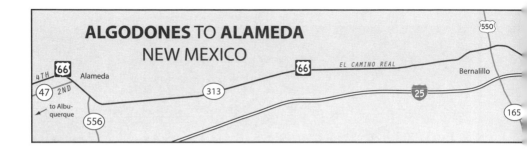

ALGODONES

You will pass through the communities of Algodones, the **Pueblo de Santa Ana**, and El Llanito. Road signs designate this stretch as both El Camino Real and Pan American Central Highway. Just south of El Llanito is the town of Bernalillo.

BERNALILLO

Behind the Sandoval County Courthouse sits a **nineteenth-century stone jail** (1500 Idalia Rd. NE) that once served the area. Also in town is **Silva's Saloon** (955 S. Camino Del Pueblo), which opened the day after Prohibition ended in 1933 and has been run by the same family ever since. There is plenty of memorabilia displayed on the walls—over seventy years' worth—including a hat collection.

Just a mile or so northwest of Bernalillo by way of NM 44 (co-numbered U.S. 550) is the **Coronado**

Bernalillo, New Mexico.
GPS: 35.30226,-106.55020

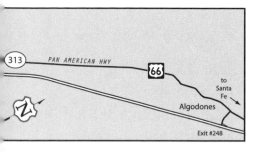

State Monument (485 Kuaua Rd.). The famous Spanish explorer is said to have stayed here during his 1541–1542 expedition. Today, there is a park overlooking the Rio Grande here, as well as a river walk and museum gallery. Parts of the village of Kuaua were excavated here as part of a WPA project in 1936, and there is a self-guided trail taking you through the ruins, which include a kiva and a pre-Columbian mural.

FURTHER AFIELD

Bernalillo is also your launch pad for a terrific detour: the **Jemez Mountain Trail National Historic & Scenic Byway**. Take NM 44 northwest from Bernalillo to San Ysidro. From here, NM 4 is the Jemez Mountain Trail. The "Scenic Byway" designation means that the trail has scenic, historical, and cultural importance, and is one of only a handful in the state. It winds through 5,000 years of human history, millions of years of geologic time, and four climatic zones. The trail takes you to Jemez Pueblo, Jemez Springs, Jemez State Monument, Soda Dam, Battleship Rock, and Bandelier National Monument. Jemez Pueblo features a visitor's center that is a destination in itself. Jemez Springs is known for its mineral waters and bath houses (some of which are clothing-optional), and features a number of galleries for you to stop into and enjoy. Jemez State Monument is the prehistoric site of the Pueblo of Giusewa ("boiling waters"), which includes the ruins of the seventeenth-century Church of San Jose de los Jemez. Marvel at the walls of these ruins, some of which are eight feet thick. Soda Dam is a natural dam formed on the Jemez River from mineral deposits built up over thousands of years. The river emerges through a hole in the dam, forming a waterfall. Further north is Battleship Rock, which towers over you as you wend your way through rugged terrain formed by volcanic activity ages ago. Bandelier

National Monument is one of the most-visited collections of American Indian ruins in the nation. Miles of trails leave the visitor center and radiate outward to dozens of cliff dwellings.

Nearby is Los Alamos, America's "Secret City" and birthplace of the nuclear age. It was here that the Manhattan Project was undertaken during World War II in order to develop the atomic bomb. You can learn more about it at the **Bradbury Science Museum** (1350 Central Ave.).

About halfway between Bernalillo and Alameda, but on the opposite side of the Rio Grande from you, is the community of Corrales. This community was named Sandoval (the same name as the county you are now in) at the time my 1957 atlas was printed. There is an old church there, the **Old San Ysidro Church** (966 Old Church Rd.), that is a favorite subject for painters and photographers. Built in 1868, it now serves as a community center. Nearby is **Casa San Ysidro** (973 Old Church Rd.)—also known as the Gutiérrez-Minge House—which is a restored Spanish-Colonial ranch house now operated by the Albuquerque Museum.

Corrales, New Mexico. GPS: 35.23213,-106.61173

South of Bernalillo, and just east of the old highway, is the Sandia Pueblo.

ALAMEDA

As you approach the northern outskirts of Albuquerque, you will pass through a community called Alameda. The highway will split here; take the 4th Street branch, which is old 66, into Albuquerque. On the way, you'll encounter the city's **Madonna of the Trail monument** (Marble Ave. and 4th St.).

See the description for Albuquerque below, following the Flying C-to-Tijeras narrative.

 The loop of old Route 66 that passes through Santa Fe is a rather circuitous route necessitated by the challenging terrain and limited road-building budgets and equipment of the time. However, it was recognized very early on that a more direct route to Albuquerque from Santa Rosa should someday be achieved. In 1934, Clyde Tingley, the governor of New Mexico at the time and a personal friend of President Roosevelt's, secured a number of New Deal projects for the state. Among those projects was the straightening of Route 66. That new alignment opened in 1937, running into Albuquerque along Central Avenue, and leaving the state capital high and dry.

Taking the newer alignment, you'll proceed due west out of Santa Rosa and continue straight ahead (on I-40) past the U.S. 84 junction.

If you took the newer alignment by passing up exit #256/U.S. 84, then you need to use exit #234, the location of the Flying C.

BOWLIN'S FLYING C RANCH

Bowlin's Flying C Ranch (7164 U.S. 70 N) is of course not a town in the traditional sense, but it is certainly pure Route 66. At exit #234 you'll find

Iconic sign at the Flying C Ranch.
GPS: 34.99590,-105.37761

At the crossroads that is called Clines Corners,
New Mexico. GPS: 35.00947,-105.66752

a distinctive sign and what's left of a once-proud roadside complex that offered cross-country motorists food, fuel, lodging, and entertainment.

CLINES CORNERS

Clines Corners is just that—an intersection. Today, there is an enormous gift shop here that purveys such classics as rubber tomahawks, beaded belts, and cedar gewgaws of every description.

Further west, I-40's exit #203 is the **Longhorn Ranch** interchange. The Longhorn Ranch has been characterized as the ritziest, glitziest former tourist trap on the route. It was once a full-blown compound including a motel, gas station, museum, curio shop, restaurant, and bar. The whole operation was packaged in the guise of a Wild West movie set. Most of the structures are gone now, and some of what remains is fenced off.

There's just a short fragment of Route 66 here, so you'll need to rejoin the interstate.

 Leave I-40 at exit #197 and follow NM 333.

Part of what remains of the Longhorn Ranch tourist complex west of Clines Corners. GPS: 35.00509,-105.91599

MORIARTY

The town of Buford shows up on some early maps of the area, but today it has been taken over or absorbed by the modern-day Moriarty.

The sign at **El Comedor de Anayas** (1009 Hwy M) in Moriarty was fortunate to be the target of neon restoration work several years ago. Described as a rotosphere, the sign consists of two halves of a ball rotating in different directions, with numerous Sputnik-style spikes protruding all around.

MORIARTY ATTRACTIONS

The Moriarty Airport is home base for the Albuquerque Soaring Club. The group chose this area for its unbeatable thermal conditions that result in many flights in excess of 250 miles each year. The airport is also home to the **U.S. Southwest Soaring Museum** (918 Historic Rte. 66). At this point, you're within the "Albuquerque Box," a favorable wind

Moriarty, New Mexico.
GPS: 35.00640,-106.05521

This building originally housed Moriarty's first fire station.
GPS: 35.00514,-106.05278

pattern that has also made this area home to one of the largest ballooning communities in the world.

Moriarty calls itself the Pinto Bean Capital—there's a **pinto bean festival** held here in the fall. In November, the town plays host to an annual meeting of the Sherlock Holmes Society. This, in spite of the fact that there is no known connection between the town's name and that of Holmes's notorious rival.

The **Moriarty Historical Society Museum** (202 S. Broadway) is located in the town's civic center/library complex. The museum used to be housed in the town's first fire station; there is still a **Route 66-themed mural** (777 Historic Rte. 66 SW) on the building.

 Stay on NM 333 as you leave Moriarty and head toward Edgewood.

EDGEWOOD

At Edgewood is the **Wild West Nature Park** (87 N. Frontage Rd.), a

122-acre facility harboring non-releasable wildlife, including deer, coyotes, and mountain lions. The park is a project of the New Mexico Wildlife Association, and most of the structures were built by members and volunteers of the state's Youth Conservation Corps.

TIJERAS

Somewhere in the Tijeras Canyon area was **Balanced Rock**, a distinctive rock formation destroyed by the highway department in 1951. The reasoning was that the vibrations brought about by passing traffic posed the danger of toppling the formation; however, it's been widely reported that the job took considerably more explosives than anyone predicted, and so it may have endured for quite some time, had it been left alone. At one time there was a painted sign on the rock directing the passing motorist to **Queens Rest Camp** (6200 Central Ave.), six miles ahead in Albuquerque.

FURTHER AFIELD

A great side trip from Tijeras is the **Turquoise Trail** (NM 14), a beautiful scenic byway that runs northward towards Santa Fe and takes the traveler through turquoise mining country, complete with three revived ghost towns: Golden, Madrid, and Cerrillos. Madrid, established in 1914, was a ghost town for many years until, in the 1970s, it was re-settled by artists. A few miles farther north is Cerillos, which fits the bill as the stereotypical Old West town—it had over twenty saloons at one time. That Western atmosphere has been exploited by the film industry, with *Shoot Out* (1972) and *Outrageous Fortune* (1987) being filmed in the area. Cerrillos is also home to the **Casa Grande Trading Post** (17 Waldo St.), which also houses a Turquoise Mining Museum and a petting zoo.

Just off the Turquoise Trail via NM 536 is **Sandia Crest**, with an elevation of over 10,000 feet. The view is spectacular, and you can hike the

Tinkertown is an old-fashioned family-run attraction. Sandia Park, New Mexico. GPS: 35.16954,-106.36739

numerous trails in the Sandia Mountain Wilderness, which treat you to one gorgeous view after another. You can either drive to the top of Sandia Peak or take the thirty-minute chair lift from the Sandia Peak ski area. The adventurous may also bring (or rent) mountain bikes and ride down from the observation area on a fifteen-mile trail. Alternatively, there is a popular tram ride that departs from Albuquerque, the longest of its kind at 2.7 miles, with spectacular views of the Land of Enchantment.

From NM 536 in the Sandia Crest area, you can follow Highway 165 north toward Placitas. About halfway to Placitas is the site of an archaeological dig where evidence of very early man has been discovered. This **Sandia Man Cave** is the earliest known archaeological site in the southwest (20,000 B.C.).

Also on NM 536 is the town of Sandia Park. This is the home of **Tinkertown** (121 Sandia Crest Rd.), the creation of a man named Ross Ward. Tinkertown consists of twenty-plus rooms depicting the world in miniature, including an animated miniature Western town, a tiny three-ring circus, and other dioramas, all surrounded by a collection of over 50,000 glass bottles. The slogan at Tinkertown: "We did all this while you were watching TV."

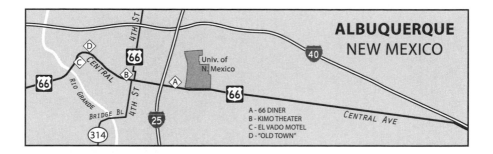

ALBUQUERQUE
NEW MEXICO

A - 66 DINER
B - KIMO THEATER
C - EL VADO MOTEL
D - "OLD TOWN"

ALBUQUERQUE

As explained elsewhere, there are essentially two Route 66 alignments in Duke City: east-west Central Avenue, and north-south 4th Street. The latter only lasted until the mid-1930s, when Santa Fe was cut off from the route.

Albuquerque's **Central Avenue** is the nation's longest main street, at eighteen miles from east to west. Decades ago, the city must have appeared almost oasis-like to the traveler who had just come the 100-plus miles from Santa Rosa, the last stopover of any size. There is a huge array of vintage motels on Central Avenue along the eastern approach to the city, though more and more of them are being demolished every year. Keep your eyes peeled for **Kelly's Brew Pub** (3222 Central Ave. SE), which is housed in a restored Streamline Moderne-style auto dealership dating from 1939.

Albuquerque is the hometown of the fictional Ethel Mertz (in fact, Vivian Vance actually lived here for a time herself). It is also home to the New Mexico Route 66 Association, which is headquartered at the **66 Diner** (1405 Central Ave.

Albuquerque, New Mexico.
GPS: 35.08184,-106.63100

Downtown Albuquerque. GPS: 35.08472,-106.65261

NE), a 1940s-era Streamline-style structure. The 66 Diner burned down in 1995, but fortunately for all of us, it has been lovingly restored to its full glory.

Architecturally, the city is marked by fine examples of Pueblo Revival architecture, including several examples at the **University of New Mexico** (even the UNM campus is on Central). The city also boasts the **KiMo Theatre** (423 Central Ave. NW), which was built circa 1927 and designed by Carl and Robert Boller, the same team of architects that conceived the one-of-a-kind Coleman Theatre in Miami, Oklahoma (see page 193). Its design, sometimes referred to as Pueblo Deco, is intended to reflect the three major cultural influences in the area: American Indian, Hispanic, and Anglo. Details include painted murals and terra-cotta buffalo skull wall sconces. Some say that the KiMo is haunted by the ghost of a small boy who died there in 1951, when a hot water heater exploded.

If you want to take a self-guided walking tour of Pueblo Deco architecture, I suggest beginning at the KiMo Theater (see above) and also taking in **Maisel's Indian Trading Post** (510 Central Ave. SW), **Wright's Indian Art** (2677 Louisiana Blvd. NE), the **J. A. Skinner Building** (722 Central Ave. SW), and several others.

The old **Monte Vista Fire Station** (3201 Central Ave. NE), built circa 1936, has been converted to a restaurant. The **Hotel Andaluz** (125 2nd St. NW) was formerly a Hilton and one of Albuquerque's most prestigious hostelries. It was here that Conrad Hilton married Zsa Zsa Gabor on April 10, 1942. The hotel also includes a 1930s-era coffee shop.

Be sure to check out Albuquerque's Old Town, where the city was first settled around 1706. The area is actually believed to have been inhabited prehistorically. The 300-year-old **San Felipe de Neri Church** (2005 N. Plaza St. NW) stands at the corner of the plaza. Nearby is the 1912 **Bottger Mansion** (110 San Felipe St. NW), which once played host to Machine Gun Kelly and his gang. It's now a bed and breakfast. Free maps are available in Old Town for self-guided walking tours. There is also a tour company offering seventy-six-minute motor tours of the city in an open-air trolley.

If you enter Albuquerque on the pre-1937 alignment from Santa Fe, watch out for one of the **Madonna of the Trail monuments** (4th St. and Marble Ave. NW).

ALBUQUERQUE ATTRACTIONS

Petroglyph National Monument (6510 Western Trail NW), with thousands of ancient examples of rock art on thousands of acres, is near the western edge of town, north of I-40. Visitors can hike several trails of varying difficulty to view the rock art, which is strung out along some seventeen miles of volcanic escarpment.

The **National Museum of Nuclear Science & History** (601 Eubank

Albuquerque, New Mexico.
GPS: 35.09531,-106.67426

MADONNA OF THE TRAIL

In the 1920s, the National Society of the Daughters of the American Revolution (DAR) commissioned the design, casting, and placement of twelve monuments commemorating the spirit of the pioneer woman. All twelve monuments were placed alongside the National Old Trails highway between Washington, DC, and Los Angeles, California. Originally, the ambitious plan called for more than 3,000 individual mile markers approximating the route of the National Road, the Santa Fe Trail, the National Old Trail, and others. Working with the National Old Trails Road Association, which at the time was headed by Judge Harry S. Truman of

Madonna of the Trail monument, 4th Street, Albuquerque, New Mexico. GPS: 35.09293,-106.64999

Independence, Missouri, the groups finally settled on the idea of one marker being placed in each of the twelve states through which the route passed.

The monuments were dedicated at: (from east to west) Bethesda, Maryland; Beallsville, Pennsylvania; Wheeling, West Virginia; Springfield, Ohio; Richmond, Indiana; Vandalia, Illinois; Lexington, Missouri; Council Grove, Kansas; Lamar, Colorado; Albuquerque, New Mexico; Springerville, Arizona; and Upland, California.

Blvd. SE), formerly known as the National Atomic Museum, has replicas of Fat Man and Little Boy on display, as well as films and other exhibits on atomic energy in both peace and war.

The **Unser Racing Museum** (1776 Montaño Rd. NW) celebrates four generations of a family that has become a household name in auto racing. There's even a section of wall from the Indianapolis Motor Speedway on display.

Pimentel & Sons (3316 Lafayette Dr. NE) have been crafting handmade custom guitars for more than fifty years. Each is made by one craftsman, and typically includes inlay made especially for the individual customer. The Pimentels say that the New Mexico air is like a kiln, and perfectly seasons the wood in ten to fifteen years.

The **American International Rattlesnake Museum** (202 San Felipe St. NW) has a sizable collection of captive-born rattlesnakes. The museum is the largest of its kind ever developed, and its specimens include the rare albino rattlesnake. A helpful sign reminds the visitor that this is "not a petting zoo."

The **Turquoise Museum** (2107 Central Ave. NW) is an immersive experience. You'll enter the exhibit area through a mock mine tunnel, just as if you were prospecting for the semi-precious stone yourself. There are even daily demonstrations on preparing the stone for use in jewelry, and they've got a huge specimen on display in the shape of George Washington's profile.

The **Albuquerque Skateboard Museum** (1311 Eubank Blvd. NE) is housed in Skate City Supply. Lots of models are on display, including the Skee Skate of the 1950s.

The **Telephone Museum of New Mexico** (110 4th St. NW) has

three floors of telephone history on display—photographs, literature, and physical exhibits—dating back to 1876 and covering well over a century of telephone development. See the actual switchboard that was used to warn of the attack by Pancho Villa in 1916, or place a call to the Elvis novelty phone to hear how it rings.

Exhibits at the **New Mexico Museum of Natural History and Science** (1801 Mountain Rd. NW) include full-scale dinosaur models, an Ice Age cave, a walk-through volcano, and a saltwater aquarium.

The **Institute of Meteorites** (221 Yale Blvd. NE), in Northrop Hall on the University of New Mexico campus, was established more than thirty years ago as an educational resource for the state. In its permanent collection is one of the largest stone specimens on record. Also on display, on long-term loan from the Field Museum in Chicago, is a spectacular 1,600-pound iron meteorite.

Ernie Pyle, the famous World War II news correspondent, once lived in Albuquerque. His former residence has been converted into the **Ernie Pyle Memorial Branch Library** (900 Girard Ave. SE), which houses a small museum dedicated to the Pulitzer Prize winner who was killed in action in Okinawa.

The **Anderson-Abruzzo International Balloon Museum** (9201 Balloon Museum Dr. NE) is a scholarly presentation of the history of ballooning, with an emphasis on notable scientific and record-setting endeavors. For example, the collection includes the gondola from the first solo trans-Atlantic balloon flight in 1984. The museum is named for Albuquerque balloonists Ben Abruzzo and Maxie Anderson, who made the first nonstop gas balloon crossing of the Atlantic in 1978.

The **Kodak Albuquerque International Balloon Fiesta** is held the first two weekends in October, and is considered one of the world's most-photographed events. Balloon entries have mimicked boats, bottles, houses, and animals ad infinitum.

Since 1988, Albuquerque has been home to the **National Fiery Foods & Barbecue Show** every March. This show is for both the trades and the public, and participants include retailers, wholesalers, growers, and just plain aficionados. There are product and cooking demonstrations—anything goes, if it's even remotely chili-related.

On the western edge of Albuquerque is the Rio Grande (Spanish for "Large River"). It was here, on the east bank of the river and the south side of old 66, that there was a sort of neighborhood bathing pool called **Tingley Beach** (1800 Tingley Dr. SW), which originated during the New Deal era and was named for city commissioner (later state governor) Clyde Tingley. Nowadays, Tingley Beach is a public park featuring fishing ponds and other recreational features very near the defunct **El Vado Motel** (2500 Central Ave. SW). As you cross the Rio Grande, you are finally leaving the old territory of the Republic of Texas that you entered in western Oklahoma all those miles ago.

West of Albuquerque, the highway begins its climb up out of the Rio Grande Valley and onto the Colorado Plateau. The plateau continues until about halfway across Arizona. The hill on the horizon is **Nine Mile Hill**, so named because its summit is located that many miles from the town center of Albuquerque.

It should be noted here that the early alignment of the route, which

EL VADO COURT
ALBUQUERQUE, N. M.

U. S. Highway 66

20 Blocks From Center of Town - Albuquerque, N. M.

entered Albuquerque from the north via Santa Fe, continued southward out of Duke City and passed through Isleta Pueblo, Los Lunas,
and Correo. The later alignment heads due west toward Rio Puerco. To
drive the older alignment, leave Central Avenue at 4th Street and turn
left (south). Then turn right (west) onto Bridge Boulevard, cross the Rio
Grande, and follow the signs for NM 314 to Los Lunas. There, turn west
on NM 6, which is Los Lunas's Main Street. The two alignments will
come together again near the village of Mesita.

     What immediately follows is the narrative for the older
alignment that left Albuquerque heading southward. If you choose the
more modern alignment headed due west, you can pick up that thread
below at Rio Puerco.

> **Head south on 4th Street. Then turn right (west) onto Bridge Boulevard,
> cross the Rio Grande, and follow the signs for NM 314 to Los Lunas via
> Isleta Pueblo.**

ISLETA PUEBLO

The **mission church** (71 Tribal Rd. 35) at Isleta Pueblo is a heavily
buttressed structure built about 1613, making it one of the oldest in
New Mexico. It was partially destroyed during the Pueblo Rebellion,
and then restored after the 1692 re-conquest. Since that time it has been
in constant use.

Isleta Pueblo is where Thomas Edison made the very first mo-
tion picture, a short piece called *Indian Day School*, using his newly
invented Kinetoscope around 1898. These days, the pueblo engages
in several commercial enterprises, including a casino and golf course.

LOS LUNAS

The **Luna-Otero Mansion** (110 Main St. SW) is an elegant former

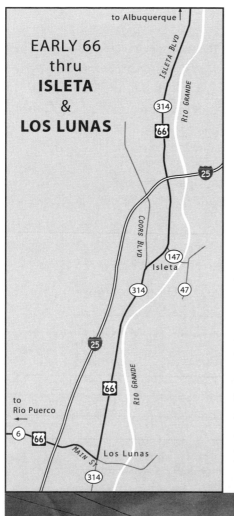

EARLY 66
thru
ISLETA
&
LOS LUNAS

to Albuquerque

ISLETA BLVD

RIO GRANDE

314

66

25

COORS BLVD

147

Isleta

314

47

25

66

RIO GRANDE

to
Rio Puerco

6 66

MAIN ST

Los Lunas

314

residence on the National Register that is now a restaurant and bar.

Blues/rock and roll musical legend Bo Diddley lived in Los Lunas for most of the 1970s.

The **Santa Fe Railroad Depot** (410 S. Guadalupe St.) was constructed in 1879, making it one of the very oldest in the state.

The **Los Lunas Museum of Heritage and Arts** (251 Main St. SE) is dedicated to local history and art, and is housed in the Agustin Archuleta house under the town's water tower.

West of Los Lunas via NM 6 is Mystery Mountain, at the base of which is **Mystery Rock**. The rock itself—actually a large boulder with an estimated weight of more than eighty tons—is also known as Ten Commandments Rock and the Los Lunas Decalogue Stone. The rock carries an inscription, said to be a variation of the Ten Commandments, in a Paleo-Hebrew form of writing. Its origin is a matter of some dispute and contention.

Isleta, New Mexico.
GPS: 34.91199,-106.69360

FURTHER AFIELD

Just south of Los Lunas is the town of Belen. In Belen is a **Harvey House** (104 N. 1st St.) that has been turned into a museum operated by the Valencia County Historical Society (VCHS). A walking/driving tour of the city, sponsored by the VCHS, includes such features as the **Central Hotel** (114 Becker Ave.), which figured prominently in the 1970 film *Bunny O'Hare*.

 Join NM 6 in Los Lunas, and turn west.

CORREO

Correo is a Spanish word meaning "mail." The community used to be known as Suwanee.

 There is a three-way intersection here; make a left turn from NM 6 onto "Old U.S. Highway 66" to head toward Mesita. The road is somewhat primitive, but is quite passable under most conditions. If you prefer, you can stay on NM 6 and join I-40 at exit #126 instead.

 If you chose to follow the modern route west out of Albuquerque, you'll cross the Rio Grande on Central Avenue and continue straight ahead for several miles. You'll cross to the north side of I-40 at exit #149 and continue west on the north frontage road.

RIO PUERCO

You'll actually cross the Rio Puerco ("Pig River") on I-40 at exit #140. The older 66-era truss bridge, though no longer bearing traffic, has been preserved.

**Vintage bridge over the Rio Puerco west of Albuquerque, New Mexico.
GPS: 35.03373,-106.94113**

MESITA

At Mesita, use the north frontage road to follow old Route 66. If you've been driving on I-40, take exit #117. If you've been following the more primitive road out of Correo, then you'll cross over I-40 a little southeast of Mesita and join up with the north frontage road (called Old Route 66 Road in this area) pretty seamlessly. The actual village of Mesita is a little

Near the entrance to the village of Mesita. GPS: 35.01900,-107.31577

Owl Rock, on old
66 west of Mesita,
New Mexico.
GPS: 35.03408,
-107.33810

to the north and east of I-40's exit #117 (see the reference map).

Just a short distance to the west is **Owl Rock**, an outcropping very close to the side of the road which has been pictured on many a postcard over the years.

Mission church at Laguna, New Mexico.
GPS: 35.03488,-107.38819

LAGUNA

Laguna is the site of a very photogenic church up on a hill—the **Saint Joseph of the Lake Mission Church**. This is where Kirk Douglas's character hurriedly picked up a priest in the movie *Ace in the Hole*, aka *The Big Carnival*.

PARAJE

Route 66 once passed the old, long-abandoned Paraje Trading Post here. However, it has since been demolished.

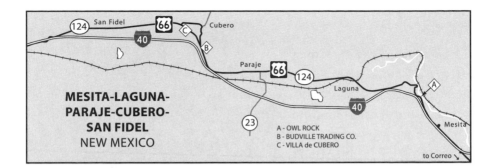

MESITA-LAGUNA-
PARAJE-CUBERO-
SAN FIDEL
NEW MEXICO

A - OWL ROCK
B - BUDVILLE TRADING CO.
C - VILLA de CUBERO

FURTHER AFIELD

On the highwayside west of Paraje, New Mexico.
GPS: 35.05099,-107.50597

From here, a side trip to **Acoma Pueblo** is possible, about thirteen miles or so to the south. Acoma Pueblo, or "Sky City," has been called the oldest continuously inhabited pueblo in America. These days, only about fifty individuals live here full time, but many more gather on traditional feast and festival days. Guided tours are available that take visitors to the pueblo atop Enchanted Mesa (about 350 feet up). There is a mission church there, the **Mission de San Esteban Rey**, which is the setting for Willa Cather's book *Death Comes to the Archbishop*. The church was constructed in 1629, and all of the materials were carried to the mesa top by the builders. This includes the roof beams, which have been traced to Mount Taylor, some thirty miles away. Until a road was built to the top of the mesa in the 1950s, the only access was by way of a steep stone staircase.

BUDVILLE

The **Budville Trading Company** still stands here: a former gas station, garage, and general store, dating from the 1930s. The tiny community was named for H. N. "Bud" Rice, who started a business hereabouts in 1928.

Budville, New Mexico. GPS: 35.06906,-107.52524

CUBERO

Cubero proper was an early victim of bypassing sometime in the 1930s. Afterward, a cluster of enterprises at the new highway junction appeared, including tourist court, café, etc. The **Villa de Cubero Trading Post** found itself host to a number of no-

Old tourist room at Cubero, New Mexico. GPS: 35.08436,-107.54179

table events: the filming of *Desert Song* took place here; Lucy came and stayed here after leaving Desi; and Papa Hemingway came to stay awhile and wrote *The Old Man and the Sea* while he was a guest here.

 Continue on NM 124/old 66 toward San Fidel.

SAN FIDEL-McCARTY'S

Just to the west of San Fidel, the route approaches I-40, at which point you and NM 124 will shift to the south frontage road and into the

McCarty's, New Mexico. GPS: 35.06548,-107.67687

vicinity of McCarty's. Up on a nearby hillside is the **Santa Maria Mission**, a 1933 Spanish-Colonial church that is a half-sized replica of the church at Acoma.

About five miles west of McCarty's is the interchange for NM 117. South of here is the eastern access to **El Malpais National Monument** (11000 Ice Caves Rd.). Covering about 400,000 acres, El Malpais, or "badland," is the largest contiguous lava flow in the U.S. Features include the Sandstone Bluffs Overlook, Big Tubes, and the Chain of Craters. Also here is La Ventana, one of the Southwest's largest freestanding natural arches. El Malpais can also be accessed via NM 53 south of Grants. The city of Grants also offers an **El Malpais Information Center** (620 E. Santa Fe Ave.). Wear rugged footgear if you go, as the lava is very hard and sharp.

East of exit #89, old 66 passes beneath I-40 and continues on to the city of Grants.

GRANTS

First settled in 1872, Grants is referred to as "Place of Friendly Smoke" by the local natives because of a peace pact that was reached here between

Grants, New Mexico.
GPS: 35.15284,-107.85481

Kit Carson and Chief Manuelito. In 1887, American Indians robbed a Santa Fe train of about $100,000 that was never recovered. Some think it may be buried somewhere in the area. In more modern times (1950), uranium was discovered nearby at a place called Haystack Mountain.

It was outside Grants in 1958 that Liz Taylor's then-husband, Michael Todd, met his death in a plane crash.

Here, Route 66 is called Santa Fe Avenue, and it's the main drag through Grants. It's lined with a number of vintage motels and other structures. The sign for the defunct

Downtown Grants, New Mexico.
GPS: 35.15073,-107.84995

Los Alamitos Motel is still standing. However, one of my personal favorites, the Grants Motel, was demolished several years ago.

GRANTS ATTRACTIONS

The **New Mexico Mining Museum** (100 Iron Ave.), said to be "one of the few" uranium mining museums in the world, includes a simulated underground mine allowing visitors to explore underground tunnels and get a taste of the mining experience.

Be sure to stop by the **Northwest New Mexico Visitor Center** (1900 E. Santa Fe Ave.), located in Grants just south of I-40 at exit #85.

FURTHER AFIELD

Some forty-odd miles southwest of Grants is **El Morro National Monument** (NM 53). Also known as Inscription Rock, the main feature is a 200-foot sandstone cliff rising from the valley floor and bearing inscriptions dating back centuries. The rock sits along an ancient east–west trail that has been frequented by travelers since prehistory. The earliest "European" inscription belongs to Juan Oñate, the first colonial governor of New Mexico, who made his mark in 1605. But there are petroglyphs that are, of course, a great deal older. A half-mile trail takes the visitor on a tour of the inscriptions, and a longer trail takes one to the top of the mesa where there is a pueblo ruin. Interesting, isn't it, that once graffiti gets old enough, it's considered a cultural treasure?

On the way to El Morro is the **Bandera Volcano and Perpetual Ice Caves** (NM 53). It's said that Zuni guides brought Coronado here, and that the place has been a destination ever since. A study in contrast, this privately held attraction includes the 500-foot extinct volcano with hiking trail, as well as nearby caves that glisten with ice year-round. Trails begin at the historic **Ice Cave Trading Post**.

MILAN-BLUEWATER-PREWITT

 Route 66 is marked as NM 122 in these parts.

Heading west out of Grants, you'll pass through country that, in the time of Rittenhouse, was a major carrot-producing area covering thousands of acres between here and Bluewater.

Imposing sign for the now-defunct Bluewater Motel. GPS: 35.24821,-107.95586

Milan is immediately northwest of Grants, and you'll be hard-pressed to tell when you've passed from one into the other.

You'll know Bluewater by the enormous **Bluewater Motel** sign that still stands. A friendly couple lives in the small collection of buildings beneath the sign.

Farther along, south of Prewitt, are the remains of one of the **Bowlins Trading Posts**. This one is covered in hand-painted vignettes depicting

Former trading post, Prewitt, New Mexico. GPS: 35.28386,-107.98481

American Indian traditional scenes.

As for Prewitt, I once saw a matchbook cover for sale on eBay that advertised **Justin's Western Shop & Fountain** "on Highway 66" in Prewitt. It looked as though it was printed in the 1940s. The telephone number, believe it or not, said "phone Prewitt No. 2."

Continue on old 66/NM 122, which soon sidles up very closely to the north side of I-40.

THOREAU

Thoreau, New Mexico.
GPS: 35.39730,-108.22594

Originally named Mitchell, but later re-named for the author Henry David Thoreau, this town is home to the **Zuni Mountain Trading Company** (15 2nd Ave.) and also to **Maynard Buckles** (23 Bluewater Ave.), manufacturer of trophy belt buckles for rodeo champions and other traditional accessories.

FURTHER AFIELD

North of Thoreau is the town of Crownpoint, which is famous for its monthly Navajo rug auctions, held at the local elementary school. Crownpoint is also a potential launching pad for an excursion to **Chaco Culture National Historic Park**, although this is not the preferred approach (it is more advisable to access the park from the north). Chaco Canyon is one of the key sites in the Four Corners region that exemplifies prehistoric culture in America. There are dozens of impressive sites here, two of the major ones being

Pueblo Bonito and Chetro Ketl; the area was settled as early as the ninth century, and the culture reached its apex around A.D. 1150. Archaeologists have determined that these people established a network of roads connecting them not only with the other villages in this canyon, but with a broader community extending for many miles. The complexity of architecture, community, and social organization is astonishing. Chaco Canyon is quite isolated—plan on bringing plenty of food and drink if you go.

Continue out of Thoreau on NM 122 (the north frontage road) for a short distance to the Continental Divide.

CONTINENTAL DIVIDE

Around five miles west of Thoreau is a small service community named after the backbone of the North American continent. There is a sign here explaining how rainwater that falls west of this dividing line flows westward to the Pacific, while that which falls to the east flows toward the

Continental Divide. GPS: 35.42285,-108.30923

Atlantic via the Gulf of Mexico. This was formerly home to Top O' the World, a dance hall, bar, tourist court, and boarding house.

The **Continental Divide National Scenic Trail** crosses Route 66 here as it wends its way along the divide from the Mexican border in the south all the way to the Canadian border north of Glacier National Park, a distance of more than 3,000 miles.

About fifteen miles or so west of Continental Divide is the turnoff for **Fort Wingate** (NM 400) to the south. Fort Wingate was established in 1862 at a site near San Rafael (south of Grants). It was used as a base for Colonel Kit Carson's campaigns against the Navajos, when he rounded up thousands and marched them 300 miles to Fort Sumner in what has become known as the "Long Walk." The fort was moved to its present site in 1868, the same year Carson died. He is buried near Taos.

About four miles west of the Fort Wingate turnoff is the turnoff for **Kit Carson Cave**, which is a few miles north of old 66 via NM 566.

Leaving Continental Divide, you'll need to join I-40 here at exit #47. Continue to exit #36, then follow the north frontage road, which parallels a set of railroad tracks (on your right) all the way into Gallup, where it becomes Business Loop 40.

GALLUP

Old Route 66 through Gallup is unmistakable; it parallels the railroad tracks, which are only yards away.

The jewel of Gallup is the **El Rancho Hotel and Motel** (1000 E. Hwy 66). Boasting the "Charm of Yesterday and the Convenience of

Gallup, New Mexico.
GPS: 35.52633,-108.74550

Gallup, New Mexico. GPS: 35.52992,-108.72577

Tomorrow," the El Rancho is truly one of a kind. The lobby decor is extraordinary, and the guest rooms are all named after Hollywood personalities who used to stay here in the glory days of filmmaking, when Gallup was a sort of Hollywood Southwest: Clark Gable, John Wayne, Claudette Colbert, and dozens of others are enshrined here. Photographs

El Morro Theatre, downtown Gallup, New Mexico. GPS: 35.52715,-108.74275

of stars line the walls. There is also a restaurant, lounge, and gift shop on the premises.

Downtown Gallup invites pedestrian exploration in an area of several blocks, including old Route 66 and Coal Street (formerly part of 66), which is one block to the south. Check out the **Rex Museum** (300 W. Rte. 66), the **McKinley County Courthouse** (207 W. Hill Ave.), and the **El Morro Theatre** (207 W. Coal Ave.), which underwent extensive renovations before reopening in 2006.

Downtown Gallup.
GPS: 35.52762,-108.74399

GALLUP ATTRACTIONS

The **Gallup Cultural Center** (201 E. Hwy 66) is located in a restored Santa Fe railroad depot. A project of the Southwest Indian Foundation, the center hosts a variety of events and includes a gallery, cinema, museum, bookstore, gift shop, and café.

The **McKinley County Courthouse** (201 W. Hill Ave.) contains what is believed to be the largest WPA-sponsored mural still in existence.

The Gallup Historical Society operates the **Rex Museum** (300 W. Hwy 66), which specializes in railroad and mining history of the area.

The **Navajo Code Talkers' Room** (103 W. Hwy 66) is housed in the chamber of commerce building. Here you can learn their fascinating story of war heroism (see sidebar).

Red Rock State Park, just east of town, is home to the **Intertribal Indian Ceremonial** gathering in August and the **Red Rock Balloon Rally** in December. More than thirty tribes from throughout North America participate in the intertribal gathering, which has been held since 1922 and is the largest gathering of its kind, attracting some 50,000 visitors.

CODE TALKERS

The Navajo language proved to be an important strategic advantage to the American forces in the Pacific during World War II. The U.S. Marine Corps employed some 400 Navajo speakers to transmit messages that would be undecipherable to the Japanese. This was possible mainly because the Navajo language has no alphabet and is extremely complex, unwritten, and spoken only in the American Southwest. At the outbreak of World War II, it was understood by no more than thirty or so non-Navajos—none of them Japanese. For decades following the war, the U.S. military kept this part of history largely under wraps in case they might need to use the language again. In 1992, the information was finally made public and the hundreds of code-talkers so vital to the war effort were recognized and honored for their unique contributions. In 2002, MGM released a feature film on the subject, *Windtalkers*.

Near the entrance to the park is **Mr. Wilson's Red Rock Trading Post** (3111 W. Chandler Blvd.), a National Historical Landmark. The park's red cliffs have been the setting for many movie productions over the years, including *Sea of Grass*, starring Spencer Tracy and Katharine Hepburn in 1946.

FURTHER AFIELD

Gallup sits at the junction of U.S. Routes 66 and the former 666. The highway which carried the apocalyptic designation (now known as 491) heads north out of Gallup toward the Four Corners region of the country.

About eighty miles or so north of Gallup lies the town of Shiprock. It was named for the very distinctive remains of an **extinct volcano** situated

a few miles outside of town that resembles a many-masted sailing ship. From Shiprock, access to a huge wealth of **ancient ruins** throughout the Four Corners region is possible. These spectacular Anasazi sites include Salmon Ruins, Aztec National Monument, Chaco Canyon, Mesa Verde National Park, Hovenweep National Monument, Canyon de Chelly, and many lesser-known archaeological treasures. There is also the **Four Corners Monument** itself, right at the juncture of New Mexico, Arizona, Utah, and Colorado, where one can actually stand in four states at once. Straddling the Arizona-Utah border is **Monument Valley**, with an array of interesting geological features many of us recognize immediately from having seen John Ford westerns.

 At the west end of Gallup, continue straight ahead onto NM 118 as you pass beneath I-40.

DEFIANCE-MANUELITO

At Defiance, NM 118 takes a left turn to pass beneath I-40, where you'll continue on the south side of the freeway for a few miles.

Prior to reaching Manuelito, you'll once again cross I-40 (to the north side).

West of Manuelito and just before the Arizona state line, the old highway passes the 1950 filming site of *The Big Carnival* (aka *Ace in the Hole*). The caves are in the cliffs on the north side of the highway. Many years ago, there was a sign near the border as one headed east advertising "Cliff Dwellings" one-half mile east of the state line.

ARIZONA

Quietly, New Mexico gives way to Arizona as you continue to motor west. The character of the land here is harsher than any you've seen earlier in your journey. There certainly are green

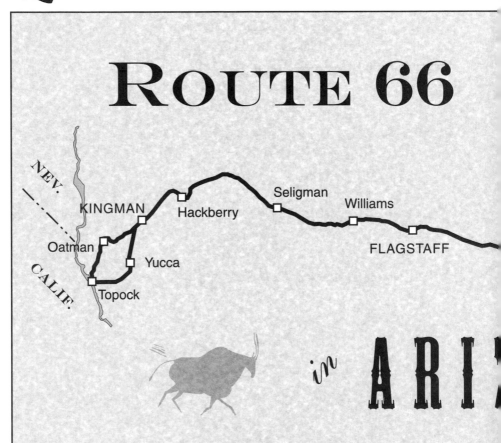

and inviting places in Arizona, but at this moment you could be forgiven for not believing it.

And yet, there are many who are profoundly drawn to this place. I first glimpsed it myself many years ago in what is called the Arizona Strip, that northwestern portion of the state that is cut off from the rest by the Grand Canyon. There, far from the bright lights of any metropolis, I lay on the ground one evening and saw more stars in the sky than I had ever thought possible—I could swear they overlapped.

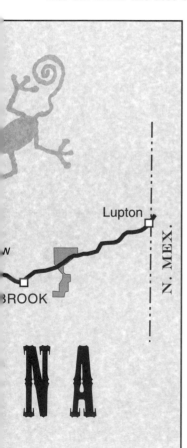

Water, that most precious of commodities, is in short supply. You could say that water in this area is an acute condition, rather than a chronic one—you will see a great many dry stream beds which gush to life on only a few occasions during the year. The lack of a reliable supply of water through much of this territory has shaped Arizona's history and destiny. Early inhabitants, such as the Anasazi, were likely forced to move elsewhere when weather patterns made their already-marginal existence untenable; more recently, the path of the railroads was dictated in part by the same limitations.

In this minimalist landscape, the austere is beautiful, and the beautiful is sublime. This land is a canvas bearing the strokes of Mother Nature the artist, for whom a millennium is no more than a moment. Red rock country, a painted desert, and the scar from a meteoric collision all await you in a place where trees turn to stone and volcanic eruptions shape the countryside.

Just across the New Mexico-Arizona border you'll encounter the community of . . .

LUPTON

 You'll cross the state line on the north frontage road, but quickly switch to the south side at exit #359.

From Route 66, Lupton looks to be mostly a sort of "strip" comprised of **trading posts** offering tourist-oriented souvenirs. The most notable thing about these trading posts is their garish appearance, including bright primary colors and replicas of teepees. At least one of them features a wooden American Indian chief standing outside. This area is an excellent place to pick up that bullwhip or rubber tomahawk you've been wanting.

Lupton, Arizona. GPS: 35.36021,-109.04966

About twenty-five miles or so to the north of here via Highway 12 is Window Rock, a natural feature consisting of an aperture carved in a large sandstone formation by the forces of wind, dust, and water. There is a viewing area at the **Window Rock Tribal Park** (Hwy 12.) The nearby community of Window Rock has been the official capital of the Navajo nation since 1938. There is a museum nearby on Highway 264.

Traveling Route 66 in Lupton, you will quickly cross to the south side of I-40 for the run toward Sanders. Here you'll see what remains of the former **Ortega's Indian Galeria**, which was housed in a geodesic-domed building, now in derelict condition. There's a similar structure, also a trading post, which you'll see later at Meteor City.

Continue on the south frontage road to Allentown at exit #351 and cross to the north frontage road.

HOUCK

At Houck is something called **Fort Courage**, built as a replica of the fort used in the 1960s television series *F Troop*. Nearby is an old **coffee house** in a sort of Googie-wannabe style.

This tourist attraction tapped into the popularity of the *F Troop* television comedy.
GPS: 35.28316,-109.20755

Continue on the north frontage road toward Sanders. At exit #346, this becomes Querino Dirt Road. If conditions are good, continue ahead. If not, enter the interstate here and then use exit #339 for Sanders.

If you took Querino Road, then at the end of it you'll need to join the interstate (exit #341). Leave I-40 at exit #339.

SANDERS

At mile marker 339 is the village of Sanders. The former **Route 66 Diner** (Arizona Park Ests. #26), housed in a building manufactured by the renowned Valentine, is in the portion of town

This Valentine-brand diner has seen much better days. Sanders, Arizona. GPS: 35.20965,-109.32856

south of the interstate. To find it, go south on 191, left on Navajo, then right on E. Butte.

 Leave Sanders on the north frontage road heading west.

CHAMBERS-NAVAJO

You'll meet up with U.S. 191 North at Chambers.

FURTHER AFIELD

About thirty-seven miles north of Chambers via U.S. 191 is the village of Ganado and the **Hubbell Trading Post National Historic Site** (1/2 AZ-264). Established in the 1870s, this is the oldest continuously operating Navajo trading post, now run by the National Park Service. John Hubbell's grave overlooks the site from nearby Hubbell Hill.

Thirty-six miles north of Hubbell's Trading Post is the **Canyon de Chelly National Monument**, which contains probably the most-photographed ruin in the United States: the White House ruin. The ruin is reached by an arduous trail, about 2.5 miles round-trip, which may leave you breathless on the ascent, but it is well worth the effort. The trail goes past an active farmstead and across a small stream before reaching the bottom of the canyon, where the ruin is built into the canyon wall. This is the only ruin in the park that is accessible without a guide.

Continuing on Route 66, you'll need to join the interstate here at Chambers (exit #333) due to the fact that the Mother Road remnants in this area are rough, impassable, or come to dead ends. Continue on I-40 to exit #303.

PETRIFIED FOREST

No longer accessible from what remains of old 66, the Painted Desert and the Petrified Forest, a pair of natural attractions straddling the highway, must be reached from I-40 (at exit #311). However, in this vicinity you can use the I-40 overpasses to look at the adjoining terrain and pick out where the Highway 66 pavement used to run. The paving was pretty thoroughly removed in this area, but out here scars are slow to heal, and you

A Portion of the Painted Desert lies within the Boundaries of Petrified Forest National Monument

Logs of Stone, in the Petrified Forest

can often spot differences in the color and character of the soil and vegetation signaling where the old roadbed was. Keep alert and you'll see what I mean.

The **Petrified Forest National Park** is about twenty-six miles east of Holbrook. It was established in 1906 during the Theodore Roosevelt

Rock shop at exit #303, near Adamana, Arizona. GPS: 35.00212,-109.89702

administration, and designated a national park in 1962. This area was once a dense and humid forest eons ago, and conditions were such that fallen trees transformed into mineralized versions of themselves. The agate and quartz that comprise these fossils still exhibit the visible characteristics of wood, such as grain and growth rings. The park includes natural formations, such as undisturbed fallen trees, as well as some man-made structures like the Agate House, a pueblo that is fashioned from the rare material. Other features include the Puerco Indian Ruin, a 100-room pueblo dating from about A.D. 1300, and Newspaper Rock, which is covered in petroglyphs.

The **Painted Desert** is just north of the highway and connects with the Petrified Forest to the south. Plenty of photo opportunities are provided by the colorful mineral deposits that give the area its name. These are particularly impressive in early-morning or pre-dusk light. The **Painted Desert Inn** (1 Park Rd.), at Kachina Point, was built in the 1920s and then restored in the '30s by the Civilian Conservation Corps. Later, it became a part of the Harvey House chain.

Both the Petrified Forest and the Painted Desert are bona fide Route 66-era attractions, so be sure to take advantage of this opportunity to experience them.

HOLBROOK

Take exit #289/Business Loop 40 into Holbrook (Navajo Boulevard), which follows the course of old Route 66, including a turn to the west on Hopi Drive.

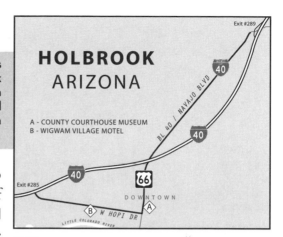

Holbrook is well-known to 66 travelers as the home of the **Wigwam Village Motel** (811 W. Hopi Dr.). There were at one time seven such villages, all built between 1933 and 1950, with the original one in Horse Cave, Kentucky. The sister set of units near San Bernardino was the last to be built. Each

Ambience at the Wigwam Motel, Holbrook, Arizona. GPS: 34.90287,-110.16864

Holbrook, Arizona. GPS: 34.90493,-110.15810

Holbrook, Arizona. GPS: 34.90172,-110.15908

Holbrook, Arizona. GPS: 34.90295,-110.17098

village consists of several individual room units designed to resemble American Indian teepees. Furthermore, all units of each village originally had pay-per-listen radios, the receipts of which were forwarded to the originator of the concept, Frank Bedford, as a sort of royalty fee.

HOLBROOK ATTRACTIONS

The old **Navajo County Courthouse** (Navajo Blvd. and E. Arizona St.), built in 1898, now houses a museum and visitor center and includes the original Old West jail. The jail has preserved some old inmate artwork on the walls. You can also pick up a copy of Holbrook's self-guided walking tour of various points of interest at the museum. Included is the Blevins House, where an Old West shootout occurred in 1887.

There are numerous purveyors of petrified wood and other exotic minerals in Holbrook, some of which include some campy dinosaur figures as décor.

Rejoin I-40 at the west end of town (exit #285 interchange).

If you haven't had your fill of petrified wood yet— or if you skipped the Petrified Forest completely—you might want to exit at Geronimo (exit #280), where the trading post has what they boast is the **World's Largest Petrified Log** on display.

Geronimo's, west of Holbrook, Arizona.
GPS: 34.91954,-110.25513

JOSEPH CITY

Leave I-40 at exit #277 to enter the town of Joseph City.

This community was originally established by Mormons circa 1876— America's centennial year, and exactly fifty years before the establishment of U.S. 66 and the rest of the federal highway system.

West of the town proper is the famous **Jackrabbit Trading Post** (3386 Historic Rte. 66). The billboard proclaiming "HERE IT IS" has to be one of the best-known sights along the route. I for one find myself transported back in time whenever I see it. Aside from the billboard, the Jackrabbit is also famous for its slogan: "If you haven't been to the Jackrabbit, you haven't been in the Southwest." Lots of travelers over the years have had their photographs taken sitting astride the giant

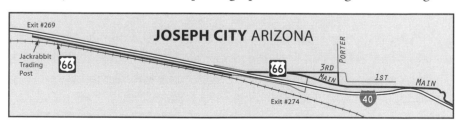

ROADSIDE MARKETING AT THE JACKRABBIT

Anticipation. That's something that comes to mind when I think of the Jackrabbit Trading Post. Sure, the big billboard exclaiming, "Here It Is!" is unique and impressive and known the world over. But the marketing strategy for the Jackrabbit is all about anticipation. And when it's done right, anticipation is one of the hardest things to resist.

In addition to the renowned billboard pictured, the Jackrabbit posted smaller signs up and down the highway in both directions giving progress reports. When you were eighty-seven miles away, you'd see a simple sign with a jackrabbit silhouette stating: "87 miles."

Jackrabbit Trading Post, Joseph City.
GPS: 34.96765,-110.43054

Several miles later, there'd be exactly the same graphic, but with the enticing figure: "69 miles."

As you, the Route 66 motorist, approached ever closer, the signs would appear more and more frequently: 26 miles . . . 18 . . . 14 . . . 11 . . . .

It's no wonder, then, that by the time the family arrived, everyone in the car—including dear old dad—was *desperate* to pull over and find out for themselves just what all the fuss was about. And we still do pull over, even today.

Here It Is: the most famous billboard on all of Route 66, Joseph City, Arizona.
GPS: 34.96765,-110.43054

jackrabbit figure on the premises. To find the Jackrabbit, you can either cross to the south side of I-40 at exit #274 and then turn west, or you can take the interstate west to exit #269 and then double back on the south frontage road.

 After visiting the Jackrabbit, rejoin I-40 at exit #269 just to the west. Continue until you reach exit #257.

MANILA-HIBBARD-HOBSON

Manila shows up plainly as a town directly on Route 66 in my 1957 road atlas, as does Hibbard. By that time, Hobson had already been bypassed, and it appeared just south of the route. Hobson is still down there, right on the railroad tracks, as befits a very old alignment. The memory of Hibbard persists thanks to the I-40 exit sign—exit #264 is called Hibbard Road. Today, the community at this exit is called Havre.

If you have a rugged vehicle and are feeling adventurous, take the

Hibbard Road exit, go to the north side of the interstate, and follow the road west. You will lose the pavement for most of the way, but you will pass through what was once a well-traveled piece of back country. At the Highway 87 junction, cross to the south side of I-40 for the run into Winslow.

WINSLOW

As you enter Winslow from the east, the highway splits into east-bound and west-bound portions. As always, when the highway splits like this through any town, I rec-

Downtown Winslow, Arizona. GPS: 35.02334,-110.69812

ommend that you double back after you've passed through town in order to see what's on the other side.

Winslow received mention in the Eagles' song "Take It Easy" many years ago, and the town has latched onto this bit of trivia for all it's worth. Go check out the **"corner in Winslow, Arizona"** yourself, where you'll see a sign quoting the famous line, a bronze statue, and a mural that includes a girl in a flatbed Ford (Kinsley St. and 2nd St.).

WINSLOW ATTRACTIONS

The **Old Trails Museum** (212 N. Kinsley) houses a collection of Winslow historical artifacts and Route 66 memorabilia in a former bank building that includes many of its original features.

Winslow's **1st Street Pathway**, which runs a half-dozen blocks or so, was only the first phase in a project to revitalize the downtown area, collectively referred to as "Renaissance on 66." In phase two, five blocks of 2nd and 3rd Streets had new streetlamps installed, Route 66 banners hung, and brick inlays added to the crosswalks and intersections. The pathway links two of the town's most historic landmarks: the La Posada Hotel and the Hubbell Trading Post.

The **La Posada Hotel** (303 E. 2nd St.) is a former Harvey House property created in 1928 by top-tier architect Mary Colter, widely regarded today for being far ahead of her time. Offering a modest number of guest rooms in a space larger than the Hearst Castle, this Spanish hacienda-style jewel was restored in the late 1990s and features a museum, gardens, and meeting spaces.

The **Hubbell Trading Post** (1/2 AZ-264) is part of an extensive network of stores once operated in the Southwest by the Hubbell family. This one was established in 1924, before Route 66 became a reality. The building has recently been renovated in order to house historical exhibits, as well as a new visitor center and offices for the local chamber of commerce.

Winslow's **Remembrance Garden** (E. 3rd St. and Transcon Ln.) is a memorial to the lives lost in the September 11 terrorist attacks. On display are some beams from the World Trade Center wreckage.

La Posada Hotel, Winslow, Arizona. GPS: 35.02168,-110.69511

FURTHER AFIELD

Just outside Winslow is **Homolovi Ruins State Park** (AZ 87). This is a 4,000-acre preserve with more than 300 archaeological sites and numerous petroglyphs. *Homolovi* is a Hopi word meaning "place of the little hills." The four major pueblo sites here are thought to have been occupied from A.D. 1200 to 1425. The park is an active archaeological site; archaeologists work here Monday through Friday in June and July, revealing agricultural features and pit houses.

  Leave Winslow on Old 66/W. 3rd and join I-40 again at exit #252 at the west end of town.

LEUPP CORNERS-DENNISON

According to my trusty 1957 atlas, Leupp Corners was a small community at the Route 66 junction with a gravel road going north to the town of Leupp. That road (or the closest thing to it) is marked today as State Highway 99.

METEOR CITY

Leave I-40 at exit #239 for Meteor City.

This is **Meteor City**, a geodesic-dome-style trading post by the side of the highway. When I first started traveling Route 66, this was still an active business, but not long after, the folks running it pulled up the stakes. Now, it's in a deplorable state with probably no hope of ever being active again.

  Rejoin I-40 until exit #233.

Former site of the Meteor City Trading Post. GPS: 35.09439,-110.93550

RIMMY JIMS

Rimmy Jim was the moniker of the man who originally ran the **Meteor Crater concession**. The crater itself is about six miles south of I-44 here at exit #233. The meteor was traveling at 45,000 mph when it hit earth; the impact resulted in a crater 570 feet deep, one mile across, and three miles in circumference. Today, you'll find a gift shop, snack bar, interpretive exhibits, and observation platforms at the site. You can hike around

Former observation tower near Meteor Crater, Arizona. GPS: 35.10464,-111.03123

the crater via guided tour, but you cannot enter it. Since the object causing the crater originated in outer space, there is also a sort of Astronaut Hall of Fame on the premises. Fun fact: a segment of

Meteor Crater, 5 Miles South of U. S. Highway 66 between Flagstaff and Winslow

This Huge Pit dug by a Meteor Thousands of Years ago is 600 Feet Deep and a Mile across

1984's *Starman* was filmed at the crater.

Nearby, on an unused stretch of old 66, is the stone ruin of a primitive observation tower used in the old days, the **Meteor Crater Observatory** (Meteor Crater Rd.). It's on private property and lately has been fenced off from explorers like you and me.

TWO GUNS

You may or may not be able to gain access to Two Guns (exit #230), due to the fact that it rests on private property. It has gone through cycles where it has been posted against trespassing, and periods where visitors have been at least permitted, if not encouraged, to enter. Two Guns was a town only in the loosest sense; it was actually a made-to-order tourist trap, with several cages of captive animals, such as coyotes and mountain lions, to lure the motorist off the highway. This is the stuff that lasting memories are made of, for young boys traveling with mom and dad.

TWIN ARROWS

Twin Arrows, at exit #219, is an abandoned tourist complex featuring a café, trading post, and fuel station. It's distinguished by a pair of

Part of the vast tourist complex at Two Guns, Arizona. GPS: 35.11507,-111.09106

enormous arrows sticking out of the ground. I've been hoping for years that someone would make a go of it here, but so far those hopes have not been answered. Now that this property belongs to the American Indian group running the casino on the opposite side of the

Twin Arrows, Arizona. GPS: 35.16144,-111.27924

freeway, I'm sure it'll never happen.

WINONA

 From Winona, you have a choice to make regarding your approach to Flagstaff (see the reference map).

This is the place made somewhat famous for its reference in Bobby Troup's classic song, in which he exhorts: "Don't forget Winona." There's not a great deal to see in Winona, other than the big, gleaming **vintage trestle bridge** that used to carry the highway. From Winona, you can take an early alignment to Flagstaff by using Townsend-Winona Road, then turning south at Highway 89. To use the later alignment, return to the interstate and exit at Walnut Canyon Road/Historic 66 (exit #204).

COSNINO

Once the Townsend-Winona Road loop mentioned above was bypassed, Route 66 took a slightly more direct path toward Flagstaff, passing through the village of Cosnino, near today's exit #207.

FLAGSTAFF

 You'll enter Flagstaff from the northeast. Route 66/BL-40 is also U.S. 89 in town.

Nestled at the feet of the San Francisco Peaks, Flagstaff enjoys nearly the same elevation as Denver, and so has a considerable skiing season in the winter months. The same slopes in summer make for excellent hiking, affording views that sometimes extend into neighboring Utah to the north. There is a Flagstaff anecdote that says that Cecil B. DeMille almost made Flagstaff the center of filmdom instead of Hollywood.

On Route 66 in Flagstaff. GPS: 35.21387,-111.59956

However, the day he arrived from the east there was snow falling, and so he decided to stay on the train and continue to California and sunnier climes. The rest, as they say, is history.

Entering Flagstaff from the east, prior to arriving downtown, you'll see a vintage roadhouse known as the **Museum Club** (3404 E. Rte. 66). Built in 1931 to house a taxidermy collection and other artifacts, it was originally called the Dean Eldridge Museum. Later it evolved into a honky-tonk nicknamed the Zoo because of all the animal trophies on display, and it has seen the likes of some top-tier performers over the years. There are a few stories of ghost hauntings here; one of the former owners committed suicide in front of the fireplace. Look for the guitar-shaped neon sign out front.

In downtown Flagstaff you'll find a lot of vibrancy, mixed together with a lot of vintage architecture and still-working neon. The **Hotel Monte Vista** (100 N. San Francisco St.) first opened its doors on January 1, 1927, and has played host

Flagstaff, Arizona.
GPS: 35.19627,-111.64852

The former Santa Fe railroad depot now serves as the town visitor center. Flagstaff, Arizona. GPS: 35.19746,-111.64897

to the likes of Jane Russell, Spencer Tracy, Humphrey Bogart, Theodore Roosevelt, and many, many others of similar celebrity. It's said that Zane Grey did some of his writing here at the hotel. The adjoining bar has a neon marquee that says simply: COCKTAILS.

Route 66 runs right alongside the railroad tracks through Flagstaff, so you'll see the old **Santa Fe depot** (1 Historic Rte. 66) as well. It has been spruced up and turned into a visitor center with a gift shop.

There is also a lively commercial district along old 66/Santa Fe Avenue, San Francisco Street, and Aspen Avenue.

FLAGSTAFF ATTRACTIONS

Walnut Canyon National Monument (3 Walnut Canyon Rd.), established in 1915, is home to the ruins of a small Sinagua community. The thirteenth-century community is comprised of some 300 rooms. There is a steep, self-guided walking trail here that meanders through the canyon past numerous cliff dwellings.

The world-famous **Lowell Observatory** (1400 W. Mars Hill Rd.), established in 1894, is where astronomers discovered Pluto in 1930; the telescope used at the time is still on display. Also here is the original twenty-four-inch refractor used in the 1890s. Guided tours and lectures are available.

Riordan Mansion State Historic Park (409 W. Riordan Rd.) features the forty-room Riordan Mansion, built in 1904 in the Arts and Crafts style. The architect, Charles Whittlesey, also designed the Grand Canyon's El Tovar Lodge. This house was built for two close-knit families; the Riordan brothers married two sisters from another prominent family, and both couples lived and raised their own families here. The house features log-slab siding, volcanic stone archways, and hand-split wood shingles. Interior appointments include handmade furniture and stained-glass windows. A truly unique feature of the house is the set of photographic windows in the Rendezvous Room. A prominent photographer, John K. Hillers, was commissioned by the owners, and his photographic transparencies were fused to panes of translucent glass, so that the photos are illuminated by the incoming sunlight. These windows were painstakingly restored in the 1990s using his original glass negatives found at the Smithsonian Institution.

The Arizona Historical Society's **Pioneer Museum** (2340 N. Fort Valley Rd.) is located north of town in a building that served as a hospital for the indigent from 1908 until 1938. Also on the grounds are a barn and root cellar that were utilized by the hospital, and a cabin that was moved to the site in 1967 from elsewhere in Flagstaff. From November

Flagstaff, Arizona. GPS: 35.19681,-111.65067

to February each year, the museum presents "Playthings of
the Past," an exhibit of toys
from the 1880s through the
1960s. Every June, they host a
Wool Festival featuring sheep,
goat, and llama shearings, as
well as wool spinning, dyeing,
and weaving demonstrations.

Here at Flagstaff, Route 66
crosses paths with the **Arizona
Trail**, a hiking path spanning
the state from the Utah state
line in the north all the way
to the Mexican border in the
south. Conceived by a Flag-

Flagstaff, Arizona. GPS: 35.19493,-111.64916

staff schoolteacher, the 820-mile trail earned its designation in 2009 as a
National Scenic Trail after decades of effort. You can get more information about the trail at **City Hall** (211 W. Aspen Ave.).

FURTHER AFIELD

About fifteen miles north of Flagstaff (take U.S. 89) is the **Sunset
Crater Volcano National Monument** (6082 Sunset Crater Rd.). This
cinder cone was formed around A.D. 1064, and was active intermittent-
ly for the next 200 years or so. The Lava Flow Nature Trail begins at the
visitor center and consists of a forty-five-minute walk that traverses some
of the lava flows and affords some nice views. For the stout of heart, the
Lenox Crater Cinder Cone Trail is steep and strenuous.

From Sunset Crater, a paved road crosses the lava flow and connects
with **Wupatki National Monument** (25137 N. Wupatki Loop Rd.). Established in 1924 by Calvin Coolidge, Wupatki is composed of several
ruins on 35,000 acres thought to have been inhabited by ancestors of

the Hopi. Most impressive is the Tall House, a 100-room complex with a nearby amphitheater and ball court. Self-guided walking trails take the visitor through each of the ruins.

To the south of Flagstaff (thirty miles) is Sedona. A sort of New Age sanctuary, Sedona is famous for its red rock scenery, which changes in appearance throughout the course of each day. The nearby **Red Rock-Secret Mountain Wilderness** is a red-hued landscape filled with canyons, pinnacles, cliffs, ruins, and rock art. Sedona also hosts an **International Film Festival** every March.

Beyond Sedona, but still on ALT 89, is the old mining community of Jerome. This town, perched on the side of Cleopatra Hill, was just about gone until it was resurrected as a sort of art colony. Today, the town bustles with guests browsing the assortment of galleries, shops, and historic buildings. Just walking the streets of Jerome is an enjoyable experience. While you're in town, check out the old **Douglas Mansion** (100 Douglas Rd.) at Jerome State Historic Park. The museum traces the history of Jerome and the Douglas family in particular, through photos, minerals, and artifacts. Very close to Jerome is the **Tuzigoot National Monument** (25

Jerome has a mining heritage.

Tuzigoot Rd.). Here you can tour a pueblo once inhabited by the Sinagua people that rests on a ridge some 120 feet above the surrounding valley.

Southeast of Jerome and Sedona, near I-17, are the **Montezuma Castle National Monument** (Montezuma Castle Rd.) and **Montezuma Well** (E. Beaver Creek Rd.). Named by early explorers who assumed it was Aztecan in origin, the castle structure is about ninety percent intact and is at the end of a paved trail, which makes for an easy stroll. The well is about eleven miles away and consists of a spring at the bottom of a canyon-like depression. The sides of the depression are filled with small pueblo ruins.

Farther south of Jerome on ALT 89 is the city of Prescott (pronounced "press kit"). Prescott is a destination in itself, offering a beautiful historic downtown district ideal for walking around. Prescott has more Victorian-era buildings than any other community in Arizona. The **Sharlot Hall Museum** (415 W. Gurley St.) alone has twelve buildings on three acres evoking the flavor of territorial Arizona. Included are the old Territorial Governor's Mansion, Fort Misery Cabin, and the Bashford House, considered a premier example of Western High Victorian style. Prescott also is home to the country's oldest **rodeo**, which has been held consistently since 1888. And, if you appreciate Western art, don't miss the **Phippen Museum** (4701 AZ-89), named for the founder of the Cowboy Artists of America.

Back on Route 66 heading west out of Flagstaff, the road will eventually force you back onto the interstate between exits #191 and #190. Leave the interstate again at exit #185.

BELLEMONT

The name Bellemont literally means "pretty mountain." Here at exit #185 are some **fragments of old 66** on both sides of today's I-40, both paved and unpaved, and going in both directions from the exit. I recommend that you explore the area and make good use of the tips you learned in the "How to Find Route 66" chapter in the front portion of this book.

Parks, Arizona. GPS: 35.25996,-111.94834

PARKS

This tiny town at exit #178 (formerly called Maine) was severely damaged by the construction of the interstate. It includes the **Parks in the Pines General Store** (12963 Historic Rte. 66), established in 1921, years before the highway was designated Route 66.

From Parks, I recommend that you stay away from I-40 for a while by taking Parks Road/Historic 66 westward. It becomes Wagon Wheel Road, and will lead you to **Deer Farm** (6769 Deer Farm Rd.), a petting zoo that includes several varieties of deer, plus some more recent acquisitions.

OLD 66 WEST OF **PARKS** ARIZONA

 Jump back onto I-40 near Deer Farm (see the reference map) for the run to Williams. Then use exit #165, which will take you into town along Grand Canyon Avenue (old 66). If you take a quick right after the "Williams – Gateway to the Grand Canyon" sign onto Rodeo Road, you'll find the Canyon Motel & RV Park here on the east edge of town. More details follow.

WILLIAMS

> **Highway 66 through Williams is divided into eastbound and westbound portions; don't forget to turn around when you reach the end of town so you can drive it in the other direction.**

Williams was the last town to be bypassed by the construction of the interstate in 1984. It therefore had the last active stretch of Route 66 and the last stoplight on I-40.

The town is named after Bill Williams, a prominent fur trapper who is widely believed to be the first white man in the area. There is a mountain south of town also bearing his name, as well as the **Bill Williams Trail**, also to the south of town.

Williams has a very nice stretch of vintage 66 running through town, lined with small motels and other tourist-related businesses. Williams, though small, was very well-developed for the motoring public, due in large part to its proximity to the Grand Canyon. Williams is the traditional jumping-off point for Grand Canyon National Park, which lies about sixty miles or so to the north. You should explore this town thoroughly.

WILLIAMS ATTRACTIONS

The renovated **Fray Marcos Hotel** (235 N. Grand Canyon Blvd.) was formerly a Harvey House and acts as both museum and depot for the Grand Canyon Railway, perhaps the most tradition-rich method of getting to the canyon. The railway was established in 1901, and from then until 1927, more than half of all canyon visitors came by train. Today, you can get a taste of the Old West by taking the train from Williams. The **Grand Canyon Depot**, at the end of the run at the canyon's south rim, is one of only three remaining log-constructed depots in the U.S., and is

You can spend your night in a railroad car in Williams, Arizona. GPS: 35.25821,-112.17099

Route 66 spirit is alive in Williams.
GPS: 35.25018,-112.18941

Williams, Arizona. GPS: 35.25166,-112.18500

on the National Register. It was built out of rustic logs in 1909 to complement the adjoining Ponderosa pine forest. At the Grand Canyon, facilities are plentiful, including a laundromat, post office, general store, and bank. The 1905 **El Tovar Hotel** (Apache St. and Center Rd.) is also nearby. Activities at the Grand Canyon include hiking, camping, mule rides to the bottom of the canyon, helicopter tours, and white-water rafting.

Notable businesses in Williams include the **Turquoise Teepee** (114 Historic Rte. 66) and **Rod's Steak House** (301 E. Rte. 66), a fixture on the route since 1945. The **Williams and Forest Service Visitor Center** (200 W. Railroad Ave.) has brochures to guide you on a historic walking tour of the city.

If you like unusual accommodations, be sure to check into the **Canyon Motel & RV Park** (1900 Historic Rte. 66) east of town. Besides the standard motel rooms and campsites, you can choose from a small collection of cabooses and other railcars.

At the west end of town, you'll need to rejoin I-40 at interchange #161. Between here and Ash Fork there are some Mother Road fragments back in the woods that are suitable for hiking or mountain biking. They get a pretty thorough treatment in Jerry McClanahan's *EZ66 Guide for Travelers*. For this narrative, we're going to stay with I-40 until exit #146 (Ash Fork).

ASH FORK

This is the self-proclaimed Flagstone Capital of the World. As we've seen in a number of other towns, Route 66 splits itself into eastbound and westbound portions, separated by a city block. Make sure to turn around and check out the eastbound portion before you move on. You'll need to enter I-40 at the west edge of town, but not for long (see below).

Ash Fork, Arizona. GPS: 35.22437,112.48345

DeSoto's Salon (314 W. Lewis Ave.) has a pretty well-preserved old car planted on its roof. On an older dead-end alignment of 66 is the local **historical museum** (Pine Ave.), which includes a detailed diorama depicting the town in its Route 66 heyday.

IMPORTANT: Between Ash Fork and Seligman is the Crookton Road exit (#139). This is the route to take in order to cruise the longest unbroken section of old 66 remaining: Seligman to Topock. From now on, and all the way to the California border (see the reference map), you will remain on old Route 66 and won't have to use any interstate highway at all. Yay! This stretch was so completely bypassed by I-40 that, today, it is as unspoiled as any section of the road anywhere, all the way to the Colorado River.

SELIGMAN

As you know, earlier alignments of Route 66 tended to cling close to the railroad tracks in town. So don't fail to explore Railroad Avenue, which is a block or so away from the official I-40 Business Loop (Chino Street). Both streets are genuine Route 66.

Seligman is home to the Delgadillo brothers, Angel and Juan. These brothers had a lot to do with the resurgence in interest in the old highway after its "final" demise. Angel used to run the barber shop in Seligman, and Juan (now deceased) operated the **Snow Cap Drive-In** (301 AZ-66). Juan's son now continues the tradition at the drive-in.

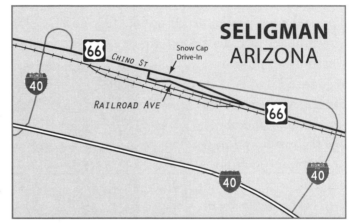

Snow Cap Drive In, Seligman, Arizona. GPS: 35.32622,-112.87302

Whether the place is open or closed, be sure to get out of your car and do some exploring on the grounds of the Snow Cap. It is chock-full of interesting artifacts, humorous signs, and other surprising touches.

A little ways past the Snow Cap is Angel's **Route 66 Gift Shop**

Seligman, Arizona. GPS: 35.32678,-112.87579

Seligman, Arizona. GPS: 35.32631,-112.87342

Seligman, Arizona.
GPS: 35.32689,-112.87654

and Visitor Center (22265 Historic Rte. 66) where, if you're lucky, Angel can share a few stories and you can stock up on Mother Road merchandise.

A little farther along is what's known as **Historic Seligman Sundries** (22405 Historic Rte. 66), in a building that was once home to a roadside store called Ted's at the Flagpole, as evidenced in an old postcard from that era.

Route 66, west of Seligman. GPS: 35.42061,-113.04711

AUDLEY-PICA-YAMPAI

This is a series of small communities strung out along Route 66 when the predecessor to the alignment you are now driving was still current. They are all just southwest of the modern-day road.

GRAND CANYON CAVERNS

Here's a good old-fashioned roadside attraction. Called Coconino Caverns on some old maps—and later, Dinosaur Caverns—the **Grand Canyon Caverns** (115 Mile Marker AZ-66) are accessed by an elevator that takes you twenty-one stories underground. Aside from the normal cave formations, attractions below include a mummified bobcat. Outside, you'll see dinosaur replicas lining the walkway to the front door. This complex has everything: motel rooms, a restaurant, a gift shop, and even an airstrip.

Grand Canyon Caverns, Arizona. GPS: 35.51770, -113.21947

 As you approach Peach Springs from the east, keep your eye on the north horizon. There is a point at which you can see all the way to the south rim of the Grand Canyon, which makes its closest approach to the highway along here.

It is possible to take Highway 18 from this vicinity (just east of Peach Springs) to a relatively untrammeled part of the Grand Canyon called **Hualapai Hilltop**. There is a rather demanding trail here that you can take down into the canyon to the remote village of Supai.

PEACH SPRINGS

The **Hualapai tribal headquarters** (941 Hualapai Way) are located here in Peach Springs. On the west side of town is **Indian Route 1**, which goes north to **Grand Canyon West Airport** (5001 Diamond Bar Rd.) and the **Grand Canyon Skywalk** (Eagle Point Rd.). The road is only partially paved. If you want to take in the Skywalk, it's best to make inquiries with Grand Canyon West to determine your best option—call (888) 868-9378.

TRUXTON

Here in Truxton is the former **Frontier Motel and Restaurant**, with a cluster of street signs standing out front. One says Will Rogers Highway, another says Historic Route 66, and a third tells us that

Truxton, Arizona.
GPS: 35.48477,-113.56337

this was the Beale Wagon Road, in use from 1857 to 1882.

CROZIER

Although the town of Crozier appears plainly on the path of Highway 66 in my 1957 atlas, Rittenhouse had already reported it as "bypassed" in 1946. It's near here that you'll

Truxton, Arizona. GPS: 35.48477,-113.56337

run across **Keepers of the Wild** (13441 AZ-66), a nonprofit sanctuary for rescued exotic animals.

VALENTINE

A scene from the movie *Easy Rider* was filmed here in Valentine on the south side of the highway, just west of the **Indian Agency** (13067

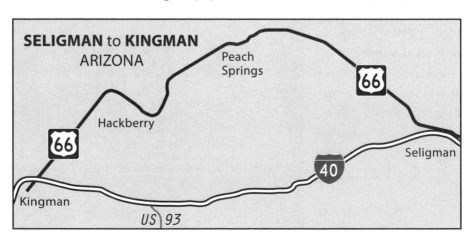

E. Hwy 66). In the movie, Peter Fonda fixes a flat tire in the background while a cowboy shoes a horse in the foreground, demonstrating that some things really don't change.

On the grounds of the Hackberry General Store. GPS: 35.37471,-113.72298

HACKBERRY

The **Hackberry General Store** (11255 AZ-66) is a must-stop. The old advertising signs and other assorted artifacts make it obligatory to get out of your vehicle and have a look around. Several years ago, this location was home to Bob Waldmire's International Bioregional Old Route 66 Visitor Center.

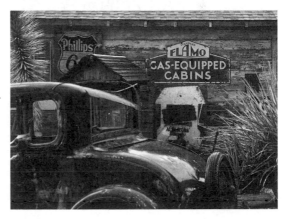

Hackberry, Arizona. GPS: 35.37471,-113.72298

KINGMAN

Follow Andy Devine Avenue all the way through town. There's a small park near the western edge of town that includes a retired steam locomotive from the Santa Fe line. It's there that you'll need to bear left in order to take the old Route 66 alignment into the hills toward Oatman.

This settlement was named for Lewis Kingman, a civil engineer with the Santa Fe railroad, in 1880. Today there's no mistaking Kingman, thanks to the huge beige-colored tower that's been painted with these words:

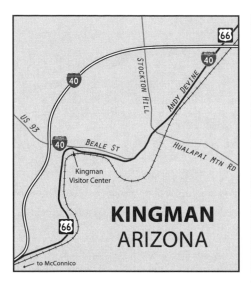

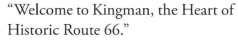

Public art in downtown Kingman, Arizona. GPS: 35.18887,-114.05309

"Welcome to Kingman, the Heart of Historic Route 66."

Kingman is the hometown of the well-known character actor Andy Devine, who grew up at the **Beale Hotel** (325 E. Andy Devine Ave.), which his parents used to run. Every September, the city throws **Andy Devine Days**, a week-long celebration in Devine's honor that includes a rodeo, parade, and various other events. Clark Gable and Carole Lombard got married at the local **Methodist Church** (1730 Kino Ave.) here in Kingman, and then raced down Route 66 to honeymoon in nearby Oatman. In the downtown area, one block from the

Kingman, Arizona. GPS: 35.18865,-114.05312

route, there is a nice neon sign at the **House of Hops** (312 E. Beale St.), formerly the Kingman Club.

Nightlife in Kingman, Arizona. GPS: 35.18972,-114.05400

KINGMAN ATTRACTIONS

The **Kingman Visitor Center** (120 W. Andy Devine Ave.) houses a Route 66 museum, including a theater showing short films and an extensive gift shop. You can also pick up a walking tour map here to historic sites in the city.

The **Bonelli House** (430 E. Spring St.) is a two-story mansion built in 1915, on the site of an earlier dwelling that burned down. Therefore, this structure was built of locally quarried tufa stone, a material valued for its fire resistance and its insulating, cool-in-the-summer characteristics. The home is maintained by the **Mohave Museum of History and Arts** (400 W. Beale St.), which also includes items relating to the town's favorite son, Andy Devine.

The **Kingman Army Air Field Museum** (4540 Flightline Dr.) is adjacent to the modern-day airport. This base in Kingman was one of a handful of sites assigned to dispose of thousands of warplanes at the close of World War II.

FURTHER AFIELD

South of Kingman is **Hualapai Mountain Park** (6230 Hualapai Mountain Rd.). Established in the 1930s, the park has several cabins constructed by the Civilian Conservation Corps. The scenery is beautiful, and there are several trails for hiking, as well as a campground.

North of Kingman is the near-ghost town of **Chloride**, founded in

1862. To reach Chloride, take U.S. 93 North. A sign will direct you to turn right on a county road to the small, now-quiet town of Chloride.

Also north of Kingman via U.S. 93 are **Lake Mead**, the **Boulder Dam**, and **Las Vegas**. Opinions on Las Vegas, Nevada, are generally of two kinds: love it, or hate it. I count myself among the few who don't feel strongly one way or the other. I don't care for the casino scene, but what I do like about Las Vegas is its location. My wife and I have used Vegas as a convenient launching pad for a number of other destinations. Easy day trips out of Las Vegas include **Death Valley**, **Zion National Park**, the ghost town of **Rhyolite**, and— of course—Route 66.

Vegas's other redeeming feature for Route 66 fans, at least as I see it, are its **signs and architecture**. If you think the Mother Road has some wild and kitschy signs and architecture, then Las Vegas has to be the record-holder. In Vegas, there are casinos and other businesses that mimic Hawaiian islands, pirate ships, castles, pyramids, miniature cities of the world, and much, much more, most of them open twenty-four hours a day and brightly lit all through the night. If Las Vegas should fall into disuse over the next generation or two, as Route 66 has, then it will make for some fine exploration one day for the ruin-hunters among us.

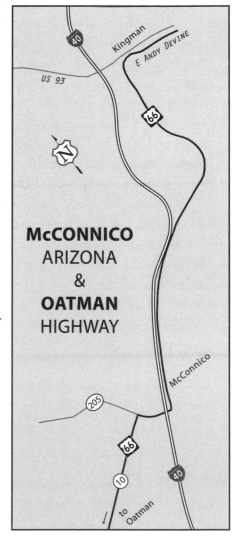

McCONNICO
ARIZONA
&
OATMAN
HIGHWAY

ROUTE 66 TV SERIES

In the fall of 1960, the CBS television network launched a weekly series called *Route 66*. On the show, two young men (portrayed by Martin Milner and George Maharis) traveled around the country in a Corvette and became involved in the lives of the people they met in each episode.

Although only a small number of the 100-plus episodes were actually filmed on Route 66, the series is notable for a number of reasons. The early 1960s were a transitional period in America, and the series took on themes that were unconventional—even daring—for the time. The two protagonists came into contact with a runaway heiress, a dying blues singer, and a heroin addict, to name just a few. They tackled issues such as gang violence, racism, labor unions, and mental illness at a time when most television shows stayed on safer ground.

Also notable about the program were the logistical challenges involved. The series was shot on location throughout the country (even in Canada) and required a crew of fifty to sixty people, along with two tractor-trailers full of equipment. It was probably the largest mobile filming operation in television history up to that time.

Guest stars on the show included some fading film stars such as Joan Crawford, but more interesting in retrospect is the roster of up-and-coming talent featured, including such now-familiar names as Rod Steiger, Suzanne Pleshette, and Robert Redford.

Returning to Route 66: Soon after leaving Kingman on old 66 near **Locomotive Park** (310 W. Beale St.) and the **Kingman Visitor Center** (120 W. Andy Devine Ave.), the scenery and terrain begin to change. Be mindful of the conditions out here; there are lots of dusty, gravelly switchbacks and plenty of low places in the road where flash flooding can occur.

McCONNICO

According to my 1957 atlas, roughly at McConnico there was a fork in the road, and today there still is. The older stretch of road went on to Oatman from here, but that alignment had already been bypassed. By 1957, official Route 66 went southward through Griffin and on to Yucca, Haviland, Powell, and Topock. That, of course, is the same alignment that was later upgraded to become Interstate 40. The narrative in this book covers the preferred route through Oatman. Begin by crossing over to the west side of I-40 at the #44 interchange, and then make a left turn onto Oatman Highway/County Road 10 (see the reference map on page 401).

About fifteen miles or so after crossing the interstate at McConnico, you'll encounter **Cool Springs Camp** (8275 W. Oatman Rd.). Not long ago it was little more than a pile of rubble, but this success story has made

Cool Springs Camp, a ruin beautifully restored, west of McConnico, Arizona.
GPS: 35.02731,-114.30879

a comeback, thanks to its caring owners. The structure was temporarily rebuilt in the early 1990s so that it could be destroyed in a scene for the film *Universal Soldier*. This time around, however, it's a keeper. About a mile or so past Cool Springs is what remains of **Ed's Camp**. After that, get ready for numerous switchbacks in the old highway.

GOLDROAD

Sitgreaves Pass, just east of Goldroad, was a very hard climb for vehicles in days gone by. Some cars and drivers had a very difficult time of it, and so there were wreckers in the area solely to haul hapless motorists over these crests. Some vehicles could make it in reverse, if not forward. The reason for this was two-fold: one, reverse is a substantially lower gear than first; and two, moving in reverse could overcome the shortcomings of early gravity-fed fuel delivery systems.

For some time, the old **Gold Road Mine** (10277 Oatman-Topock Hwy) had shut down production and was conducting public tours of the mine instead. Later, however, mining resumed and tours were discontinued when the price of gold went up enough to make mining worthwhile. They could be either mining or touring when you make your trip through here.

OATMAN

Mining was big business in this area through the 1930s and right up until the onset of World War II. The town was named after Olive Oatman, who was abducted by the Mojave Indians as a young girl and lived with them for several years.

You can't really get lost in Oatman, as there's just one road through it: old Route 66. This is a true Old West mining town that went through a ghost town phase and is now clinging to life as a tourist town. There are wooden plank sidewalks here, and the town's most celebrated inhabitants

Oatman, Arizona   *Color by Merle Porter*

are its **burros**, descendants of the beasts of burden that were brought here in the gold-mining days. There are feed dispensers scattered around town so that you can indulge them. Get out of your car and do some walking around here.

The old **Oatman Hotel** (181 Main St.) is where Clark Gable and

Oatman, Arizona. GPS: 35.02748,-114.38531

Burros really do run free in Oatman. GPS: 35.02571,-114.38286

Carole Lombard came for their honeymoon in 1939. You can view their suite (room 15) and lots more of the place just by wandering upstairs. The bar downstairs has walls that are covered in dollar bills. If you find a space, you can add one of your own.

Every July, Oatman holds an annual **Egg-Frying Contest**. Entrants use every solar-based gizmo imaginable to try and fry an egg in fifteen minutes or less. I've been told that the town's population sometimes increases tenfold for this event.

In the early 1960s, portions of *How the West Was Won* were filmed in Oatman and its environs.

GOLDEN SHORES-TOPOCK

Neither of these communities qualifies as much of a town. Golden Shores is really no more than a housing subdivision that sprouted where two roads merge. A view from the air reveals that Topock is virtually identical. *Topock* comes from the Mojave word meaning "water crossing," which is certainly appropriate.

There is an arching bridge (circa 1916) here that crosses the Colorado River, but it carries no vehicle traffic, only a pipeline. Today's Route 66 adventurer is forced to make the crossing on the I-40 bridge.

FURTHER AFIELD

Consider a side trip down Highway 95 to **Lake Havasu City**. In 1971, the London Bridge was painstakingly dismantled and re-assembled here in Lake Havasu City, piece by piece, and turned into a tourist attraction. The man who masterminded the plan originally thought he was buying London's Tower Bridge, which is much more picturesque, but after learning of his mistake, he decided to follow through with his plan anyway.

Route 66 has now passed through seven states on its journey west, and is now poised at the crossing of the Colorado River. The promised land of California awaits you on the opposite shore.

CALIFORNIA

After traversing the Illinois prairie, the Missouri Ozark country, the Indian Territory of Oklahoma, the Panhandle of Texas, the old Spanish colony of New Mexico, and the harsh landscape of

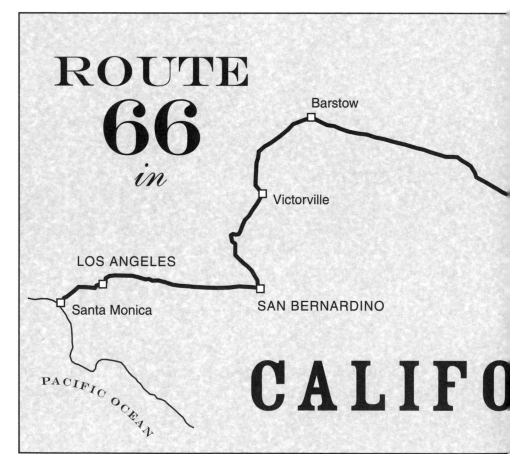

Arizona, Route 66 finally arrives at the doorstep of California.

California, the land of milk and honey; the land where dreams live, fortunes are built, and the soul longs to be. Surely this is where the end of the rainbow must lie. But Nature can be a cruel provider. Although the Colorado River, threshold to the Golden State, is a welcome sight to the traveler who has arrived after crossing the desert of western Arizona, the fabled land on the other side looks no more inviting than that which has tested him for more than 100 miles already.

How cruel it must have seemed to the Okies fleeing the Depression that even in California, the land appeared barren and forsaken. Greeting them here at the border was no Xanadu, but rather the dusty town of

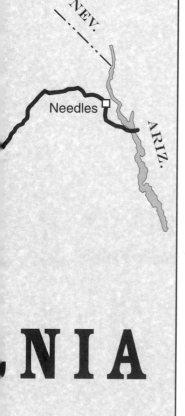

Needles and many more miles of Mojave Desert yet to be crossed. The river is not an end to the desert; it's only a reference point.

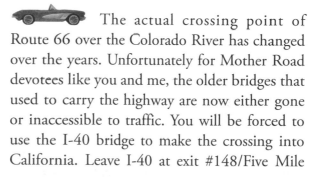 The actual crossing point of Route 66 over the Colorado River has changed over the years. Unfortunately for Mother Road devotees like you and me, the older bridges that used to carry the highway are now either gone or inaccessible to traffic. You will be forced to use the I-40 bridge to make the crossing into California. Leave I-40 at exit #148/Five Mile

Road. Turn left at the end of the ramp to cross to the west side and merge with U.S. 95 heading north.

NEEDLES

 Route 66 passes through town primarily on Broadway, but as you've learned to suspect, earlier in its life it took a path alongside the railroad tracks—in this case, Front Street.

Established in 1883 as a stop on the railroad, Needles is known for being one of the hottest places in the United States. Temperatures frequently exceed 100 degrees Fahrenheit. Named for the rocky outcroppings across the river in Arizona, Needles was once the home of *Peanuts* cartoonist Charles Schulz, who often used Needles and the surrounding desert as the setting for Snoopy's cousin Spike. The river bath scene in *The Grapes of Wrath* was filmed here in Needles back in the 1930s.

Keep an eye out for the **66 Motel** (91 Desnok St.), on the eastern outskirts of town, which has a neon sign in decent condition. As you pass through the town of Needles, there are still a number of buildings to see that are from the Route 66 era.

As you enter Needles from the east, you'll see an old **wagon** beside

On the California side of the Colorado River. GPS: 34.71542,-114.48944

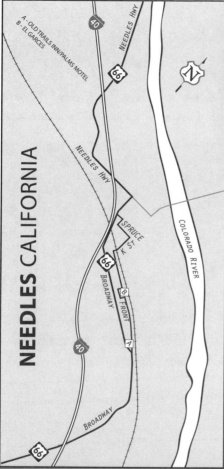

NEEDLES CALIFORNIA

One of the countless roadside businesses named for the highway that brought customers to their doorsteps. Needles, California. GPS: 34.83331,-114.59623

the road that is said to be the same twenty-mule-team wagon used in the old *Death Valley Days* television show, which starred Ronald Reagan. Just across from it is a former motel that was known variously as either the **Old Trails Inn** or the **Palms Motel**.

This authentic wagon welcomes the westbound traveler to Needles, California. GPS: 34.83646,-114.60017

The colonnaded rail depot in Needles was named El Garces. GPS: 34.84020,-114.60658

Needles, California. GPS: 34.83637,-114.60019

On Front Street, an older alignment of Route 66 that goes through Needles, sits **El Garces** (149 G St.). This Santa Fe depot and hotel was built shortly after an earlier structure was destroyed by a fire in 1906. It was designed with distinctive columns and balconies, which are unusual for this part of the country. Near El Garces is the **Needles Chamber of Commerce** (100 G St.), whose staff can furnish you with information about the surrounding area.

 Historic 66 crosses over I-40 in the northeastern part of town, and becomes River Road/Bernardino County Road 66. Veer left onto National Trails Highway. When it comes to a "T," turn left and join I-40 at Interchange #139.

HOMER-GOFFS-FENNER

Exit I-40 with U.S. 95 (exit #133) in order to experience less interstate and more Route 66. In about six miles, and just prior to crossing the railroad tracks, turn west on Goffs Road/San Bernardino County Road 66.

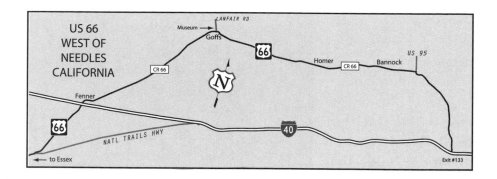

The loop that includes Homer, Goffs, and Fenner was cut off from Route 66 at an early date. The later alignment took a more direct path, from Needles straight to Essex. You won't see much evidence of Homer other than Homer-Klinefelter Road, which you passed while on U.S. 95.

Goffs is situated right at the edge of the **Mojave National**

Goffs, California. GPS: 34.92091,-115.06705

Preserve. The crown jewel is a schoolhouse dating from 1914 that was meticulously restored by the **Mojave Desert Heritage & Cultural Association** (37198 Lanfair Rd.) from 1998 to 1999. The association maintains what must be the largest collection of Mojave Desert historical materials anywhere. Aside from the ma-

Old schoolhouse, Goffs, California.
GPS: 34.92091,-115.06705

terials and exhibits displayed within the schoolhouse, there are dozens of artifacts, including vehicles, mining equipment, and a tiny portable courthouse, all on display outside in a self-guided tour format. In 2008, the association also installed the **Dennis G. Casebier Memorial Library**, which is a replica of the Goffs Santa Fe Railway Depot that graced the town from 1902 to 1956. Operating hours at the complex are limited, but you can call ahead at (760) 733-4482.

Fenner is nothing more than a small set of travelers' service stations offering fuel and snacks where Goffs Road crosses I-40. Continue past I-40 on Goffs Road toward Essex.

ESSEX

It was here in the Mojave Desert near Essex that U.S. troops under General Patton trained for desert conditions in preparation for the anticipated confrontation with General Erwin Rommel's (the Desert Fox) troops in North Africa. There is a **public well** (now dry) here that once offered free drinks of water to Route 66 travelers generations ago.

Essex, California. GPS: 34.73475,-115.24594

From Essex, and virtually all the way to Amboy, there is an intermittent **berm**, or small bank, along the north side of the highway. Individuals have placed small stones and other detritus here to spell out words, make outlines, or otherwise communicate with future passersby. Among the symbols are peace signs, various initials, a Route 66 shield, and many more that are difficult either to describe or to comprehend. One can easily become entranced by looking at this artwork for mile after mile through the side window.

DANBY-CADIZ SUMMIT

There is a cluster of **old buildings** in the former community of Danby, including a fuel station and/or market, that are now cut off from the

Ruins at Cadiz Summit. GPS: 34.56971,-115.48523

Former tourist complex at Chambless, California. GPS: 34.56196,-115.54433

highway by a chain-link fence.

At Cadiz Summit, you'll find the remains of a small **tourist complex**, the ruined buildings now festooned with graffiti.

CHAMBLESS

At Chambless, you'll see the remains of a **tourist complex** with several boarded-up cabins. Also, the remains of a huge **restaurant sign with a roadrunner logo** are baking in the desert a little farther west.

Chambless, California. GPS: 34.56148,-115.57298

AMBOY

For many years, the property owners here tried to capitalize on the isolated highwayside atmosphere here in Amboy. I saw some magazine ads extolling the virtues of the place for location filming, commercials, and so forth. I agree; in fact, I think this would make an excellent setting for an episode of *The Twilight Zone*. The **Roy's Motel & Café** complex (87520 National Trails Hwy) definitely has that certain something. The large, circa-1959 sign is one of the most iconic on all of Route 66.

A new owner promises that Amboy, California, is on the rebound.
GPS: 34.55863,-115.74277

Roy's Motel, Amboy, California.
GPS: 34.55863,-115.74277

In 2005, the whole town was bought by a new owner—lock, stock, and barrel. The goal is to once again have Amboy humming with tourists stopping for fuel and other traveler's needs. Stop in and see how things are progressing.

Amboy Crater. GPS: 34.55704,-115.78097

FURTHER AFIELD

Amboy Crater is just a mile or two south of the highway. There is a turn-off to the dormant volcano just west of Amboy proper. The crater itself is accessible via a three-mile trail (round-trip) from the parking area.

For the truly adventurous, south of Amboy near Twentynine Palms is **Joshua Tree National Park**. Featured are a number of hiking trails, including one about four miles long leading to the largest group of palms. A shorter trail (less than two miles) takes you to an oasis at Fortynine Palms Canyon. There is also a restored ranch within the confines of the park, where park rangers offer guided tours.

BAGDAD-SIBERIA

Bagdad is the inspiration for the name of the movie *Bagdad Café*, though the film was actually shot a little farther down the highway in Newberry Springs (see page 419). At one time, there actually was a Bagdad Café here, with a changing cast of road-weary travelers making up its clientele, but it's long gone. Satellite photos show evidence that there were structures here in the past, but nowadays you'll be hard-pressed to see much of anything from the vantage point of your car.

Siberia seems an odd name for a community in the Mojave Desert, but it's somewhat in keeping with the community of Klondike nearby (a short distance off of 66). I suppose one name inspired the other. Today, only a few building foundations remain in Siberia.

LUDLOW

This town was established circa 1882 by the Ludlow Mining Company. Most of the Mother Road-era part of town is now privately owned by the railroad and is slowly wasting away. The old **Ludlow Mercantile Company building**, which was constructed in 1908, is now partially collapsed and no longer as photogenic. The old **Ludlow Café** has burned to the ground. The town hasn't completely died off, however, thanks to an I-40 interchange.

When it's time to depart Ludlow, don't jump onto the interstate. Instead, cross I-40 and take the north frontage road. Cross the interstate again (to the south side) at Lavic Road (overpass). My 1957 map of the region shows no community by that name, only the **Lavic Dry Lake** to the south. A little farther west and just south of Route 66 is another extinct volcanic crater—**Pisgah Crater** (Pisgah Crater Rd.)—in case you missed the one near Amboy.

NEWBERRY SPRINGS

In Newberry Springs, there's an old Whiting Brothers station behind a fence named **Dry Creek Station** (46731 Historic Rte. 66). There are some wonderful old pumps standing out front.

Former Whiting Brothers station, Newberry Springs.
GPS: 34.81884,-116.64014

The **Bagdad Café** (46548 National Trails Hwy) is also here (formerly named the Sidewinder). As mentioned earlier, this is where the 1980s movie of the same name was filmed.

 The highway will cross to the north side of I-40. At about where Barstow-Daggett Airport is on your right, old 66 picks up on the opposite side of the railroad track. You can either turn right at Hidden Springs Road to take that early alignment into town, or you can do as I do, which is continue straight into town and then, as part of my routine exploration, turn east on Santa Fe Street to see that section that formed the early eastern approach to Daggett.

Just before you reach town, to the north of the highway, you'll see what is called a **Solar Concentrator**. This is one of the latest high-tech methods for converting solar light and heat into useful energy.

DAGGETT

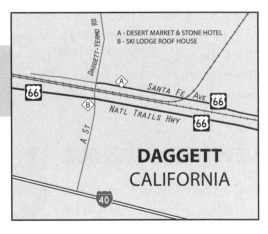

Don't miss out on the older alignment of Route 66, Santa Fe Street, north of the railroad tracks.

In Daggett stands the **Stone Hotel**, frequented in its day by the likes of Tom Mix, Death Valley Scotty, and John Muir. The hotel was constructed in the 1880s (some sources say even earlier), and has walls that are some two feet thick.

Also in town is the **Desert Market** (35596 Santa Fe Ave.), built in 1908, which in its day was the place local miners came to exchange their findings for legal tender.

In Daggett there is a building with an unusual shape to its roof that

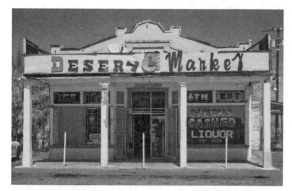

Daggett, California. GPS: 34.86340,-116.88528

This unusual building dates from 1926, the same year Route 66 was established. Daggett, California. GPS: 34.86276,-116.88849

is locally known as the **Ski Lodge Roof House** (Historic Rte. 66 and Daggett-Yermo Rd.). It originally opened as a visitor information center in 1926, the same year our beloved highway was designated as "Route 66."

The **Daggett Museum** (33703 2nd St.) includes a collection of railroad china and Navajo code-talkers' memorabilia.

FURTHER AFIELD

North of Daggett, near the small town of Yermo, is the **Ghost Town of Calico** (36600 Ghost Town Rd.), a true Old West silver-mining town dating from 1881. Calico was also a source of borax, a mineral known to mankind since ancient times that can be used for pottery glazing as well as an ingredient in fertilizers and detergents.

One-third of Calico's buildings are original, with the rest being carefully recreated to evoke the late nineteenth century. The town site covers about sixty acres, and includes a downtown business district, miners' quarters, tours of an actual mine, and an operating narrow-gauge railroad. The town has been a filming location for numerous television shows and movies over the years, thanks to its authentic look and feel. It also holds a number of festivals throughout the year, notably the

At the tourist-oriented "ghost town" of Calico, California. GPS: 34.94799,-116.86502

Calico Spring Festival in May, which includes a chili cook-off, music festival, and the World Tobacco Spitting Championship. **Calico Days** occurs every October and features a parade, burro races, and the National Gunfight Championship.

A little to the east of Yermo and the ghost town is the **Calico Early Man Archaeological Site** (Minneola Rd.). This archaeological dig, begun in 1964 by Dr. Louis Leakey, has pushed back the date for the presence of man on this continent by thousands of years. Stone tools have been found here as much as 200,000 years old, making it one of the oldest tool-bearing sites in the Western Hemisphere. Public tours of the facility are available year-round.

 Back on 66: After just a short distance on National Trails Highway, you'll be forced to join I-40 briefly in order to get around the U.S. Marine Corps base. Exit again at E. Main Street (exit #2).

BARSTOW

Enter town on E. Main/National Trails Highway/Business Loop 15.

Named in 1886 for the president of the Santa Fe Railroad at the time, Barstow has a number of vintage Route 66-era signs and buildings to make you slow down and explore. Not the least of these is the **El Rancho**

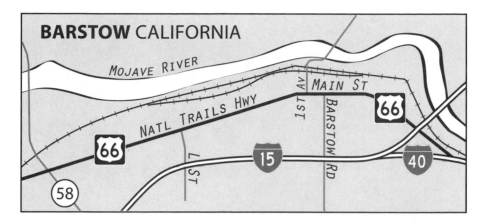

BARSTOW CALIFORNIA

Barstow Motel (112 E. Main St.), with its 100-foot-tall neon sign supported by twin towers. Much of the motel was constructed using discarded railroad ties from the defunct Tidewater & Tonopah Railroad.

Around 1940, Barstow was visited by avant-garde musician and part-time hobo Harry Partch, whose composition, "Barstow," was inspired by some hitchhiker markings he saw on a highway railing on the outskirts of town.

Downtown Barstow, California.
GPS: 34.89874,-117.02633

BARSTOW ATTRACTIONS

Barstow is home to another fine example of the Harvey House hotels from the glory days of rail travel: the **Casa del Desierto** (685 N. 1st Ave.). Located inside are the Barstow Route 66 Mother Road Museum and the Western America Railroad Museum.

This railroad depot in Barstow now houses the Route 66 Mother Road Museum and the Western America Railroad Museum. GPS: 34.90504,-117.02544

There are several history-oriented murals in Barstow known collectively as the **Main Street Murals**. Subjects for the artwork include the local Harvey House, the Mormon Trail, and Route 66. You can take a guided walking tour of the murals, or you can go all out and view them from atop a wagon pulled by a pair of Belgian draft horses. For advance tickets and other information, call (760) 257-1052.

The **Mojave River Valley Museum** (270 E. Virginia Way) is dedicated to the history and culture of the area. Their collection includes local newspapers going back to 1911 and more than 20,000 photographs.

The **Desert Discovery Center** (831 Barstow Rd.) has on display the second-largest space rock ever found in the United States. The Old Woman Meteorite is about three feet across and weighs about three tons.

Barstow, California.

LENWOOD

 From Lenwood through Helendale, Oro Grande, and some miles beyond, you'll be far away from the interstate, so the driving will be super easy. Just keep following National Trails Highway to Victorville.

Lenwood is just west of Barstow, and seems in danger of losing its identity due to its proximity to its larger neighbor. Lenwood Road, however, and several businesses do use "Lenwood" in their names.

HELENDALE

Most of Helendale is off the highway, on the other side of the railroad tracks, but you will see the landmark **Helendale Market** (26428 National Trails Hwy) alongside 66. The empty lot next door features an antique Polly Gasoline sign.

HELENDALE ATTRACTIONS

About halfway between Helendale and Oro Grande is a veritable **forest of bottle trees** (24266 National Trails Hwy)—the creation of Elmer Long, who lives on the property and has been fashioning his brand of

Helendale, California. GPS: 34.73006,-117.32739

Elmer Long's forest of "bottle trees" awaits today's traveler just west of Helendale, California. GPS: 34.69057,-117.33925

folk art since about 2000. Some of the bottles are old and dusty, while others are quite new and shiny, revealing the fact that this is indeed a work in progress.

ORO GRANDE

Oro Grande has a very small former business district right on the highway. The most notable structures in Oro Grande are an enormous **cement plant** and a small **building with a curved facade** that has changed uses over the years.

Part of the Oro Grande business district. GPS: 34.60031,-117.33759

VICTORVILLE

The highway will cross beneath I-40 and become Victorville's D Street. Turn right on 7th and pass through downtown.

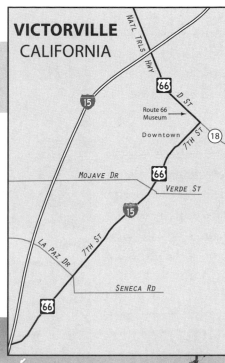

VICTORVILLE
CALIFORNIA

You need to stop and spend a little time in Victorville. Here, you'll find the **California Route 66 Museum** (16825 D St.), located in a former roadhouse that was known as the Red Rooster Café. The folks here are friendly and knowledgeable, so you can gather whatever

Route 66 Museum, Victorville, California. GPS: 34.53751,-117.29455

materials and tips you'll need for the remainder of your journey.

Formerly here in Victorville was the Roy Rogers Muse-um, which moved to Branson, Missouri in 2003 and later closed permanently. You can still see a hint of the museum's influence, though, in the sign at the nearby **New Corral Motel** (14643 7th St.). The rearing Palomino in the motel sign is a distinct echo of a figure of Trigger that used to stand in front of the museum.

Downtown Victorville. GPS: 34.53382,-117.29568

Decades-old business on the east side of Victorville, California. GPS: 34.54071,-117.29849

Leaving Victorville via 7th Street on the west edge of town, you'll need to enter Interstate 15 southbound and take it for several miles.

CAJON PASS AREA

At the Oak Hill exit (#138) is the **Summit Inn** (5970 Mariposa Rd.), which has been operating at this location since 1952. Not only is this

Cajon Summit. GPS: 34.35945,-117.43511

Monument erected In 1917, Cajon Junction. GPS: 34.30631,-117.46678

an authentic stop from the Route 66 era, there are also a number of relics on display outside, including some old vehicles and several items of antique gas station equipment. Inside, the menu includes such exotics as bison and ostrich burgers, and you can take your chances asking questions of a fortune-telling machine similar to one featured in a well-known *Twilight Zone* episode starring William Shatner.

It's in this vicinity that Route 66 crosses the **Pacific Crest Trail**, a hiking trail that runs all the way from the Mexican border to the Canadian border, a distance of more than 2,600 miles. This trail was established at the same time as the more well-known Appalachian Trail in the east, and covers much more rugged terrain. It passes beneath I-15 along here.

The narrow Cajon Pass has several sets of railroad tracks passing through it, as well as traces of **old Route 66 alignments**. Unfortunately, most are difficult or impossible to gain access to. You have to try pretty hard just to spot some of them.

A little past the Summit Inn is a spot called **Cajon Junction,** the

**Cajon Boulevard, just outside San Bernardino.
GPS: 34.15565,-117.33369**

junction with State Highway 138, at exit #131. Here you'll find a small obelisk-shaped marker a short distance to the south, on the east service road. The inscription reads: "Santa Fe and Salt Lake Trail 1849. Erected in honor of the brave pioneers of California in 1917 by pioneers." West on Highway 138 from this same exit, if you choose to explore the area, are some weathered rock formations known as **Mormon Rocks**, with a few hiking trails.

You'll need to return to I-15 and then leave it again at exit #129/Cleghorn Road. Follow Cajon Boulevard, which parallels the freeway on its western side. Rejoin I-15 at Kenwood Rd./exit #124. Shortly after, I-15 splits into I-15 and I-215—you'll want to use I-215. Exit #54 is what you want, but there may be serious roadwork in this vicinity that might make this impractical. You can continue a bit further to exit #50 for the continuation of Cajon Boulevard toward San Bernardino.

Just prior to reaching the city

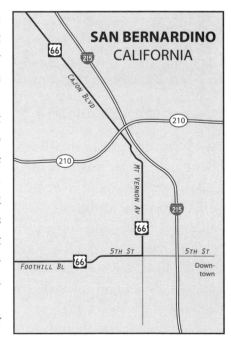

you can see the remains of two old 66-era motels, the **El Cajon Motel** and the **Palms Motel**. They are in very bad shape, but the old neon signs are still legible.

SAN BERNARDINO

Enter the city outskirts on Cajon Boulevard, which parallels some railroad tracks on your left. Just after passing beneath Highway 210, bear right onto Mt. Vernon Avenue. If you miss it, you'll actually have a second chance moments later, so don't sweat it. Mt. Vernon will take you to 5th, where you'll turn right and head westward (the road will become Foothill Boulevard). Note that Route 66 pretty much misses most of San Bernardino, so consider whether you want to break away from the highway for a while and investigate some of the listed attractions.

San Bernardino, California.
GPS: 34.13376,-117.31390

The County of San Bernardino is the largest in the nation—you've been in it ever since crossing the Colorado River from Arizona!

Once you reach San Bernardino, the pace of the road quickens noticeably, even though you are not traveling on the interstate; you might say that there's a sea change. You are beginning to enter the Southern California megalopolis, or what is euphemistically referred to as Greater L.A. From now on, you will be hard-pressed to observe everything you want to and still drive safely. You're getting a taste of what happened to Route 66 and the other major highways like her, a development that led to widespread

San Bernardino, California. GPS: 34.10645,-117.29546

public support to replace them with limited-access superhighways.

It was here in San Bernardino, in 1948, that the McDonald brothers sounded the first death knell for mom-and-pop hamburger joints everywhere. What began as the very first McDonald's restaurant is now the **Original McDonald's Site and Museum** (1398 N. E St.). Part of the structure is dedicated to displays pertaining to the history of the McDonald's fast-food empire, and part of it is filled with photos, highway signs, and other memorabilia associated with the Mother Road.

SAN BERNARDINO ATTRACTIONS

San Bernardino is home to the **California Theater** (562 W. 4th St.), a 1928 Spanish Colonial Revival showplace. It was at this theater that Will Rogers made his last public appearance—to benefit the Salvation Army—prior to his death in Alaska a couple of months later. The California Theater was an early "soundie," outfitted for sound even though *The Jazz Singer* had only been released about one year prior. Today, the restored California Theater hosts live stage performances, including opera and symphony.

The **San Bernardino Historical and Pioneer Society Museum** (796 N D St.), which is located in an 1891 mansion, includes a primitive iron jail cell on its grounds that some historians claim was built around 1860.

Perris Hill Park (1135 E. Highland Ave.) has several interesting concrete picnic tables that were salvaged from a defunct roadside picnic area on Route 66 called Camp Cajon.

FURTHER AFIELD

Southeast of San Bernardino is the city of Redlands, which is home to a mission dating from 1819, the **Asistencia Mission de San Gabriel** (26930 Barton Rd.). Also in Redlands are: the **Marmalade Mansions** (1 E Blvd.), a large number of Victorian homes from the era when "citrus was king"; the **Historical Glass Museum** (1157 Orange St.), which features American glassware from the early 1800s; and the world's tallest water slide, at **Splash Kingdom Waterpark** (1101 California St.).

East of San Bernardino is Big Bear Lake. Once known as Southern California's favorite mountain getaway, this area offers trails for hiking and mountain biking, and seasonal skiing in the surrounding San Bernardino National Forest. Big Bear Lake has also been called Hollywood's Backlot. Numerous films have been shot here, including such well-known classics as *Birth of a Nation*, *Kissin' Cousins*, *The Parent Trap*, *Dr. Doolittle*, and *Creature from the Black Lagoon*. In May, Big Bear Lake hosts the **Trout Classic**, during which some 400 contestants participate in trophy trout fishing. In the summertime the area hosts **Old Miners' Days**, with a chili cook-off, parade, and cowboy shoot-out. A motorcycle rally, called the **Ladies of the Harley Mountain Fun Run**, takes place each August. To get to Big Bear Lake, you can choose between two very scenic highways: Route 18 (Rim of the World Drive) or Route 38. Each includes scenic overlooks of the area.

RIALTO

Since you're now in one of those "Greater Metropolitan" areas, you probably won't notice the transition as you drive out of San Bernardino and into Rialto. The name of the street doesn't change, either—it will remain

Wigwam Village Motel, Rialto, California. GPS: 34.10698,-117.34996

Foothill Boulevard for some time.

Here in Rialto is the sister to the Wigwam Village we saw earlier in Holbrook, Arizona. This one, now called the **Wigwam Motel** (2728 E. Foothill Blvd.), was lovingly restored in 2004, after new owners took over and reversed years of neglect. In recognition of this enormous effort, they were presented with the Cyrus Avery Preservation Award in September of 2005.

The **Rialto Historical Society** (205 N. Riverside Ave.) claims to be "the best-kept secret in Rialto." Based in a picturesque old Christian church, the historical society has converted the adjoining church school building into a museum of local history.

FONTANA

The notorious Hells Angels Motorcy-cle Club was founded in Fontana in 1948. The name, which officially no longer contains an apostrophe, was originally used by U.S. air squadrons during both World Wars, and is also the title of a Hollywood film star-ring Jean Harlow. The **Hells Angels**

Roadside orange vendors were once common on this part of Route 66. Fontana, California. GPS: 34.10652,-117.46922

Clubhouse (19th St. and Medical Center Dr.) is here in Fontana.

The Deco-inspired **Center Stage Theater** (8463 Sierra Ave.) underwent a full renovation before its grand reopening in 2008. It now hosts a live dinner theater.

Be on the lookout for an old orange stand outside the long-established **Bono's Restaurant** (15395 E. Foothill Blvd.). The inscription over the window reads "Bono's Historic Orange." You are in what was once the heart of citrus country.

RANCHO CUCAMONGA

Cucamonga is thought to be a Shoshone word meaning "sandy place." This really was a large ranch at one time, and the area eventually found itself awash in vintners. At the corner of Foothill and Vineyard, there used to be an old wine barrel with an inscription declaring that this was once the

site of the oldest vine-
yard in California.

The **Sycamore Inn** (8318 E. Foothill
Blvd.), which dates
from 1848, served
as a stagecoach stop
in the days before
motorized travel. In
the eighteenth cen-
tury, Spanish visitors
named this area Ar-
royo de los Osos, or
Bear Gulch, and to-

In the heart of wine country, Rancho Cucamonga,
California. GPS: 34.10679,-117.61084

day there is a small stone monument out front featuring a bear sculpture.

Just a little farther west is the **Magic Lamp Inn** (8189 E. Foothill
Blvd.). The neon sign out front, which is shaped like Aladdin's lamp,
actually spouts a gas flame when the sign is illuminated each evening.

The **Sam Maloof Residence, Workshop, and Gardens** (5131
Carnelian St.) is located just north, in the neighboring community of
Alta Loma. Maloof was a highly regarded designer and maker of fine

Rancho Cucamonga, California. GPS: 34.10671,-117.59414

This figure stands in front of the Sycamore Inn, Rancho Cucamonga, California.
GPS: 34.10530,-117.62411

This establishment began life as a stagecoach stop. Rancho Cucamonga, California.
GPS: 34.10510,-117.62355

furniture. He passed away in 2009, and today his hand-built residence and adjoining workshop are open for tours.

UPLAND

In Upland is the twelfth and final **Madonna of the Trail monument** (N. Euclid Ave.), signifying the end of the National Old Trails Highway.

The **Cooper Historical Museum** preserves and interprets the heritage of Upland and its surrounding communities. Their displays can be found in two separate locations: the main

One of a series of monuments marking the old National Trails Highway. Upland, California. GPS: 34.10710,-117.65106

location at 217 E. A Street, and another at 525 W. 18th Street. The building on A Street was designed in the Art Moderne style, built in 1937 by the Ontario-Cucamonga Fruit Exchange.

South of Upland, in Chino, is the **Planes of Fame Air Museum** (7000 Merrill Ave.), featuring WWII aircraft and memorabilia.

CLAREMONT

This city is home to the Claremont Colleges, a collection of several affiliated colleges in a park-like setting spanning some 300 acres.

The old Claremont High School building has been converted into a small retail and office center called the **Old School House** (Foothill Blvd. and Indian Hill Blvd.). There is some decorative tiling around the main entrance in the Art Nouveau style.

The **PFF Bank & Trust** (393 W. Foothill Blvd.) sports a decorative mural facing Route 66.

The **Folk Music Center Museum** (220 Yale Ave.) houses a collection of

Claremont, California.
GPS: 34.10713,-117.72101

musical instruments accumulated since the center's establishment more than fifty years ago. They also sponsor a folk music festival every spring.

Claremont Heritage (840 N. Indian Hill Blvd.) administers a collection of maps, photographs, postcards, and citrus growers' materials in a historic former residence. They can also provide you with a brochure for a self-guided walking tour of local points of interest.

LA VERNE

La Verne has an "old town" section known as **Lordsburg**, which has an interesting walking tour featuring a town square, public murals, and such varied architectural gems as an Armenian college, a residential row characterized by Craftsman bungalows, and a distinctive water filtration plant. Details are available at the **La Verne Chamber of Commerce** (2078 Bonita Ave.).

SAN DIMAS

San Dimas, though not well-known as a Route 66 town, was the setting for the cult film classic *Bill and Ted's Excellent Adventure*, with comedian George Carlin in a key supporting role.

The real San Dimas is a former citrus-growing region that is quite equestrian-oriented today. A large equestrian center is

San Dimas, California. GPS: 34.10668,-117.80761

**Historic residence now serving as a restaurant, San Dimas, California.
GPS: 34.10717,-117.80711**

visible from the highway and yellow "horse crossing" warning signs dot the roads. There is also a very nice old **downtown district** that is worth visiting, with late-nineteenth-century commercial buildings and plank sidewalks. To find the downtown area, leave 66 at San Dimas Avenue, turn south, and drive several blocks to Bonita Avenue. There is also a small 1930s-era Santa Fe depot in the downtown area that now houses the **San Dimas Historical Society** (121 N. San Dimas Ave.). In front of the depot is a water fountain and trough built to serve "both man and beast."

On San Dimas Avenue, just north of Bonita, is a very large residence known as the Walker House. According to the San Dimas Historical Society, it is the last standing railroad hotel in California, and was later used as a residence by Mr. J. W. Walker, a prominent local citizen. In 2009, a full restoration was completed, and the building has recently started a new life as a restaurant, **Lucabella at the Walker House** (121 N. San Dimas Ave.).

Right about where San Dimas transitions to Glendora is the **Pinnacle Peak Steak House** (269 W. Foothill Blvd.). There is a covered wagon out front to attract your attention.

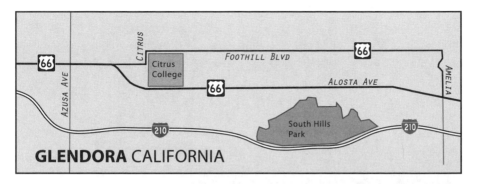

GLENDORA

Glendora has two Route 66 corridors. The later alignment (formerly Alosta, but renamed "Route 66") is the better-known of the two, but it's really more of a bypass route. To explore the earlier alignment, turn right at Amelia Avenue, which will then take you left onto old Foothill Boulevard. Along this older route are lots of classic bungalows for your inner architect to enjoy.

Glendora, California. GPS: 34.12888,-117.84283

AZUSA

Azusa calls itself "Canyon City." How the name Azusa came about is the subject of some debate. One explanation I've read (which I assume to be tongue-in-cheek) is that it came from a local general store that was said to provide "everything from A to Z in the USA." A more serious explanation states that the area was at one time inhabited by a group of Shoshoneans calling themselves Asuksa-gna.

Azusa, California, also calls itself "Canyon City." This relic of a sign has since been replaced. GPS: 34.13352,-117.91191

The **Azusa Foothill Drive-In** (675 E. Foothill Blvd.) was still operating when I drove through here for the first time. In 2001, however, the nearby Azusa Pacific University acquired the property and obtained permission to demolish the theater. The old marquee, however, still stands.

Azusa's business district is just north of Foothill on Azusa Avenue. Just north of the business district is a residential area lined with extremely tall, slender **palm trees** that remind me of the introductory footage from the *Beverly Hillbillies* television series. See if you agree.

DUARTE

In Duarte is **Justice Brothers, Inc.** (2734 E. Huntington Dr.), a manufacturer of automotive products since shortly after

The Capri Motel has been replaced by a residential complex. GPS: 34.13982,-117.95245

the Second World War, with a history of building and sponsoring race cars. Today, you can see the racing museum they've assembled right here at their world headquarters.

The Duarte Historical Society operates the **Duarte Historical Museum** (777 Encanto Pkwy). The building is a former residence that was moved to the location in 1990. Exhibits include an extensive collection of local-area fruit crate labels.

MONROVIA

In Monrovia is a very old **gasoline station** (Shamrock Ave. and Walnut Ave.) that, so far, has avoided the wrecking ball (see the reference map).

The **Aztec Hotel** (311 W. Foothill) was built in 1925—just in time for the inauguration of Route 66—and is on the National Register. The hotel is designed in a style the architect termed "Mayan Revival," but it was named the Aztec Hotel because it was thought that Americans would consider it less obscure and would more readily identify with it.

Old Town Monrovia is an area of several blocks, centered at the intersection of Myrtle Avenue and Lime Avenue, featuring small businesses, theaters, galleries, and restaurants. You can park at the curb and wander around, enjoying the small-town neighborhood feel. They even have street parties every Friday for most of the year.

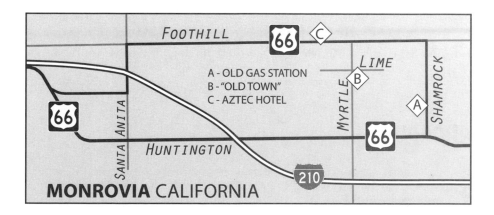

Vintage filling station on old 66, Monrovia, California. GPS: 34.14384,-117.99079

Monrovia, California. GPS: 34.15137,-118.00574

You can also visit author and activist **Upton Sinclair's residence** (464 N. Myrtle Ave.) in Monrovia, where he lived for more than twenty years.

ARCADIA

 In Arcadia, Huntington Drive splits just before Santa Anita Park (the race-track). You'll need to take the right-hand fork (Colorado Boulevard) in order to follow Route 66.

In Arcadia, the **Santa Anita Park racetrack** (285 W. Huntington Dr.) is widely regarded as an architectural treasure, exhibiting design elements of Art Deco, Spanish Revival, American Colonial, and New Orleans styles. It was designed by Gordon Kaufmann, the same architect who designed the massive Hoover Dam on the Colorado River. Out front is a bronze statue of the racehorse Seabiscuit, whose most famous comeback race occurred here at this track. Santa Anita was also the setting for the Marx Brothers film classic, *A Day at the Races*. During WWII, it was used as a detention center for Japanese Americans, including George Takei of *Star Trek* fame.

Just east of the racetrack is a **Denny's restaurant** (7 E. Huntington Dr.) that has a Dutch-style windmill dominating its roofline. Today's **Arcadia County Park** (405 S. Santa Anita Ave.) served as a U.S. Army balloon training facility during the First World War.

The **Gilb Museum of Arcadia Heritage** (380 W. Huntington Dr.) opened its doors in 2001 as a joint venture of the City of Arcadia and the Arcadia Historical Society.

Enter Pasadena on Colorado Boulevard. From this point onward, following Route 66 becomes difficult for a number of reasons. First, there is the fact that traffic picks up exponentially because Route 66 was "improved" early on in this area so that it became more of the type of highway we are accustomed to today. Secondly, Route 66 was re-routed many, many times over the years, so there are several true paths for you to choose from. I recommend lots of exploration here in Southern California, and lots of patience, too. As a byproduct of all of this complexity, one of our road warrior brethren, Scott Piotrowski, has assembled a detailed guide to help clear up the confusion (see the bibliography).

One of the many paths you can follow from here to the coast is Colorado Boulevard–Figueroa Street–Arroyo Seco Parkway–Sunset Boulevard–Santa Monica Boulevard. Also be aware that the earliest path of Route 66 went only as far as downtown Los Angeles, to the corner of Broadway and 7th (see the Greater Los Angeles reference map). The highway was extended to Santa Monica in the 1930s.

PASADENA

As early as 1890, "games" were held here in Pasadena that included foot races, tugs of war, and burro races. There were even what might be called "floats" in those early days. Later, these festivities became known as the **Tournament of Roses**, and in 1902 a football game was added to the program. Those traditions, of course, continue to the present day.

The city of Pasadena is architecturally blessed, particularly for those of us with a weakness for Mission or Art and Crafts style. The most outstanding example is the **Gamble House** (4 Westmoreland Pl.), designed by Charles and Henry Greene in 1908. For a tour of some fine architecture, drive along Oak Knoll and San Rafael and into the hills near the Rose Bowl. The **Colorado Street Bridge**, which crosses the Arroyo Seco River, was completed in 1913.

In 1924, at Pasadena's Rite Spot Restaurant, grill chef Lionel Sternberger concocted the world's first cheeseburger, which at the time he dubbed the "cheese hamburger." Today, the location has been taken over by **800 Degrees pizzeria** (2 E. Colorado Blvd.).

One of the earliest transcontinental auto trips originated in Pasadena way back in 1908. Jacob Murdoch loaded his son, two daughters, and 1,200 pounds of supplies into his Packard for a twenty-five-day expedition

from Pasadena to New York City. Packard later published a publicity booklet about the adventure entitled *A Family Tour From Ocean to Ocean*.

In 1939, Pasadena managed to capture first place in Columbia University's Quality of Life Competition.

PASADENA ATTRACTIONS

The **Tournament House** (391 S. Orange Grove Blvd.), is a sort of museum of Rose Bowl memorabilia in a former home of millionaire William Wrigley, Jr. It also serves as the headquarters for the annual parade festivities.

The **Pasadena Museum of History** (470 W. Walnut St.) is housed in the Fenyes Mansion, constructed in 1905 in the Beaux-Arts style. Its rooms are furnished with authentic period pieces. Also on the grounds is the Finnish Folk Art Museum, with exhibits including handmade furniture, utensils, and sundry decorative arts.

Castle Green (99 S. Raymond Ave.) built in 1898 as an annex to the Hotel Green, was architecturally state-of-the-art in its day, and exhibits an odd combination of styles the owners call "stunningly original." Today, Castle Green is reserved for special events, and has appeared in numerous films.

Displayed among more than twenty alleys that crisscross **Old Pasadena** are about forty plaques memorializing the area's earliest settlers and merchants.

The **Old Mill** (1120 Old Mill Rd.) dates from 1816, and is therefore the oldest surviving building in Southern California. Originally built as a gristmill for the San Gabriel Mission, it later served as a golf clubhouse and even a residence. It now houses historical exhibits, an art gallery, and native gardens.

Bungalow Heaven is a fairly compact area of Pasadena containing about 800 examples of California Bungalow architecture, all constructed from 1900 to the 1930s. The neighborhood is bordered on the north and south by Washington Boulevard and Orange Grove Boulevard, and on the east and west by Hill Avenue and Lake Avenue.

Candace Frazee and Steve Lubanski invite you to tour their home, otherwise known as the **Bunny Museum** (2605 Lake Ave.). These folks are crazy for bunnies; their collection (over 20,000 strong) includes celebrity bunnies such as Bugs Bunny, Peter Rabbit, Thumper, and the Trix rabbit, along with more obscure cousins from the hare family, such as "Elvis Parsley." Of course, they also have several "real" bunny pets wandering the house. It all started years ago when Steve made Candace a present of a small plush rabbit. A tradition began, and now they have the Guinness-recognized, record-setting collection. Come tour the fruits of an obsession.

LOS ANGELES

Entire books have been written about Los Angeles, and that's not what this book is about. Lots of major cities around the world consider themselves the center of the known universe, but L.A. probably more so than most. Say what you will about L.A., but it's true that Western culture pushes its envelope here, takes chances here, and subsequently affects the rest of the modern world.

Depending on the air quality on the day of your visit, you can catch

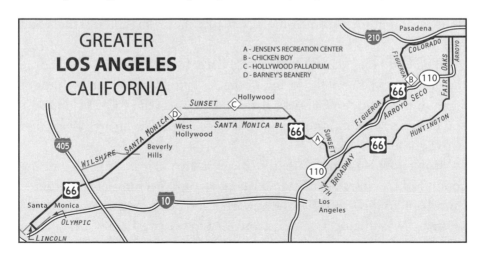

Vintage postcard featuring Los Angeles
City Hall.

The Los Angeles Theater stands
just steps away from Route 66's
original terminus in downtown L.A.
GPS: 34.04588,-118.25257

some excellent views of the city from the observation deck of **Los Angeles City Hall** (200 N. Spring St.). The city hall, built in 1928, might be familiar to you due to its countless appearances on television's *Dragnet*.

LOS ANGELES ATTRACTIONS

The Highland Park neighborhood includes **El Alisal** (200 E. Ave. 43), the hand-built home of artist and preservationist Charles F. Lummis, which now houses the Historical Society of Southern California. The **Mannings Coffee Store** rooftop sign (5707 N. Figueroa St.) is the last remaining example of more than a dozen that used to dot the Los Angeles area. The building is currently occupied by Las Cazuelas restaurant.

This neighborhood is also justifiably proud of the 1924 **Highland Theater** (5604 N. Figueroa St.), which sports a classic rooftop sign that was restored and ceremonially relit in May 2011. Also in Highland Park stands **Chicken Boy** (5558 N. Figueroa St.), a huge human-chicken hybrid creature that once graced a fast food outlet. In 2010, Chicken Boy was honored with a California Governor's Historic Preservation Award, and in 2016, *Time Out* Los Angeles named it "L.A.'s Most-Loved Local Culture."

The former Highland Park police station has been converted to the **Los Angeles Police Museum** (6045 York Blvd.), operated by the Los Angeles Police Society. On display are antique squad cars, vehicles used in crimes, and information about some of the area's most notorious cases.

The old Los Angeles neighborhood of Echo Park prides itself on its history. Thankfully, that means they've preserved something that lovers of unique signs will love. Atop **Jensen's Recreation Center** (1706 Sunset Blvd.) is a seventeen-by-twenty-eight-foot animated sign of a man bowling strikes, a holdover from the days when there was actually a bowling alley—and pool hall—on site.

Los Angeles's **Union Station** (800 N. Alameda St.) is a combination of Art Deco, Streamline Moderne, and Spanish Revival styles that was completed in 1939. A 125-foot-tall clock tower is incorporated into the design, and the interior appointments include mahogany and black marble.

Jensen's Rec Center, Los Angeles.
GPS: 34.07734,-118.25867

The **Bradbury Building** (304 S. Broadway) is on the National Register. Its modest-looking exterior masks an expansive Victorian-style inner courtyard, which features marble stairs, open-cage elevators, and copious amounts of ornamental metalwork. The Bradbury is the oldest commercial building remaining in Los Angeles's central business district.

Located in the Wells Fargo Center is the **Wells Fargo History Museum** (333 S. Grand Ave.). This museum recounts Western history in general, and the development of the Wells Fargo Company in particular. Visitors can climb aboard an authentic stagecoach and hear a firsthand account of the journey west from St. Louis, Missouri, which took three weeks.

The **Grammy Museum** (800 W. Olympic Blvd.) celebrates music in all its genres, and is part of a relatively new arts and entertainment complex known as L.A. Live.

The **Watts Towers** (1727 E. 107th St.) is one of only nine works of "folk art" listed on the National Register of Historic Places. They were built by an Italian immigrant, Simon Rodia, over the course of more than thirty years, using steel, wire mesh, mortar, and embedded pieces of tile and glass.

The **African American Firefighter Museum** (1401 S. Central Ave.) is housed in old Fire Station No. 30, parts of which were constructed in 1913. The station served as one of two segregated fire stations in Los Angeles between 1924 and 1955 (roughly the same thirty-year period that the Watts Towers, above, were constructed).

The **Autry National Center** (4700 Western Heritage Way) pays homage to the Old West—both in the historical sense (as in the Gold Rush days) and the romantic sense (as in Hollywood's notions of the era). The current name was adopted after the merger of the Autry Museum of Western Heritage, the Women of the West Museum, and the Southwest Museum of the American Indian (which is in a separate location, at 234 Museum Dr.).

Open again following extensive renovations is the **Griffith Observatory** (2800 E. Observatory Rd.). This was the location for a climactic fight scene in the James Dean film *Rebel Without a Cause*.

Forest Lawn Cemetery (6300 Forest Lawn Dr.), has such stars as Buster Keaton, Stan Laurel, and George "Gabby" Hayes among its tenants. Forest Lawn is even evolving into a sort of theme park, with such attractions as *The Birth of Liberty*—the world's largest historical mosaic —and a reproduction of Boston's Old North Church.

In Hancock Park is the Page Museum at the world-famous **La Brea Tar Pits** (5801 Wilshire Blvd.). About 10,000 to 40,000 years ago, during the last Ice Age, extinct creatures such as saber-toothed cats and mammoths roamed the Los Angeles area. There is a museum containing many of the fossil finds from the vicinity, as well as a viewing area where you can see fresh excavations taking place.

The **Petersen Automotive Museum** (6060 Wilshire Blvd.) is where Herbie the Love Bug lives. The museum features an ever-changing program of exhibits, and over 300,000 square feet of exhibit space means there's something of interest for everyone.

The **Murphy Sculpture Garden** (Charles E. Young Dr. E.), on the campus of UCLA, covers about five acres with sculptures by such notables as Matisse and Rodin.

Near the UCLA campus is the very tony community of Bel Air. Several stars still live here, but one of the things that hits home for a lot of people is the ***Beverly Hillbillies* mansion** (750 Bel Air Rd.) that was used in the television series.

Los Angeles, California. GPS: 34.07730,-118.25700

FURTHER AFIELD

In Glendale is another **Forest Lawn Cemetery** (1712 S. Glendale Ave.). You can pick up a guide to the more notable gravesites at the office. These include Humphrey Bogart, Walt Disney, and W. C. Fields. There is also a marriage chapel called the Wee Kirk o' th' Heather, where Ronald Reagan and Jane Wyman were wed in 1940.

The **Museum of Neon Art** (216 S. Brand Blvd.) in Glendale features both modern and vintage neon art. On permanent display is an animated sign that once stood in front of Steele's Motel in Van Nuys. You can sign up for an eight-week neon art workshop at MONA, which also sponsors the highly regarded Neon Bus Cruises of Los Angeles.

Nearby Anaheim is home to the original **Disneyland** (1313 Disneyland Dr.), which opened its gates on July 17, 1955. An employee who was there on opening day says it was a near disaster—someone had counterfeited tickets, so there were around three times the number of visitors in the park as there were tickets sold. Not only that, but the day was warm and the new asphalt still soft, so ladies' heels were continually getting stuck in it.

Near Anaheim is Buena Park, home of the world-famous **Knott's Berry Farm** (8039 Beach Blvd.). Knott's has the tallest and longest roller coaster west of the Mississippi—the Ghost Rider—and also the world's tallest water ride within its 113-acre water park, called Soak City, USA. Knott's Berry Farm had the country's first log flume ride way back in 1969.

In Garden Grove is Robert Schuller's famous **Crystal Cathedral** (13280 Chapman Ave.). Dr. Schuller is well-known for having come to Southern California in the 1950s, and soon thereafter conducting Sunday services from the roof of the snack bar at the local Orange Drive-In Theater.

The city of Gardena is the home of the former **Ascot Park**. The Ascot was the starting point for the Great Transcontinental Footrace, also known as the Bunion Derby, on March 4, 1928. This was a promotional footrace from Los Angeles to New York City, which was won by

Andy Payne of Foyil, Oklahoma. Automobile races were being held at this track as early as the 1910s.

Long Beach is where the **Queen Mary** (1126 Queens Hwy) is berthed. The Queen Mary was one of the largest passenger liners ever built, and has been restored as a first-class hotel. Featured in over 200 films, the Queen Mary nowadays hosts the Annual New Year's Eve Ship-walk Party celebrations. Also in Long Beach is the **Toyota Grand Prix**, held every April on city streets.

Nearby Huntington Beach is known as Surf City, USA, and hosts more than fifty surfing events every year, making it the obvious home for the **International Surfing Museum** (411 Olive Ave.). Huntington Beach also features a **Surfing Walk of Fame** (Pacific Coast Hwy).

Catalina Island is a retreat that Angelenos have long treasured. Catch the ferry from either San Pedro, Long Beach, or Marina Del Rey and spend the day here. There are glass-bottomed boats to ride, and a herd of 400 buffalo roam the island. There is also a mansion on Catalina that was built by the Wrigley Gum fortune; author Zane Grey used to make his home here, too. What is now the Avalon Ballroom was originally a gambling casino built by Mr. Wrigley shortly after he first acquired the island back in 1911.

HOLLYWOOD

Now officially a district within Los Angeles, Hollywood was for many years an independent city.

HOLLYWOOD ATTRACTIONS

Notable sites in Hollywood are extremely numerous. Most tourists make a pilgrimage to the Mecca of Tinseltown—Grauman's Chinese Theatre, now named the **TCL Chinese Theater** (6925 Hollywood Blvd.). This is where they began collecting footprints (and later, other imprints) of Hollywood celebrities in the concrete out front. That tradition started in

1927 with Norma Talmadge, who was soon followed by Douglas Fairbanks and Mary Pickford.

Just across the street from the TCL is the **El Capitan Theater** (6838 Hollywood Blvd.), where the premiere of Citizen Kane was held in 1941.

Over 2,500 bronze-inlaid stars stud the sidewalks of the **Hollywood Walk of Fame**, which runs along Hollywood Boulevard between Gower and Sycamore, and on Vine between Sunset and Yucca.

The **Hollywood Bowl** (2301 Highland Ave.) includes the Hollywood Bowl Museum, which features exhibits on the many famous performers who have played here. Some of those include the Beatles, Elton John, Jimi Hendrix, and the Doors. The Bowl is the home of the Los Angeles Philharmonic and the Hollywood Bowl Orchestra.

The **Hollywood Heritage Museum** (2100 N. Highland Ave.), across the street from the Bowl, is housed in the 1895 Lasky-DeMille Barn. It features memorabilia from movies of all stripes, and is housed in the birthplace of Paramount Pictures, where Cecil B.

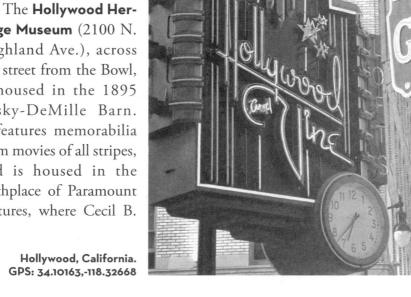

Hollywood, California.
GPS: 34.10163,-118.32668

Greetings from "Hollywood and Vine"   Color by Bert Phillips

Postcard featuring one of our country's most famous intersections.

DeMille filmed *The Squaw Man* in 1913.

The **Hollywood Museum** (1660 Highland Ave.) is housed in what was formerly the Max Factor Museum, and the original Max Factor salon. Items in the collection are extremely varied, including a spaceship model used in the filming of *Flash Gordon* episodes in the 1930s, costumes worn by such stars as Marilyn Monroe, Barbara Stanwyck, and Jane Russell, and the actual bathroom from Roddy McDowell's personal residence.

Packed into a single block of busy Hollywood Boulevard are the **Ripley's Believe It Or Not Museum** (6780 Hollywood Blvd.), the **Guinness World Records Museum** (6764 Hollywood Blvd.), and the **Hollywood Wax Museum** (6767 Hollywood Blvd.).

The **Hollywood Palladium** (6215 W. Sunset Blvd.) has seen just about everything. Opening in 1940, this music venue featured such acts as Frank Sinatra. In the 1960s, it hosted the Grateful Dead, the Rolling Stones, and The Who, even though the owner at that time was none other than Lawrence Welk, who broadcast his show from here for a time.

The *Blues Brothers* concert sequences were filmed here, too.

The **Capitol Records tower** (1750 Vine St.) was constructed in 1954 based on a concept hatched by Nat King Cole and Johnny Mercer: it is designed to resemble a stack of records on a spindle (remember 45s?). There is a pulsing light atop the tower that is rumored to spell out "Hollywood" in Morse code. The lobby contains a huge array of gold records recorded by artists represented by the Capitol label.

The famous **Hollywood Sign** on the hillside originally read "Hollywoodland," which was the name of a housing development. The letters are about fifty feet tall, and are as iconic to Southern California as the Eiffel Tower is to Paris. A caretaker used to live behind one of the L's in the old days. To get a close-up view of the sign, use Mulholland Drive.

A place known as **Castillo de Lago** (6342 Mulholland Dr.) was once a gambling den run by the infamous Bugsy Siegel.

Universal Studios (8981 W. Sunset Blvd.) offers movie-making tours. Next door to Universal Studios is the **Universal CityWalk**, a sort of faux pedestrian community, which has actually received high praise from some architectural critics. Parking cost several dollars at last count, but you can easily spend a day here, and it's a safe, family-appropriate, and pedestrian-friendly area. Other movie studios in Hollywood/West

Hollywood, California.
GPS: 34.10165,-118.32585

Hollywood include Fox, Paramount, and Warner Brothers.

There's a house in Hollywood that you may recognize from somewhere—the **home of Ozzie and Harriet Nelson** (1822 Camino Palmero Dr.), both on and off the screen.

The **Sunset Strip** is a section of Sunset Boulevard known for its clubs, boutiques, and overall edginess. The television series *77 Sunset Strip*, filmed from 1958 to 1964, featured shots of **Dino's Lodge** (8524 Sunset Blvd.). There is now an office building at the location, but there is a plaque confirming the pop-culture significance of the site. The Sunset Strip runs from Crescent Heights Boulevard on the east to Doheny Drive on the west.

The **Whisky A Go Go** (8901 Sunset Blvd.) has seen its share of rock and roll history. The Doors played here regularly on their way to stardom, and it was here that the go-go girl craze of the '60s began, soon after this club began putting dancers in cages.

At **Henson Studios** (1416 N. La Brea Ave.), the front gates include a twelve-foot statue of Kermit the Frog dressed as Charlie Chaplin's Little Tramp. This was originally the location of a movie studio established by Chaplin in 1918. It changed hands several times over the years, and functioned as the A&M Record Company Studios in the 1960s, where hits by Herb Alpert were produced.

The original location of **Barney's Beanery** (8447 Santa Monica Blvd.) is in West Hollywood. Since 1920, this chili shack has been serving an eclectic blend of foods to an eclectic clientele, where international tourists and local pool sharks come together in rainbow-colored booths under a ceiling of mirrors. The menu is twelve pages long at last count, so if you can't find it here, maybe you shouldn't have it after all. Once a hangout for Jim Morrison, Barney's is reportedly where Janis Joplin did some partying the night she died.

In October of 1970, at the **Highland Gardens Hotel** (7047 Franklin Ave.), Janis Joplin died in room 105 of a heroin overdose at what was then the Landmark Hotel.

In the Hollywood Hills is a street named **Blue Jay Way**. You may have trouble finding it, because the signs keep getting stolen. This is the avenue made famous in George Harrison's song of the same name that began: "There's a fog upon L.A . . . ." George wrote the song after renting a home here in 1968.

Hollywood Memorial Park (6000 Santa Monica Blvd.) is one of the most famous "cemeteries of the stars." Hundreds of movie legends are interred here, such as Douglas Fairbanks Sr. and Rudolph Valentino. There is also the grave of one Carl Morgan Bigsby, whose marker is a replica Atlas missile. Mel Blanc's simple granite headstone states flatly: "That's all, folks."

The **Tail o' the Pup hot dog stand** (451 N. La Cienega Blvd.), shaped in the form of a hot dog between two halves of a bun, was a popular local eatery for many years, and was even forced to move more than once in response to "progress." At this writing, the iconic structure is still in storage, but plans are in place to re-open it at the address above.

BEVERLY HILLS

Formerly called Morocco Junction, Beverly Hills is synonymous with movie stars and other rich-and-famous types. You can buy a "Map of the Stars' Homes" here, but you're more likely to spot a gardener than you are a celebrity using that strategy. If you're serious about star-spotting, buy a daily update as to where location filming is taking place in the area. Our down-to-earth friend Will Rogers served for a time as mayor of Beverly Hills in the 1920s.

BEVERLY HILLS ATTRACTIONS

The legendary Trader Vic's, now transformed into **Trader Vic's Lounge** (9876 Wilshire Blvd.), is at the Beverly Hilton.

Legend tells us that it was here in Beverly Hills, at **Lawry's Prime Rib Restaurant** (100 N. La Cienega Blvd.), that toppings were first added to a baked potato in 1938.

Gangster Bugsy Siegel, of Las Vegas fame, was gunned down at the

home of his girlfriend (810 Linden Dr.), Virginia Hill, in 1947.

The **Sharon Tate murders** took place at a Beverly Hills residence (10050 Cielo Dr.) in 1969. The killers then followed that grisly crime with the **LaBianca murders** at another Los Angeles home (3301 Waverly). Charles Manson is still behind bars for those horrors, having been refused parole several times over the years.

Don't fail to stop and see the famous **Spadena House** (516 Walden Dr.)—also called the Witch's House. The house was built in 1921 as the administration building for Willat Studios in Culver City, and it subsequently appeared in several silent movies. In 1926, it was moved to this residential neighborhood. The house is designed with exaggerated features, such as crooked shutters, an extremely steep-pitched roof, and a small moat with a bridge—as though it came straight out of a Brothers Grimm fairy tale. This is a private residence, so you'll have to content yourself with viewing the exterior from the public street.

Just off the route near Beverly Hills and Bel Air is the **Westwood Village Mortuary** (1218 Glendon Ave.). The celebrity list here includes Marilyn Monroe, Daryl F. Zanuck, Natalie Wood, Frank Zappa, and Roy Orbison.

In Studio City's residential district, just north of Beverly Hills, is the ***Brady Bunch* house** (11222 Dilling St.) used in the television series.

SANTA MONICA

As you cross Centinela Boulevard on Route 66 (Santa Monica Boulevard), you enter the city of Santa Monica. Santa Monica Boulevard—and your run to the coast—abruptly ends at Ocean Avenue (although Route 66 actually turned left at Lincoln Boulevard and terminated at Olympic). Across Ocean Avenue is **Pacific Palisades Park**, where you should stroll around and relax now that you've come to the end of your journey. There is a small monument in the park dedicated to Will Rogers, which reads in part: "Highway 66 was the first road he traveled in a career that led him straight to the hearts of his countrymen."

Popularly considered the symbolic end of Route 66, but technically blocks away, is the **Santa Monica Pier**, originally constructed in 1908. This may well be because the pier, with its large neon sign, is more

Route 66 came to an abrupt end a short distance from this recreational pier.
Santa Monica, California. GPS: 34.01135,-118.49502

photogenic than the true terminus on the nearby street corner. In keeping with the location's status as the spiritual end of Route 66, a marker was dedicated in 2009 designating it as such. In the 1920s, Santa Monica had several recreational piers along its beach. This one was at one time called Ocean Park Pier, and when it reopened in 1958 as Pacific Ocean Park, there were more opening-week visitors than there had been at the grand opening of Disneyland three years earlier. Today, the pier includes a nine-story Ferris wheel, a five-story roller coaster, other rides, and midway-style games. Also here is the venerable Looff Hippodrome, named for carousel builder Charles Looff. Since 1916, the building has housed a hand-carved carousel. The one residing here currently is a 1922 model, which was brought here in 1946. The carousel was featured prominently in the 1973 movie *The Sting*, starring Robert Redford and Paul Newman, and was refurbished in 1981. The pier, much like Venice Beach to the south, is always awash with colorful local characters.

SANTA MONICA ATTRACTIONS

Overlooking Santa Monica Canyon is the **former home of composer Ferde Grofé** (710 Adelaide Pl.). It was here that he composed his most famous work, the *Grand Canyon Suite*. The piece was originally titled *Santa Monica Canyon Suite*, but, fearing a lack of recognition, Grofé renamed it after the far more famous landmark. Grofé is also the man who wrote the world-famous orchestral arrangement of Gershwin's *Rhapsody in Blue*. Gershwin had written the piece, not for symphony, but for a small band, with blank spaces left in it for Gershwin's own piano improvisations. Grofé was at that time the chief arranger for the Paul Whiteman jazz ensemble, for whom the piece was originally written. Whiteman's famous band was also where a crooner named Bing Crosby spent his salad days as one of the "Rhythm Boys."

The **Museum of Flying** (3100 Airport Ave.) features more than thirty vintage aircraft, some of which are in flight-worthy condition, all maintained on the site where Mr. Donald Douglas built the very first DC-3.

Bergamot Station (2525 Michigan Ave.) is a collection of over twenty galleries housed in renovated warehouse spaces on approximately six acres in Santa Monica. Pieces include photography, paintings, sculpture, and more.

There's a building in Santa Monica that may look vaguely familiar. The **Santa Monica Civic Auditorium** (1855 Main St.) was the regular site of the Academy Awards from 1961 to 1968.

The **Galley restaurant** (2442 Main St.) opened in 1934 and was popular with the likes of Errol Flynn. The restaurant has a seagoing theme, and features memorabilia from the 1935 film classic *Mutiny on the Bounty*.

Shirley Temple's childhood home (924 24th St.) is also in Santa Monica.

The former **City Hall** (1438 2nd St.), built in 1873, is the oldest building of masonry construction in the city, and was designated a historical landmark in 1975.

The **Annenberg Beach House** (415 Pacific Coast Hwy) is a city-run public facility on five oceanfront acres. The facility is part of an estate originally developed by William Randolph Hearst in the 1920s, and it includes the rehabilitated guest house and pool, as well as new structures added during its conversion to public use.

The City of Santa Monica has prepared a "landmarks" tour brochure that includes a wealth of architectural sites of interest, including the **Merle Norman Building** (9130 Bellanca Ave.), the **Vanity Fair Apartments** (822 3rd St.), the **Mayfair Theatre** (214 Santa Monica Blvd.), and the Grofé residence cited above. Two-hour guided downtown walking tours are also conducted every Saturday morning at 10 AM, beginning at the Hostelling International facility (1436 2nd St.).

Standing on the grounds of the **Miramar Hotel** (101 Wilshire Blvd.) is a century-old Moreton Bay fig tree with a story. It's said that around 1890 or so there was a sailor in town with no money to pay his bar bill, so he paid the bartender with a young sapling instead. The sapling changed hands a couple of times, and then was eventually planted by the gardener of the Miramar estate, which stood where the hotel is now. The tree now stands about eighty feet tall near the corner of Wilshire Boulevard and Ocean Avenue.

FURTHER AFIELD

Just northwest of Santa Monica is the **Santa Monica Mountains National Recreation Area**, bounded by the Pacific Ocean to the south and U.S. 101 to the north. Included within this preserve is the **Will Rogers State Historic Park** (1501 Will Rogers State Park Rd.), which includes the home Rogers lived in from 1928 until his death seven years later. There is also a visitor center, nature center, corral, stable, polo field, and hiking trails on the grounds. Adventurous hikers and bikers can take the Backbone Trail into the Santa Monica Mountains. The trail goes all the way to Point Mugu, some seventy miles away.

South of Santa Monica is Venice Beach. This area is prime habitat for surfers, down-and-outers, muscle builders, skateboarders, and an abundance of other species. Venice was the brainchild of one Abbot Kinney, who envisioned cloning Venice, Italy, right here in Southern California. Canals were dug throughout the area from 1904 to 1905, and two dozen black, silver-prowed gondolas were imported from Italy to ply the waters here. A tourist in 1906 observed: "The architecture was the grandest, an intricate blend of Italian columns, porticoes, and balustrades, only slightly marred by the presence of guess-your-weight machines." At some point, the Board of Health declared the canals a health hazard and ordered that they be filled in. In the 1950s, Venice had deteriorated to the point that Orson Welles used the area as the backdrop for the film *A Touch of Evil*.

If you've now successfully completed a journey of the entire length of Route 66, then you've just had an experience that—whether you realize it right away or not—will change your life.

BIBLIOGRAPHY & RECOMMENDED READING

Barth, Jack. *Roadside Hollywood*. Chicago: Contemporary Books, 1991.

Basten, Fred E. *Santa Monica Bay*. Los Angeles: General Publishing Group, 1997.

Cantor, George. *Pop Culture Landmarks: A Traveler's Guide*. Detroit: Gale Research, Inc., 1995.

Chicago Tribune Staff. *Chicago Days*. Lincolnwood, IL: Contemporary Books, 1997.

Debo, Angie. *The WPA Guide to 1930s Oklahoma*. Lawrence, KS: University Press of Kansas, 1986. Originally published by the University of Oklahoma Press, 1941, under the title *Oklahoma: A Guide to the Sooner State*.

Duncan, Glen. *Images of America: Route 66 in California*. Charleston, SC: Arcadia Publishing, 2005.

Foreman, Julie and Rod Fensom. *Illinois Off the Beaten Path*. Old Saybrook, CT: Globe Pequot Press, 1996.

Fugate, Francis L. and Roberta B. *Roadside History of Oklahoma*. Missoula, MT: Mountain Press Publishing Co., 1991.

Goddard, Connie and Bruce Boyer. *The Great Chicago Trivia & Fact Book*. Nashville, TN: Cumberland House, 1996.

Howard, Rex. *Texas Guidebook*. 4th ed. Grand Prairie, TX: The Lo-Ray Co., 1962.

Jenkins, Myra E., and Albert H. Schroeder. *A Brief History of New Mexico*. Albuquerque, NM: University of New Mexico Press, 1974.

Kelso, John. *Texas Curiosities*. Guilford, CT: Globe Pequot Press, 2000.

Mangum, Richard and Sherry. *Route 66 Across Arizona*. Flagstaff, AZ: Hexagon Press, 2001.

McClanahan, Jerry. *EZ 66 Guide for Travelers*. 3rd ed. Lake Arrowhead, CA: National Historic Route 66 Federation, 2014.

Miller, Arthur P. and Marjorie L. *Trails Across America*. Golden, CO: Fulcrum Publishing, 1996.

N.Y. Public Library. *Book of Popular Americana*. New York: MacMillan, 1994.

Piotrowski, Scott. *Finding the End of the Mother Road: Route 66 in Los Angeles County*. Pasadena, CA: 66 Productions, 2005 (Revised Second Printing).

Rittenhouse, Jack. *A Guide Book to Highway 66*. Albuquerque, NM: University of New Mexico Press, 1998. Facsimile of the 1946 First Edition.

Ross, Jim. *Oklahoma Route 66*. 2nd ed. Arcadia, OK: Ghost Town Press, 2011.

Scott, David L. and Kay W. *Guide to the National Park Areas: Western States*. Old Saybrook, CT: Globe Pequot Press, 1999.

Scott, Quinta and Susan Croce Kelly. *Route 66*. Norman, OK: University of Oklahoma Press, 1988.

Simmons, Marc, and Joan Myers. *Along the Santa Fe Trail.* Albuquerque, NM: University of New Mexico Press, 1986.

Snyder, Tom. *Route 66 Traveler's Guide and Roadside Companion.* New York: St. Martin's Griffin, 2000.

Sonderman, Joe. *Images of America: Route 66 in the Missouri Ozarks.* Charleston, SC: Arcadia Publishing, 2009.

Taylor, Nelson. *America Bizarro.* New York: St. Martin's Griffin, 2000.

Usner, Don J. *New Mexico Route 66 On Tour: Legendary Architecture From Glenrio to Gallup.* Santa Fe, NM: Museum of New Mexico Press, 2001.

Wallechinsky, David. *David Wallechinsky's 20th Century: History with the Boring Parts Left Out.* New York: Little, Brown & Co., 1995.

Wallis, Michael. *Route 66: The Mother Road.* New York: St. Martin's Press, 1990.

Yonover, Neil S. *Crime Scene USA.* New York: Hyperion, 2000.

Young, Don and Marge. *America's Southwest.* Edison, NJ: Hunter Publishing, 1998.

INDEX